Strategies for Rapid Climate Mitigation

To keep the global average temperature from rising further than 2°C, emissions must peak soon and then fall steeply. This book examines how such rapid mitigation can proceed – in the scale and speed required for effective climate action – using an analogy provided by the mobilisation for a war that encompassed nations, World War II.

Strategies for Rapid Climate Mitigation examines the wartime–climate analogy by drawing lessons from wartime mobilisations to develop contingency plans for a scenario where governments implement stringent mitigation programmes as an 'insurance policy' where we pay for future benefits. Readers are provided a picture of how these programmes could look, how they would work, what could trigger them, and the challenges in execution. The book analyses in detail one plausible approach to a crucial issue – an approach built upon knowledge of climate science and on proven and demonstrated mitigation measures. The book is meshed with a social and political analysis that draws upon narratives of mobilisations during the war to meet a transnational threat, while also addressing the shortcomings of the analogy and its strategies.

The book will be of great interest to scholars, students, and practitioners of public policy, climate policy, energy policy, international relations, and strategic studies.

Laurence L. Delina conducts research at the Frederick S. Pardee Center for the Study of the Longer-Range Future at Boston University, USA. He is also a research associate at the Center for Governance and Sustainability at the University of Massachusetts Boston, an Earth System Governance Research Fellow, and a Visiting Fellow at Harvard Kennedy School.

"The most fascinating part of this book is its close look at how wartime mobilization of our industrial sector might actually happen. People have been talking about it for years, but Laurence Delina has actually done the work to figure it out." – *Bill McKibben, founder of 350.org, USA*

"The world needs to transition to clean, renewable energy as quickly as possible to reduce the health and climate damage inflicted by the combustion age. This excellent new book examines resources and efforts needed for such a transformation, using wartime mobilization as an example. I recommend it highly for students and the public." – *Mark Z. Jacobson, Stanford University, USA*

"*Strategies for Rapid Climate Mitigation* is an important and timely contribution to the urgent debate about the actions required to drive swift and equitable decarbonisation of the global economy. The detailed and thoughtful discussion of key legislative, regulatory, financial, and labour market policies for mobilizing the resources and capabilities required to achieve emergency speed emission reductions is particularly valuable." – *John Wiseman, Deputy Director, Melbourne Sustainable Society Institute, University of Melbourne, Australia*

"In our age of catastrophe and neoliberal defeatism, this book is a beacon of hope. Laurence Delina uses his fierce intellect and bold vision to demonstrate that a global emergency mobilization against climate change, with states as central actors, is a viable strategy—indeed it may be the only one left. A must read." – *Margaret Klein-Salamon, founder and director of The Climate Mobilization, USA*

"Despite frequent calls for rapid transitions to a lower carbon economy, few people have sought systematically to build on the lessons of the past to sketch out potential scenarios for the future. The *Gendanken* (thought) experiment that lies at the heart of this book forces us to engage with historical lessons and face up to uncomfortable truths about the role of the state, finance and labour in enabling and accelerating an energy transition to a world in which climate change is more effectively addressed. It is original, provocative and deserves to be widely read." – *Peter Newell, University of Sussex, UK. Editor of* The Politics of Green Transformations *(Routledge 2015).*

"Delina asks how human societies can tackle the herculean task of recasting energy systems to meet climate change. He successfully sketches the many moving parts involved in a complex socio-technical transition. From sustainable energy technologies to public policies, and from vested interests to systemic inertia, transition looks daunting. In answer, Delina argues for reviving government as a leading agent of change, rather than relying only on the market. Using wartime mobilization history, he shows both the possibilities and limitations of government action. He calls for the creation of new, powerful institutions to help plan and superintend the widespread, rapid take-up of sustainable energy technologies. He also calls for checks on executive power, reflecting modern democratic norms. The book empowers us to imagine how we might arrive at our climate-safe future." – *Alastair Iles, University of California Berkeley, USA*

"If publics come to demand climate action, as well they might as extreme weather intensifies and surprises multiply, this book offers a model, historically grounded yet applied to contemporary, even future trends. Delina doesn't just look back for 'lessons from history' but projects forward, imagining the possibility of fundamentally challenging the self-destructive, endlessly expansionist order." – *Thomas Princen, University of Michigan Ann Arbor, USA*

Routledge Advances in Climate Change Research

Strategies for Rapid Climate Mitigation

Wartime mobilisation as a model for action?

Laurence L. Delina

Routledge
Taylor & Francis Group
LONDON AND NEW YORK

from Routledge

First published 2016
by Routledge

2 Park Square, Milton Park, Abingdon, Oxfordshire OX14 4RN
711 Third Avenue, New York, NY 10017

Routledge is an imprint of the Taylor & Francis Group, an informa business

Firstissuedinpaperback2017

British Library Cataloguing in Publication Data
A catalogue record for this book is available from the British Library

Library of Congress Cataloging in Publication Data
Names: Delina, Laurence L.
Title: Strategies for rapid climate mitigation : wartime mobilisation as a
model for action? / Laurence L. Delina.
Description: Abingdon, Oxon ; New York, NY : Routledge, Earthscan,
2016. | Series: Routledge advances in climate change research
Identifiers: LCCN 2015048759| ISBN 9781138646230 (hb) |
ISBN 9781315627663 (ebook)
Subjects: LCSH: Climate change mitigation. | Climate change mitigation--
Social aspects. | Climate change mitigation--International cooperation.
Classification: LCC QC903 .D445 2016 | DDC 363.738/746--dc23
LC record available at http://lccn.loc.gov/2015048759

ISBN: 978-1-138-64623-0 (hbk)
ISBN: 978-0-8153-6454-2 (pbk)

Typeset in Goudy
by Taylor & Francis Books

To Lucy and Rito Sr., para kay nanay kag tatay

Contents

Tables

Foreword

Hans Joachim Schellnhuber

Laurence L. Delina, the author of this book, is asking two eminently obvious questions, which are nevertheless raised by hardly anybody else. If the scientific community convincingly demonstrates that unbridled anthropogenic global warming (AGW) will create war-like harm and chaos, shouldn't humanity instigate war-like measures to avoid such a dire fate? If the answer to question 1 is yes, what should the appropriate narrative for a 'Rapid Mitigation Project' look like?

Delina not only dares to ask those questions, but also to answer them. The result is a well-informed, thought-provoking and powerful piece of work, deliberately designed as a '*Gedankenexperiment*'.

Imagine...

I am writing this foreword immediately after the historical climate summit (COP 21), where 'the spirit of Paris defeated the ghosts of Copenhagen', as I put it in several public statements. Indeed, 195 nations agreed in the French capital, which was shaken by abominable terrorist attacks just a few weeks before, to keep man-made planetary temperature rise within the range of 1.5–2.0°C. This result does not only reflect the best available risk analysis provided by the pertinent experts, but also epitomises that the world has finally grasped the immense threat associated with business-as-usual economic globalisation, which is predominantly driven by fossil fuels. Remarkably, the least developed countries have pushed hardest at the COP 21 for the aspirational 1.5°C limit to anthropogenic global warming. This limit would provide humanity with a decent chance to avoid tipping of large-scale functional components of the planetary machinery (Lenton et al. 2008) into a different mode of operation – if not into annihilation. Delina portrays those accidents as 'black-swan events', although they might be rather epitomised by grey (or even the familiar white) swans if global warming remains unchecked. Note also that global sea-level rise depends rather sensitively on global surface temperature increase: the AGW difference between 1.5°C and 2.0°C translates into at least half a meter additional sea-level rise by 2200. A margin that determines whether a small island state survives or doesn't.

So the right climate target was agreed upon in Paris, yet the multi-lateral scheme for avoiding dangerous AGW does hardly reflect the imperative need to actually succeed: climate action is still supposed to be delivered by a pledge-and-review process, which has been strengthened to a certain degree by COP 21, but is ultimately based on the sheer hope that the 195 nation states involved will somehow raise their level of ambition in good time. This is 'Realpolitik' at its best – and its worst.

So what else might be done, possibly through a major amendment of the Paris agreement? This is the central topic of Delina's book, in which he boldly delineates a concrete alternative to the pledge-and-review approach. The pathway he describes in some detail is a war-like response to a war-like challenge indeed. In order to come to grips with his topic, the author first sets out to describe what a war-like effort looks like in the first place. The military mobilisation programmes of the Allies and the Axis, respectively, during World War II, serve as a historical model for such a 'war on global warming'. Most notably, the US mobilisation in the 1942–1945 period provides the absolute showcase for what can be achieved in national economy reprogramming – if there is the political will to do so. Delina gives a fascinating account of those mind-boggling efforts, despite the fact that they were meant to maximise destruction – through direct and collateral impact.

The pathway presented by the author in this book is the mitigation counterpart of the WW II mobilisation programmes. Delina explicitly devises a global effort-sharing scheme, bluntly assigning targets and timetables to the respective countries in a top-down scheme. This may appear pathetic to many scholars, especially to the overwhelming majority of the contemporary social scientists who covet a 'realist' perception of the world. Yet it has to be appreciated that during WW II some of the combatant countries spent more than 70% of their GDP on military, and that the USA and its allies emerged as global hegemons from this epic competition for ammunition production. So, perhaps, the future hegemons will be those nations who are determined to make comparative efforts in the battle of rapid decarbonisation...

Delina does not stop at the effort-allocation level though, he also explores the funding, labour force and institutions dimensions of his approach in quite some detail. But read for yourself.

And yet, is the author writing a script for Hollywood or for Washington D.C., Bejing, New Delhi, Berlin, Lagos et al.? Is there any chance that this somewhat bewildering dream of saving the world the hard way will come true? If it remains a strictly top-down scheme, then I think that all the odds are against it. However, and Delina touches upon this crucial issue in the last book chapter, there are strong forces that may rush to help the pathway, and they are all bottom-up in character. I have portrayed them in various lectures as the main actors in a 3D drama: *D*isaster, *D*iscovery, and *D*ignity.

The *first* big driving force is Nature itself, which will teach people and politicians around the world that AGW is no joke and no fun. 'Natural' emergencies at all scales will become more and more frequent and increasingly destructive, so everybody shall be able to read the writing on the wall. The *second* big driving force is innovation by public and private institutions and companies, which will enable all sorts of small and big leaps forward. Such as batteries that will store ten times as much energy at a tenth of the cost of the contemporary devices. This is going to happen sooner than most people expect. And *thirdly*, there is that overwhelming driving force called morality as epitomised by Pope Francis' stunning encyclical *Laudato Si'*, which I had the honour to present at the Vatican last June. If we care for human dignity, we will engage in all types of social movements that help to preserve the livelihoods and the development opportunities of our sisters and brothers on Earth – especially of those, who are not yet born. The so-called divestment initiative is a shining example in this vein.

If all those motions combine to a powerful social upwelling dynamics, then it may happen that the governments of critical nations will respond to the calls to arms – in the way Delina proposes. As Nelson Mandela famously put it: 'Everything seems impossible, until it's done!'

Reference

Lenton, T.M. et al. 2008, 'Tipping elements in the Earth's climate system', *Proceedings of the National Academy of Sciences of the United States of America*, vol. 105, pp. 1786–1793.

Preface

Globally, countries have agreed to hold the increase in global temperature below 2°C by 2100. In 2015, government representatives met in Paris laying out a course to attain this objective. We know, for a scientific fact, that global emissions must peak soon and fall steeply for a chance to meet this objective. Emissions reduction targets agreed in Paris, however, do not measure up; emission trends – despite full implementation of the Paris targets – are expected to lock us in a world beyond +2°C warming. Climate action, therefore, does not stop at Paris. It is a milestone, but there is still work to be done: much more work, in fact. We still need to fall carbon emissions fast, while having some insurance that economies will not collapse. There seems to be a poverty of political will at the international stage, and inarguably at the national level as well to meet this objective; but there is no poverty of ideas.

This book is written as a *Gedankenexperiment* on how mitigation can proceed – in the scale and speed required – using an analogy provided by a mobilisation that encompassed nations, World War II.

The war metaphor has been used many times, by politicians, pundits, and even by scientists and academics, to argue for effective climate action. Nonetheless, analysis whether it is apt was not fully interrogated. Also missing in the discussion is what it would mean to be taken seriously. This book fills that gap. It examines the analogy by drawing lessons from wartime to develop contingency plans for a scenario where the state implements large-scale, aggressive, transformative, and dramatic mitigation programmes. These programmes are designed as some sort of 'insurance policy' that the present generation should 'pay' for the benefits of future generations. Readers of this book are provided with a picture of how these programmes, which I collectively call the 'Rapid Mitigation Project,' could look and how they would work.

An abundant supply of how-to-do-it literature on addressing climate change exists, but there is a dearth in terms of a book that considers the required speed and scale of mitigation. Building upon knowledge about climate science and using proven and demonstrated approaches to reduce greenhouse gas emissions, this book presents a detailed analysis of a plausible approach to this crucial issue. This book is enmeshed with social and political analysis that draws upon wartime mobilisations of resources to meet a transnational threat, while laying out the shortcomings of the analogy. Although it provides messy answers to an undeniably complex challenge, this book shows the possibility of constructing a set of strategies that could reduce emissions in a structured manner, while being applicable in policymaking. The governance aspect of this book, thus, makes it a unique read.

Mark Diesendorf, my PhD supervisor at the Institute of Environmental Studies at the University of New South Wales Australia, initiated the idea for this book. From Sydney, this book sees its completion in Boston. The Frederick S. Pardee Center for the Study of the Longer-Range Future at Boston University provided me ample space and time to finish the manuscript. Anthony Janetos, the Center director, supported me throughout. Cynthia Barakatt read portions of the manuscript and suggested improvements. Elsewhere, I learned much from Sheila Jasanoff during my Visiting Fellowship at Harvard Kennedy School in 2013 and 2016. Thoughtful conversations during this visit include those with Sir David King and Christiana Figueres. Maria Ivanova, co-director of the Center for Governance and Sustainability at University of Massachusetts Boston where I am a research associate, invited me to attend a meeting with Christiana. Elsewhere, other interlocutors include Brian Martin, Mark Jacobson, Paul Edwards, Philip Sutton, Sebastian Pfotenhauer, and Tom Bauler. I thank them all.

This book is a product of a journey. I owe great gratitude to my former teachers from Mindanao State University in General Santos City, the Philippines, Rufa Cagoco-Guiam and Macapado Muslim; and from the University of Auckland, Yvonne Underhill-Sem and Ruth Irwin. Also, Elma Lumantas, Rene Villa, Andrea Campado, Reynaldo Enrile, Inez Venus, and Nenita Paulo have shaped my interest in narratives of the past. My friends: Char Mae Andas-Kacir, Ever Piñon-Simonsson, Mary Ann Frugalidad-Latumbo, Sheila Siar, Olivia Uhr, Mae Flor Tanzo-Teves, Joannah Russell Bahian, Rima Alfafara, Allan Lao, Merlyn Jarrell, Roditt Cruz-Delfino, Alfie Maria Rio-Custodio, Rhea Venus-Dela Cruz, Cheryl Magbanua, Long Seng To, and Vipra Kumar are my life's gems. My family, whose love, care, and prayers have sustained me through the years, especially my parents Lucy and Rito Sr. who, despite our poverty in material things, imbibed in me and my siblings, Michael and Rito Jr., the great value of education. They, along with my sisters-in-law, Brendaly and May, and my nephews, Matheo and Gabriel, and nieces, Michaela, Sophia and Lorraine, are my reason for continuing in life. To them, I dedicate this work.

Climate change is indubitably the greatest challenge presented to us as a species. This decade remains a critical decade for action. As a citizen of one of the most vulnerable countries in the age of climate consequences, the Philippines, I could not just stand idly by and let catastrophic climate impacts ravage not only the livelihoods of my people, but most importantly, their lives. Although the climate issue has been elevated with many now recognising the importance of climate action, but there are still t's that need crossing and i's that need dotting. With current responses not at par with the required reductions to ensure the safety of many people's lives and live-lihoods, I offer this book as a point of departure for a reinvigorated debate and critical interrogation of plausible pathways for addressing the climate challenge in a timeframe and rate of mitigation demanded by science.

Laurence L. Delina
Boston

Abbreviations

ABC	Australian Broadcasting Corporation
AEMO	Australian Energy Market Operator
AGW	anthropogenic global warming
ANMB	Army and Navy Munitions Board, U.S.A.
AP	Associated Press
AR5	The Fifth Assessment Report of the IPCC, 2013–2014
BRICS	Brazil, Russia, India, China, South Africa
CCS	carbon capture and storage, or carbon capture and sequestration
CICERO	Center for International Climate and Environmental Research, Sweden
CO_2	carbon dioxide
COP	Conference of Parties to the UNFCCC
CSIRO	Commonwealth Scientific and Industrial Research Organisation, Australia
CSP	concentrated solar power
ENSO	El Niño Southern Oscillation
EU	European Union
GDP	Gross Domestic Product
GHG	greenhouse gas
GNP	Gross National Product
GWEC	Global Wind Energy Council
IEA	International Energy Agency
IMF	International Monetary Fund
IPCC	Intergovernmental Panel on Climate Change
IRENA	International Renewable Energy Agency
LCOE	levelised cost of electricity
MCA	Minerals Council of Australia
MEPS	minimum energy performance standard
MLP	Multilevel Perspective
MOOC	Massive Open Online Course
n.d.	undated
NASA	National Aeronautics and Space Administration

NEM	National Electricity Market, Australia
NGO	non-government organisation
NREL	National Renewable Energy Laboratory, U.S.A.
NYT	The New York Times
OECD	Organisation for Economic Co-operation and Development
OEM	Office of Emergency Management, U.S.A.
OES	Office of Economic Stabilisation, U.S.A.
OPM	Office of Production Management, U.S.A.
OWM	Office of War Mobilisation, U.S.A.
POW	prisoner of war
PV	photovoltaic
R&D	research and development
RCP	Representative Concentration Pathway
REN 21	Renewable Energy Policy Network for the 21st Century
SPAB	Supply Priorities and Allocation Board, U.S.A.
SRM	solar radiation management
U.S., U.S.A.	United States of America
U.S.S.R.	Union of Soviet Socialist Republics, Soviet Union
U.K.	United Kingdom of Great Britain and Northern Ireland
UN	United Nations
UNEP	United Nations Environment Programme
UNFCCC	United Nations Framework Convention on Climate Change
VAT	value added tax
WAIS	West Antarctic Ice Sheet
WBGU	Wissenschaftlicher Beirat der Bundesregierung Globale Umweltveränderungen, German Advisory Council on Global Change
WPB	War Production Board, U.S.A.
WRB	War Resources Board, U.S.A.
WSJ	The Wall Street Journal
WWF	World Wide Fund for Nature

Currencies

AU$	Australian dollar
AU£	Australian pound
CAD	Canadian dollar
DKK	Danish krone
EUR	euro
GBP	British pound sterling
RM	German Reichsmark
US$	U.S. dollar

Measurements

$GtCO_2e$	gigatonne of carbon dioxide equivalent
GW	gigawatt, 1 GW = 10^9 W
km^2	square kilometre
kWh	kilowatt-hour, 1 kWh = 10^3 Wh
m	metre
MtC	megatonnes of carbon, 1 MtC = 10^6 tonnes C
$MtCO_2$	megatonnes of carbon dioxide
$MtCO_2e$	megatonnes of carbon dioxide equivalent
MW	megawatts, 1 MW = 10^6 W
MWh	megawatt-hour, 1 MWh = 10^6 Wh
ppm	parts per million
PWh	petawatt-hour, 1 PWh = 1,000 TWh = 10^{15} Wh
TWh	terawatt-hour, 1 TWh = 10^{12} Wh
W/m^2	watt per square metre

Introduction

Since the beginning of the Industrial Revolution, humanity's footprint on the planet has grown large and its consequences have become visible on a global scale (Rockström et al. 2009). Considered the biggest threat, anthropogenic climate change has spawned massive ice melting in the Arctic, shrinking glaciers worldwide, acidification of ocean waters, killer heat waves, intense wildfires, huge floods, and droughts. This train of ecological disturbances is appearing more and more, with intensities increasing in scale and scope. Climate scientists have definitively linked these climate impacts to increases in anthropogenic greenhouse gas (GHG) emissions resulting in increasing global average temperatures that continue to break records (Intergovernmental Panel on Climate Change (IPCC) 2013, 2014a; National Climate Assessment 2014; Steffen and Hughes 2013; Steffen, Hughes and Karoly 2013).

The vast majority of climate scientists are confident that GHG emissions from human activities since the Industrial Revolution have been the principal contributor to global climate change (IPCC 2013, 2014a, 2014b; Gillett et al. 2012; Santer et al. 2013). As human beings turn the wheels of industrial societies, massive amounts of GHGs are emitted. According to the fifth report of the IPCC, 'Anthropogenic [GHG] emissions are mainly driven by population size, economic activity, lifestyle, energy use, land-use patterns, technology and climate policy' (IPCC 2014a: 8). With increasing atmospheric GHGs enveloping the Earth, the global mean temperature has shot upwards, disturbing the previously held safe space for life on Earth to thrive.

In response to these threats, the international community in 1992 produced a landmark agreement to collectively address increasing atmospheric GHG concentrations. Through the United Nations Framework Convention on Climate Change (UNFCCC), governments agreed 'to achieve...stabilization of [GHG] concentrations in the atmosphere at a level that would prevent dangerous anthropogenic interference with the climate system' (Article 2 of the Convention). At Copenhagen in 2009, the Parties to the Convention agreed in principle to limit warming to less than +2°C – the international and political definition of a 'safe' threshold – but failed to impose mandatory action (Copenhagen Accord 2009). Despite the set target, debates about what constitutes a 'safe' climate and the basis of establishing +2°C as the level of dangerous anthropogenic interference persist (see Victor and Kennel 2014; Hansen et al. 2013, 2008; Lenton 2011); at current warming, a host of negative impacts already occur. It also appears that, even with the Paris agreement, current emissions trajectory will most likely exceed +2°C warming.

In October 2015, the monthly mean carbon dioxide (CO_2) level reached 398.29 parts per million (ppm) (National Oceanic and Atmospheric Administration 2015). This measurement enhances our understanding that atmospheric GHG concentrations leading to +2°C warming are close to being breached. Between 2000 and 2011, emissions have grown at an average rate of 3.1% per year; a majority can be attributed to increasing use of fossil fuels (Peters et al. 2013: 4). In 2012, global emissions were estimated to be already 58% greater than 1990 levels (Peters et al. 2013). The Global Carbon Atlas (2015) shows 2013 emissions at 36,131 $MtCO_2$, a 2.3% increase from 2012. Emissions from fossil fuel combustion and industrial processes made up 78% of total emission increase (IPCC 2014b: 6) and continue to accumulate. Climate policy aimed at curbing future emissions, meanwhile, seriously lags behind.

The scientific urgency to reduce emissions swiftly is met with political sluggishness; instead of a rapid action to curb trajectories, many governments continue to provide structural and institutional support for high-carbon industrialisation, ignoring evidence-based climate science (McCright and Dunlap 2010; Washington and Cook 2011). International collaborative action is seen as so ineffective that even the widely praised 2015 Paris climate agreement is actually bereft of ambition regarding rapid emissions reduction – a challenge that consistently has been attributed to free-riding (Nordhaus 2015; Wagner and Weitzman 2015).

Vested interests also continue to obstruct effective climate policy as demonstrated by their strong influence in government policy and regulations. The vast networks of huge and powerful industries and multinational corporations carry authority over national governments, international agreements, and the media (Dunlap and McCright 2010; Washington and Cook 2011; McCright and Dunlap 2010; Oreskes and Conway 2010; Pearse 2007; Harrison 2007). These industries, which include the fossil fuel, cement, steel, aluminium and motor vehicle industries, and many large fossil-based electricity utilities, block climate legislation in Parliaments, lobby for continued fossil fuel extraction, undermine climate science, and spread disinformation in the media and public forums (Diesendorf 2009).

Vested interests had successfully introduced structural and institutional barriers into policy to obstruct climate mitigation that, along with the persistent free-riding challenge, will continue to allow atmospheric GHG concentration to increase. With these challenges for effective mitigation in place, high-carbon industrialisation could continue in many countries for many more years to come. The lacklustre targets of the Paris agreement show the continuing relevance of fossil-fuelled development. New and huge efforts to extract more fossil fuels, including from unconventional sources, are indeed proceeding at faster rates. The high-carbon pathway endures despite the series of impacts the changing climate have already brought.

The ongoing dramatic climate changes illustrate that the climate issue is a challenge facing the present generation as well as unborn future generations. These impacts are already disrupting people's lives and reordering societies in cultural, environmental, and geographic spaces and contexts, and lacklustre and ineffective climate policy only intensifies social and environmental pressures.

The basic threat to civilisation, according to Lester Brown (2009), is extreme drought. Droughts cause famines, which lead to failed states, and even resource wars (cf. Dai 2012). Modern-day Syria offers a lens to view how droughts – a closely examined impact of climate change – could act as 'threat multiplier' to social upheavals. The Syrian drought of 2007–2010, Collins et al. (2015) conclude in a study, pushed impoverished Syrian farmers to migrate into urban areas only to be shocked by high food prices. Alongside other triggers, resource-related issues helped to ignite the revolution against Bashar al-Assad and a civil war, which destabilised the region, created the conditions for the emergence of ISIS as a terror group, and sent thousands of refugees fleeing. When the crisis spilled into Europe in 2015, the largest exodus of refugees since World War II was shown extensively in news reports all over the world (Jones and Shaheen 2015).

The changes that have started reordering human societies trigger the human impulse to carry on short-term adaptation. This impulse could lead governments to maintain the integrity and security of their territorial borders as we have seen in some countries in Europe, by building seawalls, investing in warning technologies, and requiring coastal-based citizens to raise the heights of their dwellings. Such primal instincts to adapt to change, however, are only band-aid solutions that only those with ample resources can afford. Those directly affected, mostly the poor and the underprivileged, are left to suffer. While disaster response and adaptation are essential, the problem will persist in centuries and millennia unless it is rapidly and effectively addressed at its root causes.

Thus far, the climate narrative is framed as something burdensome. I think otherwise.

This book offers strategic opportunities to rapidly address the drivers of anthropogenic climate change. It avoids debilitating pessimisms and instead embarks on a *Gedankenexperiment* to design and develop the most optimistic strategies that frame climate action as one of the greatest opportunity for social, technical, political, economic and cultural change. This book argues that it is essential to engage in pragmatic ways to address climate change drivers rather than dwelling on their psychologically debilitating effects (cf. Hodder and Martin 2009; Stoknes 2015). Preventing the adverse consequences of global warming, however, can only be possible with early, rapid, and strong climate mitigation – an action that can be framed as beneficial.

This book provides policy advice and strategies to avoid future climate change impacts. Eschewing these burdens remains possible – if we act now. This book is based upon scientific findings and insights about the risks of continued high-carbon pathways, joining the call from IPCC scientists:

> Substantial emission reductions over the next few decades can reduce climate risks in the 21st century and beyond, increase prospects for effective adaptation, reduce the costs and challenges of mitigation in the longer term and contribute to climate-resilient pathways for sustainable development [without which,]…warming by the end of the 21st century will lead to high to very high risk of severe, widespread, and irreversible impacts globally *(high confidence)*.
>
> (IPCC 2014a: 17)

The message from the scientific community is clear. The longer we delay the process of shrinking anthropogenic emissions, the more drastic reductions are required to stay within 'safe' temperature levels where life-as-we-know-it can continue to thrive.

But can we still revert the Earth's temperature back to 'safe' levels?

Potentially, yes.

This book explores this potential.

What this book offers

Much of the literature on climate mitigation focuses on technological change and economic arguments in an effort to determine what policies, if any, should be adopted to drive climate mitigation (e.g. Stern 2007; Garnaut 2008, 2011; Nordhaus 1990, 2015). The economic and technical construction of climate policy, however, can be restrictive since they largely ignore the governance and social aspects – which inarguably are more challenging to navigate and address. This book offers a holistic view of mitigation strategies premised on the integrity of mainstream climate science, and built upon the urgency of social and political responses given the likelihood of extraordinary disruptions to the present and future generations to come.

Some scientists and academics (e.g. Matthew England in Cooper 2012; Delucchi and Jacobson 2011: 1178; Romm 2009), politicians (e.g. Al Gore in Webster and Pagnamenta 2009), and activists (e.g. The Climate Mobilization 2015; Gilding 2011; Wright and Hearps 2010: 3; Brown 2008: 67, 265) suggest that high emission, democratic states can rapidly mitigate climate change by adopting a wartime-like mobilisation to diffuse renewable energy technologies as they replace high carbon fossil fuels. This corpus of understanding assumes wartime mobilisation as a feasible policy model for meeting accelerated sociotechnical transitions. When markets fail to curb emissions, the wartime model assumes central role for the state in protecting citizens from harm. This book examines this claim, questions the usefulness of the analogy, and explores aspects that limit its use.

A general application of the wartime model for climate mitigation can be traced to Dennis Bartels' four-page article in *Human Ecology* in 2001. In this short piece, Bartels argues that similar Canadian war mobilisation programmes could be applied when 'widely-perceived increase in the frequency of extreme weather events leads to massive political support for an international effort to reduce [GHG] emissions' (Bartels 2001: 229). Bartels proposes generic strategies where renewable energy technologies and non-methane-producing foods rapidly replace high-carbon lifestyles.

Worldwatch Institute's Lester Brown (2008: 265) echoes a similar call in *Plan B 3.0* where he asserts

> [saving] civilization will take a massive mobilization, and at wartime speed. The closest analogy is the belated U.S. mobilization during the war. But unlike this chapter in history, in which one country totally restructured its economy, the Plan B mobilization required decisive action on a global scale.

Mark Delucchi and Mark Jacobson (2011) also refer to the rapid mobilisation of war technology in the 1940s, especially in the U.S.A., to bolster their argument for accelerated diffusion of wind, water and solar power technologies on a global scale. They suggest that a 'complete transformation of the energy sector would not be the first large-scale project undertaken in the US or world history' citing that '[during] World War II, the US transformed motor vehicle production factories to produce over 300,000 aircraft' and arguing that '[although wartime mobilisations] obviously differ in important economic, political, and technical ways from the [energy transition], they do suggest that the large scale of a complete transformation of the energy system is not, in itself, an insurmountable barrier' (Delucchi and Jacobson 2011: 1178).

Paul Gilding (2011: 125) in his book *The Great Disruption* also uses the climate-war analogy to establish an international 'crisis response plan to motivate government policymakers to dedicate adequate resources to a comprehensive version of such a plan, even if it was just a contingency.' Gilding's 'The One Degree War Plan,' an emergency response to bring warming below +1°C and atmospheric GHG concentrations below 350 ppm, consists of a massive rapid deployment of climate mitigation technologies.

This book joins this body of literature, extending these earlier discussions by reviewing and analysing what has been done to mobilise resources during the war and examining how wartime strategies can be used as blueprints for envisaging policy and strategies for rapid climate mitigation. It focuses on resource mobilisation aspects, particularly of labour and finance. Its principal contribution, however, is its examination of how resource mobilisation for rapid climate mitigation can be governed. It also offers an assessment of the analogy's shortcomings, one that is conspicuously absent in earlier works.

Following a review of wartime mobilisation, what generic non-technical strategies can the state adopt to rapidly reduce anthropogenic GHG emissions? What are the limitations and challenges of these strategies? This book is about 'looking back,' asking: what can World War II teach us about human capacities for mobilising aggressive sociotechnical changes following a large-scale societal threat? In particular, what have governments done to achieve accelerated socio-economic and technical changes in mobilising for war? It is also about 'looking forward,' asking: how can governments use the lessons provided by wartime histories in mitigating anthropogenic climate change? What are the limitations of the analogy? To produce a set of generic contingency strategies, this book centres its arguments around concepts of sociotechnical transitions and the role of 'the state' in mobilisation.

The contingency scenarios this book provides are not necessarily the best models for rapid response to climate mitigation. As I will argue, they may even be unattractive alternatives. What this book offers instead is a broad, yet critical and analytical evaluation of the wartime narrative as a model for envisioning a plausible plan for climate policy. The focus of the plan is on a staged international response by countries focusing on state-level approaches for rapid emissions reduction in the energy sector, the largest contributor to emissions. Emphasising how to accomplish an accelerated sustainable energy transition, this book frames the strategies around proven technologies to capture and distribute renewable energies and demand reduction by energy efficiency and energy conservation.

The solutions to anthropogenic climate change, however, comprise urgent, dramatic, large-scale, aggressive, and transformative changes in areas beyond how we obtain and consume energy. A comprehensive approach to effective mitigation ideally involves strategies in other industry sectors such as forestry and agriculture; a holistic approach to promoting green technologies across the economy; strategies to decelerate total global economic activity, consumption, and population which are, at one conceptual level, the other drivers of environmental destruction (Dietz and O'Neill 2013; Daly and Farley 2004; cf. Feng et al. 2015); and a rethinking of socio-political-economic paradigms that define contemporary governance arrangements (Peters et al. 2013; Anderson and Bows 2012).

This means that climate solutions should include approaches for revising ways in which societies are arranged and organised. Climate scientists Kevin Anderson and Alice Bows (2012: 640) from the Tyndall Center for Climate Change Research have stressed the need to address issues 'about the structure, values and framing of contemporary society' as part of climate solutions. Scientists at the Global Carbon Project also assert that the 'shift to a pathway with the highest likelihood to remain below 2°C above pre-industrial levels…requires high levels of technological, social and political innovations, and an increasing need to rely on net negative emissions in the future' (Peters et al. 2013; cf. Friedlingstein et al. 2011; cf. Global Energy Assessment 2012; cf. Van Vliet et al. 2012). Envisaging climate policy that encompasses these complex challenges is inarguably one of our time's most important questions.

This book does not claim to have all the answers to these big questions. Rather, it seeks to contribute to the ongoing debate about the use of a wartime analogy to frame how we think about contemporary climate mitigation strategies. It uses a *Gedankenexperiment* based on a thinking aloud protocol where historical social change events at wartime are revisited, analysed and considered to think through their consequences as a structure for social change strategies in the contemporary context. To the best of my knowledge, this book offers the first of this kind of methodology to be applied to climate policy although analysis of one or more histories for their contemporary applications has already been a staple in various fields of scientific inquiry (e.g. Hilton and Liu 2008; Liu and Laszlo 2007; Jasanoff 2005; Liu and Hilton 2005; Chang 2002; Reicher and Hopkins 2001; Schwartz 1996a; Olick and Robbins 1998; Tilly 1984a, 1984b, 1993; Skocpol 1979; Diamond 1997; Rostow 1990 [1960]).

Through the lessons of histories, this book offers two qualitative scenarios: a sustainable energy transition scenario that would lead to decarbonisation of the growth economy, and a rapid mitigation scenario using wartime mobilisation as model to govern rapid climate mitigation. The scenarios reinforce each other, and are both anticipatory, aiming to avoid climate strategies that are limited to standard responses to adaptation, crises, and disasters. In building these scenarios, I have employed an 'envisioning' process – a scenario analysis that 'use[s] the imagination to consider alternative future situations, as they may evolve from the present, with a view to improving immediate and near-term decision making' (Hughes 2009: 4).

Scenarios have been prominently used as structured ways of forethinking in contemporary policymaking and business strategising. Some of the early uses include explorations of possible consequences of nuclear proliferation after World War II (e.g. Kahn and Wiener 1967), but later uses were more prominent within the business community (e.g. Schwartz 1996b [1991]; Ralston and Wilson 2006; Shell International 2013). Another precursor to contemporary scenario analysis is systems modelling, such as the scenarios developed in the Club of Rome's *Limits to Growth* (Meadows et al. 1972) and Häfele's (1981) long-term energy options in *Energy in a Finite World*. Other streams include discussions on how to reach envisioned desirable futures in the energy field, such as Lovins' (1976, 1977) 'soft energy paths', and Robinson's (1982) backcasting studies to analyse possible future energy paths.

After the 1992 Conference on Environment and Development in Rio de Janeiro, which produced the UNFCCC, scenarios were published in the context of sustainability, including climate change models developed by Rotmans, Hulme and Downing (1994) and by Leggett, Pepper and Swart (1992). Sustainability scenarios, such as the United Nations Environment

Programme's (2012) Global Environment Outlook reports and the Millennium Ecosystem Assessment (2005), have also been produced following these traditions.

This book follows the qualitative or narrative tradition of scenario building, while complementing well-established quantitative-based scenario analysis and technical models on climate mitigation and on sustainable energy transitions. The scenarios present narratives that attempt to capture other influencers of transitions such as surprises, uncertainties, causal interactions, and social system shifts, which are impossible to account for in the quantitative tradition. By giving a voice to these qualitative elements, the scenarios in this book hope to provide a broader perspective compared to those provided by mathematical and technical models alone.

The scenarios in this book are also descriptive and normative. They are descriptive because they describe possible developments starting from what we know about contemporary socio-technical-economic-political conditions, towards articulating a plausible future development and exploring the consequences of this future. They are normative because they are constructed and aimed at a future afforded with a specific subjective value. The scenarios are organised narratives assessing the plausibility and consequences of trying to achieve beneficial outcomes, and trying to avoid the risks of costly ones. Although the subject of the scenarios is the future, they can catalyse and guide appropriate action today. The strategies needed to implement them, nonetheless, are never foolproof; this book does not claim that the scenarios represent the best, most comprehensive framework for effective climate mitigation. The readers, however, may find it useful in instigating future debates, inciting social action and activism, and spurring progressive policymaking.

Sociotechnical transitions

Sustainable energy transition to achieve the ambitious objectives of rapid mitigation involves innovations at a systemic level to change the fundamental way societies 'produce' and 'consume' energy. In essence, this transition belongs to the ambit of a multilevel sociotechnical transition – a body of scholarship that provides insights on the material, technical, institutional, and cultural processes of transition. Sociotechnical transition scholarship also highlights the ways in which technologies are embedded in a much broader and complex social context consisting of public policy, market forces, infrastructure investments, the knowledge and practices of scientists and engineers, social networks, and consumer behaviours and preferences (Rip and Kemp 1998). It is also concerned with the interactions between actors and institutions at multiple spatial levels to create 'spaces for innovation' (Sunley 2008; Amin 2002). As envisaged in this book, sociotechnical transition refers to 'a fundamental change in structure (e.g. organisations, institutions), culture (e.g. norms, behavior) and practices (e.g. routines, skills)' (Loorbach and Rotmans 2010 quoted in Lachman 2013: 270; cf German Advisory Council on Global Change (WBGU) 2011) – a dynamic pathway that explicitly provides an alternative to rapidly affect change.

In analysing the dynamics of sociotechnical transitions, the Multilevel Perspective (MLP) has received increasing attention as a salient framework. The MLP comprises an

> interplay of developments at three analytical levels: niches (the locus for radical innovations), sociotechnical regimes (the locus of established practices and associated rules that stabilise existing systems), and an exogenous sociotechnical landscape…Each 'level' refers to heterogeneous configurations of elements; higher 'levels' are more stable than lower 'levels' in terms of number of actors and degrees of alignment between the elements.
>
> (Geels 2011: 26)

The MLP describes how the three levels interact in the dynamic unfolding of sociotechnical transitions. A sustainable energy transition, in the context of rapid mitigation and following the MLP framework, occurs after a major change in a way where particular societal functions are fulfilled or, in other words, when there has been an energy 'regime' shift. Regime is a short-hand for a series of complex, nested real world phenomena, embodying the natural, physical, social, economic, cultural and cognitive elements (Rip and Kemp 1998; Geels 2002).

The MLP could be used as a conceptual tool in steering rapid mitigation through sustainable energy transition. First, MLP offers the advantages of scope – a key element in envisaging rapid mitigation strategies, since it provides a bird's eye view of transitions to guide the search for patterns, causes and impacts of different phenomena during transitions (Geels 2011). Second, it has been used to explain past (e.g. Geels 2002, 2005, 2006, 2007) and contemporary transitions (e.g. Kern 2012; Nakamura, Kajikawa and Suzuki 2012), including those in the energy sector (e.g. Yuan, Xu and Hu 2012), which is seen in this book's use of historical mobilisation to inform a sustainable energy transition. Third, it points out the importance of nurturing innovations within 'niche' spaces, such as by providing 'protection' from mainstream markets and pressures (Geels 2011). This relates to how mitigation technologies as innovative niches are to be 'protected' by public policy and regulations, and to be steered to disrupt and overtake an incumbent high carbon regime – a fundamental assumption in this book's contingency scenarios. Fourth, it informs how to influence landscape processes by shifting public attitudes, interpreting landscape trends in ways that challenge dominant regimes, and by dismantling and reconfiguring existing regimes through proposals of new visions for the future (Geels 2011). The extraordinary disruptions to the environment brought about by climate impacts and the conceptual need to redesign social paradigms are the assumed landscape disrupters for the rapid mitigation scenarios envisaged in this book.

Although the MLP provides a relatively simple, but highly flexible, framework for exploring and seeking to influence transitions in particular sociotechnical systems, it has some criticisms. A common critique revolves around MLP displaying a technological bias that makes it too functionalist, rationalist and structural in approach and, thus, inadequately conceptualises actors and agency (Genus and Coles 2008). Frank Geels (2011: 29), the framework's principal developer, however, argues that this is a misdirected criticism since MLP is 'shot through with agency, because the trajectories and multi-level alignments are always enacted by social groups.' This book also refutes this critique by drawing attention to innovations in technology and highlighting the agency of state-based actors in shaping rapid mitigation processes, and by broadly identifying and describing other actors in relation to the particular sociotechnical regime and niches under study.

Another critique of the MLP pertains to its focus on a specific regime, underplaying interactions and actors that cut across multiple regimes. Although this book is primarily focused on the energy regime, the sustainable energy transition it supports accounts for social activities that have repercussions and implications for other regimes. The scale, multilevel dynamism, and non-linearity of rapid climate mitigation through sustainable energy transition suggest that its scale, speed and endpoints could be envisaged. A key strand of this book emphasises a deliberate, yet systematic, coordination of structural changes by providing sociotechnical toolboxes, presented as generic contingency plans, to influence transition speed and direction. This coordination mechanism expects to cut across multiple regimes.

'The state' and mobilisations

This book re-affirms the significance of the state in modern polity as it coordinates and intervenes in climate policy for rapid mitigation through sustainable energy transition. States are maintaining political, economic, and social frameworks, retaining legal arrangements, collecting economic resources through taxation, expenditures for public goods and services, and administering the bureaucracy (Duit, Feindt and Meadowcroft 2016). Based on this experience, expertise, and capacity, states can be brought to the fore as principal actors in the large-scale transitions for rapid mitigation.

Through national regulations they sponsor and implement, states have been key actors in the environmental domain (Sands and Peel 2012). States are experienced in fixing market failures, and also in actively shaping new markets (Mazzucato 2015). These are key aspects that this book highlights.

States operate at multi-levels of governance, from towns to cities to states or provinces. International treaties and organisations are also largely dependent on the states that forged them. States, therefore, 'remain the most powerful human mechanism for collective action that can compel obedience and redistribute resources' (Duit, Feindt and Meadowcroft 2016: 3).

For rapid climate mitigation, this book argues that some form of executive control is needed (cf. Peters et al. 2013) and explores the various options that might work. A simplified definition of governance is about deciding who can do what, who will monitor it, and how norms and rules are modified and changed over time (Ostrom 2010). It also refers to the structures and processes that influence decisions that actors make within the system, including national and local policymakers, large firms and new entrants, consumers, and how these choices could give rise to changes to the system, in this book the climate-energy system (cf. Smith 2009).

In this book, I use a particular notion of governance to denote: (1) the politics and economics of the climate-energy system, and the interests involved in supporting or opposing rapid mitigation approaches; (2) the internal operation and management of these approaches; and (3) the interaction between climate mitigation technologies and the social organisations they create – whether they produce competition or collaboration, whether they are controlling or democratic, and whether access to them is open or closed (Coutard 1999). I use these meanings to describe the prominent role of the state in mobilisation for rapid mitigation: planning and control, which are also the basic apparatuses of welfare states.

The history of welfare states can be traced from social programmes associated with Bismarck's Germany in the 1880s to the post-war boom in welfare state expansion that came to maturity and to an end in the mid-1970s (cf. Pierson 1996). In this arrangement, the state ensures employment, economic progress, social security, health, and housing. It does this using three principal approaches: taxation and investments; state planning and economic intervention; and extending the bureaucratic apparatus for social administration (Rose and Miller 1992).

At post-war, state planning meant the central direction by the state in the interest of overall economic prosperity and social justice, which entailed nationalisation of industries, including the energy industry, and the creation of 'planned communities' (Giddens 2011). This period characterises general peace with the creation of the United Nations, the hegemony of the U.S. and its Allies, the Cold War, and the emergence of social welfare. In western democracies, the concept of welfare states meant the expanded role for the state to achieve coordination in a complex society (Kerr et al. 1960) echoing early Marxist accounts (cf. Offe 1972; O'Connor 1973).

As welfare states gained ground, the role of the state in mobilisation was evident in technological innovation – such as in research and development – and support for the massive deployment of 'new' technologies. The U.S. Apollo project for manned lunar landings (Amidon 2005; Read and Lermit 2005) and the early days of the semiconductor and computer industries and the Internet for the U.S. military (Cowan and Foray 1995) – both state-led enterprises – are some examples. Today's innovations, the Internet and GPS as two examples, would not be around if not for government funds (Mazzucato 2015).

In the mid-1970s, a shift occurred as the neoliberalism idea aligned with the proliferation of politically conservative programmes in the U.K., U.S.A., and elsewhere in Europe. In contrast with the approaches in welfare states, neoliberalism warns against big government and state interference and highlights the inefficiencies of planned economies. The strength of free markets is underscored in policies that include trade liberalisation, reduced entitlements, deregulation, and privatisation programmes in previously state-controlled institutions. The turn towards overreliance on free markets contributed to an evident long-term slump in the state's capacity to govern (Rhodes 1994). Thus, the traditional steering and coordinating roles for central governments have become increasingly ineffective. The role of the state has also changed in relation to environmental problems with many governments moving from direct regulation towards more market-based solutions (Meadowcroft 2005). The neoliberal agenda, however, shows fissures as demonstrated in the market's inability to contain the 2008 Global Financial Crisis, to address the global economic slowdown and widening inequalities. With many governments beholden to private capital, contemporary states with neoliberal orientations seem to be hampered in their ability to also address climate change.

For neoliberalism's 'catastrophic and ongoing failure…to think differently about climate change' (Anderson and Bows 2012: 640) and its failure to promote economic and social equality (e.g. Piketty 2014; Stiglitz 2003, 2013; Chang 2002), this book puts the state back at the core of public policy. In many ways, this book revitalises the state's pre-1975 apparatus of planning and control as a locus of regulation, administration, and coordination. In envisaging a reclaimed and revitalised role for the state in the mobilisation for rapid mitigation, it reinforces what is called a paradigm shift – or what Karl Polanyi (1944) referred to as 'Great Transformation' – about states, in primacy over the market, responding to the climate challenge. Polanyi (1944) argues that the embedding of innovation processes into a constitutional state, democracy, and the creation of a welfare state contributed to the success in stabilising 'modern industrialised societies.' The role for the state in rapid mitigation could, therefore, be viewed as a return to state planning (cf. WBGU 2011; Giddens 2011), a continuing evolution of modern environmental states (Duit, Feindt and Meadowcroft 2016), or some hybrid of the two (e.g. Pierre 2000).

The new politics that the state inhabits in this book's vision, however, are different from welfare states developed in the first half of the last century until the 1970s, albeit there are a number of parallels (cf. Duit, Feindt and Meadowcroft 2016). The age of climate consequences, forces of globalisation, multilevel and multi-spatial contexts, and the recognition of the morality and ethics of climate mitigation shape the social, political, and economic policy agenda of the envisioned state interventions for rapid mitigation. This is unlike the age of expansion characterising early politics of welfare.

Plan of the book

In more detail, this book is organised into the following chapters.

Chapter 1 reviews the latest available climate science and observations, as well as approaches to addressing the climate challenge. Are international targets and national climate policies adequate to ensure that warming stays within 'safe levels'? What is meant by 'safe' and what does it entail? Within current warming, what changes have been occurring? How are these changes impacting lives? What are the climate mitigation responses from governments? If 'safe' thresholds are breached, what changes can be expected? Why is there a need for rapid mitigation? What does this mean to the international community? Who are and will be most impacted? What are the characteristics of living in the age of climate consequences?

Chapter 2 offers a scenario in which governments, following a series of catastrophic climate impacts, agree on an international binding target to implement rapid mitigation. Why use catastrophe as a basis? How does psychology rationalise this assumption? What could this international agreement look like? How could the burdens of mitigation be shared among nation-states? Which countries must embark on rapid footing first? What could the timeline for accelerated climate mitigation look like? Without an international agreement, what other arrangements for international cooperation can be envisaged? Following technical models and scenarios establishing the plausibility of accelerated sustainable energy transitions as an effective solution for climate mitigation, what policies can be adopted? What technologies are included and excluded? What are the contestations and debates surrounding these technologies? Since this is a sociotechnical transition, what sociotechnical changes can be expected?

Chapter 3 presents a historical analysis of wartime mobilisation, and, based on this review, develops a contingency scenario for mobilising resources for state-led rapid climate mitigation. What does the comparison between wartime and mitigation tell in terms of scale, speed, and scope? What makes the analogy appropriate? What similarities and differences can be observed? What do these similarities and differences tell for designing contemporary climate mitigation strategies?

Chapter 4 presents how financial resources could be mobilised to meet the scale, speed and scope requirements of rapid climate mitigation following strategies provided by wartime finance. How did combatant countries mobilise wartime finance? What are the fiscal policies used? What challenges and repercussions have been encountered? In the accelerated approach to mitigation, what is the scale of finance required? Following wartime experience, how could financial resources be mobilised for rapid mitigation? What similar strategies can be adopted? What aspects make financial mobilisation for mitigation different from wartime? In light of these differences, what innovations in financial mobilisation strategies are required? What challenges need to be hurdled to meet the financial requirements?

Chapter 5 follows a similar structure and composition as Chapter 4, but focuses on labour resources.

Chapter 6 presents governance strategies developed at wartime and examines possible similar and critical strategies for governing rapid mitigation. How did states ensure efficient and effective resource mobilisations in munitions factories? What were the roles for industries and businesses in wartime? What power did governments employ? What was the role for the public? What parliamentary oversight was introduced to avoid abuse of power? What does the wartime governance experience imply for governing the mobilisation for an accelerated approach to mitigation? What institutional arrangements can work best under this envisaged scenario? What does this mean for democracy and public participation? What governance challenges need to be overcome for rapid mitigation to be effective? What aspects differentiate governing the mobilisation for climate from wartime mobilisations? What does this mean in designing contingency governance strategies for rapid climate mitigation?

Chapter 7 discusses the challenges, limitations, and uncertainties of the scenarios developed in the preceding three chapters.

The concluding chapter highlights the strengths of the contingency scenario, summarises the limitations and challenges of the approach, and presents some ways forward.

References

Amidon, J.M. 2005, 'America's Strategic Imperative: a "Manhattan Project" for energy', *Joint Forces Quarterly*, vol. 39, pp. 68–77.

Amin, A. 2002, 'Spatialities of globalisation', *Environment and Planning A*, vol. 34, pp. 385–399.

Anderson, K. & Bows, A. 2012, 'A new paradigm for climate change', *Nature Climate Change*, vol. 2, pp. 639–640.

Bartels, D. 2001, 'Wartime mobilization to counter severe global climate change', *Human Ecology*, vol. 10, pp. 229–232.

Brown, L.R. 2008, *Plan B 3.0: Mobilizing to Save Civilization*, W.W. Norton & Co., New York; London, U.K.

Brown, L.R. 2009, 'Could food shortages bring down civilization?' *Scientific American*, May, http://bit.ly/1Hc313m.

Chang, H.-J. 2002, *Kicking Away the Ladder: Development Strategy in Historical Perspective*, Anthem Press, London, U.K.

Collins, P.C., Mohtadi, S., Cane, M.A., Seager, R. & Kushnir, Y. 2015, 'Climate change in the Fertile Crescent and implications of the recent Syrian drought', *PNAS*, vol. 112, pp. 3241–3246.

Cooper, H. 2012, 'Transcript, 7.30 program', *Australian Broadcasting Corporation*, 3 December, http://ab.co/1fowzxZ.

Copenhagen Accord 2009, Decision 2/CP.15, in *Report of the Conference of Parties on its fifteenth session, held in Copenhagen from 7 to 19 December 2009*, UNFCCC, FCCC/CP/2009/11/Add.1, http://bit.ly/1kItvyE.

Coutard, O. 1999, 'Introduction: the evolving forms of governance of large technical systems', in O. Coutard (ed.), *The Governance of Large Technical Systems*, Routledge, London, U.K., & New York, U.S.A., pp. 1–16.

Cowan, R. & Foray, D. 1995, 'Quandaries in the economics of dual technologies and spillovers from military to civilian research and development', *Research Policy*, vol. 24, pp. 851–868.

Dai, A. 2012, 'Increasing drought under global warming in observations and models', *Nature Climate Change*, vol. 3, pp. 52–58.

Daly, H.E. & Farley, J. 2004, *Ecological Economics: Principles and Applications*, Island Press, Washington, D.C., U.S.A.

Delucchi, M. & Jacobson, M. 2011, 'Providing all global energy with wind, water, and solar power, part II: reliability, system and transmission costs, and policies', *Energy Policy*, vol. 39, pp. 1170–1190.

Diamond, J. 1997, *Guns, Germs, and Steel: The Fates of Human Societies*, W.W. Norton & Co., New York, U.S.A.

Diesendorf, M. 2009, *Climate Action: A Campaign Manual for Greenhouse Solutions*, University of New South Wales Press, Sydney, Australia.

Dietz, R. & O'Neill, D. 2013, *Enough is Enough: Building a Sustainable Economy in a World of Finite Resources*, Berrett-Koehler Publishers, San Francisco, California, U.S.A.

Duit, A., Feindt, P.H. & Meadowcroft, J. 2016, 'Greening Leviathan: the rise of the environmental state?' *Environmental Politics*, vol. 25, pp. 1–23.

Feng, K., Davis, S.J., Sun, L. & Hubacek, K. 2015, 'Drivers of the US CO_2 emissions 1997–2013', *Nature Communications*, doi: 10.1038/ncomms8714.

Friedlingstein, P., Solomon, S., Plattner, G.-K., Knutti, R., Ciais, P. & Raupach, M.R. 2011, 'Long-term climate implications of twenty-first century options for carbon dioxide emission mitigation', *Nature Climate Change*, vol. 1, pp. 457–461.

Garnaut, R. 2008, *The Garnaut Climate Change Review: Final Report*, Cambridge University Press, Port Melbourne, Victoria, Australia.

Garnaut, R. 2011, *The Garnaut Review 2011: Australia in the Global Response to Climate Change*, Cambridge University Press, Melbourne, Australia; New York, U.S.A.

Geels, F.W. 2002, 'Technological transitions as evolutionary reconfiguration processes: a multi-level perspective and a case study', *Research Policy*, vol. 31, pp. 1257–1274.

Geels, F.W. 2005, 'The dynamics of transitions in socio-technical systems: a multi-level analysis of the transition pathway from horse-drawn carriages to automobiles 1860–1930', *Technological Analysis and Strategic Management*, vol. 17, pp. 445–476.

Geels, F.W. 2006, 'Co-evolutionary and multi-level dynamics in transitions: the transformation of aviation systems and the shift from propeller to turbojet (1930–1970)', *Technovation*, vol. 26, pp. 999–1016.

Geels, F.W. 2007, 'Analysing the breakthrough of rock 'n' roll (1930–1970): multi-regime interaction and reconfiguration in the multi-level perspective', *Techno-logical Forecasting & Social Change*, vol. 74, pp. 1411–1431.

Geels, F.W. 2011, 'The multi-level perspective on sustainability transitions: responses to eight criticisms', *Environmental Innovation and Societal Transitions*, vol. 1, pp. 24–40.

Genus, A. & Coles, A.-M. 2008, 'Rethinking the multi-level perspective of technological transitions', *Research Policy*, vol. 37, pp. 1436–1445.

German Advisory Council on Global Change (WBGU) 2011, *World in Transition: A Social Contract for Sustainability*, WBGU, Berlin, Germany.

Giddens, A. 2011, *The Politics of Climate Change*, 2nd edn, Polity Press, Cambridge, U.K.

Gilding, P. 2011, *The Great Disruption: How the Climate Crisis Will Transform the Global Economy*, Bloomsbury, London, U.K.

Gillett, N.P., Arora, V.K., Flato, G.M., Scinocca, J.F. & von Salzen, K. 2012, 'Improved constraints on 21st-century warming derived using 160 years of temperature observations', *Geophysical Research Letters*, vol. 39, p. 5.

Global Carbon Atlas 2015, *Emissions*, The Global Carbon Project, http://bit.ly/1JCXDMC.

Global Energy Assessment 2012, *Global Energy Assessment: Toward a Sustainable Future*, Cambridge University Press and International Institute for Applied Systems Analysis, Laxenburg, Austria.

Häfele, W. 1981, *Energy in a Finite World: A Global Systems Analysis*, Ballinger, Cambridge, Massachusetts, U.S.A.

Hansen, J., Kharecha, P., Sato, M., Masson-Delmotte, V., Ackerman, F. et al. 2013, 'Assessing "Dangerous Climate Change": required reduction of carbon emissions to protect young people, future generations and nature', *PLOS One*, vol. 8, pp. e81648.

Hansen, J., Sato, M., Kharecha, P., Beerling, D., Masson-Delmotte, V. 2008, 'Target atmospheric CO2: Where should humanity aim?' http://bit.ly/1eVM0em.

Harrison, K. 2007, 'The road not taken: climate change policy in Canada and the United States', *Global Environmental Politics*, vol. 7, pp. 92–117.

Hilton, D.J. & Liu, J.H. 2008, 'Culture and inter-group relations: the role of social representations in history', in R. Sorrentino & S. Yamaguchi (eds), *The Handbook of Motivation and Cognition: The Cultural Context*, Guilford, New York, U.S.A.

Hodder, P. & Martin, B. 2009, 'Climate crisis? The politics of emergency framing', *Economic & Political Weekly*, vol. 44, pp. 53–60.

Hodder, P. 2011, 'Climate conflict: players and tactics in the greenhouse game', PhD Thesis, University of Wollongong, Wollongong, New South Wales, Australia.

Hughes, N. 2009, 'Transition pathways to a low carbon economy: a historical overview of strategic scenario planning', Joint Working paper of the UKERC and the EON.UK/EPSRC Transition Pathways Project, May, http://bit.ly/1woCQVP.

IPCC (Intergovernmental Panel on Climate Change) 2013, 'Summary for Policymakers', in T.F. Stocker, G.D. Qin, G.-K. Plattner, M. Tignor, S.K. Allen, J. Boschung et al. (eds), *Climate Change 2013: The Physical Science Basis. Contribution of Working Group I to the Fifth Assessment Report of the IPCC*, Cambridge University Press, Cambridge, U. K.; New York, U.S.A., pp. 3–29.

IPCC 2014a, *Climate Change 2014: Synthesis Report of the Fifth Assessment Report of the IPCC*, The Core Writing Team, R.K. Pachauri & L. Meyer (eds), IPCC, http://www.ipcc.ch/report/ar5/syr/.

IPCC 2014b, 'Summary for Policymakers', in O. Edenhofer, R. Pichs-Madruga, Y. Sokona, E. Farahani, S. Kadner, et al. (eds), *Climate Change 2014: Mitigation of Climate Change, Contribution of Working Group III to the Fifth Assessment Report of the IPCC, Synthesis Report of the Fifth Assessment Report of the IPCC*, Cambridge University Press, Cambridge, U.K.; New York, U.S.A.

Jasanoff, S. 2005, *Designs on Nature: Science and Democracy in Europe and the United States*, Princeton University Press, Princeton, New Jersey, U.S.A.

Jones, S. & Shaheen, K. 2015, 'Syrian refugees: four million people forced to flee as crisis deepens', *The Guardian*, 9 July, http://bit.ly/1JQOPmn.

Kahn, H. & Wiener, A.J. 1967, *The Year 2000: A Framework for Speculation on the Next Thirty-three Years*, Macmillan, New York, U.S.A.

Kern, F. 2012, 'Using the multi-level perspective on socio-technical transitions to assess innovation policy', *Technological Forecasting and Social Change*, vol. 79, pp. 298–310.

Kerr, C., Dunlop, J., Harbison, F. & Myers, C. 1960, *Industrialism and Industrial Man*, Oxford University Press, New York, U.S.A.

Lachman, D.A. 2013, 'A survey and review of approaches to study transitions', *Energy Policy*, vol. 58, pp. 269–276.

Leggett, J., Pepper, W. & Swart, R. 1992, 'Emissions scenarios for IPCC: an update', in J. Houghton, B. Callander & S.K. Varney (eds), *Climate Change 1992: The Supplementary Report to the IPCC Scientific Assessment*, Cambridge University Press, Cambridge, U.K., pp. 69–96.

Lenton, T.M. 2011, 'Beyond 2°C: redefining dangerous climate change for physical systems', *Wiley Interdisciplinary Reviews: Climate Change*, vol. 2, pp. 451–461.

Liu, J.H. & Hilton, D.J. 2005, 'How the past weighs on the present: social representations of history and their impact on identity politics', *British Journal of Social Psychology*, vol. 44, pp. 537–556.

Liu, J.H. & Laszlo, J. 2007, 'A narrative theory of history and identity: Social identity, social representations, society and the individual', in G. Moloney & I. Walker (eds), *Social Representations and Identity: Content, Process and Power*, Palgrave Macmillan, London, U.K., pp. 85–108.

Loorbach, D. & Rotmans, J. 2010, *Transition Management and Strategic Niche Management*, Dutch Research Institute for Transitions, Rotterdam, The Netherlands.

Lovins, A. 1976, 'Energy strategy: the road not taken?' *Foreign Affairs*, vol. 55, pp. 186–217.

Lovins, A. 1977, *Soft Energy Paths*, Friends of the Earth/Ballinger, New York, U.S.A.

Mazzucato, M. 2015, *The Entrepreneurial State: Debunking Public vs. Private Sector Myths*, Public Affairs, New York. U.S.A.

McCright, A.M. & Dunlap, R.E. 2010, 'Anti-reflexivity: the American conservative movement's success in undermining climate science and policy', *Theory, Culture & Society*, vol. 27, pp. 100–133.

Meadowcroft, J. 2005, 'Environmental political economy, technological transitions and the State', *New Political Economy*, vol. 10, pp. 479–498.

Meadows, D.H., Meadows, D.L., Randers, J. & Behrens, W.W. II 1972, *Limits to Growth*, Universe Books, New York, U.S.A.

Millennium Ecosystem Assessment 2005, *Ecosystems and Human Well-being: Synthesis*, Island Press, Washington, D.C., U.S.A.

Nakamura, H., Kajikawa, Y. & Suzuki, S. 2012, 'Multi-level perspectives with technology readiness measure for aviation innovation', *Sustainability Science*, vol. 8, pp. 87–101.

National Climate Assessment 2014, *National Climate Assessment*, U.S. Global Change Research Program, Washington, D.C., U.S.A.

National Oceanic and Atmospheric Administration (NOAA) 2015, *Recent Monthly Average Mauna Loa CO_2*, NOAA Earth System Research Laboratory, http://1.usa.gov/1jKojfI.

Nordhaus, W.D. 1990, 'Slowing the greenhouse express: The economics of greenhouse warming', in H. Aaron (ed.), *Setting National Priorities: Policy for the Nineties*, Brookings, Washington, D.C., U.S.A., pp. 185–211.

Nordhaus, W.D. 2015, 'Climate clubs: Overcoming free-riding in international climate policy', *American Economic Review*, vol. 105, pp. 1339–1970.

O'Connor, J. 1973, *The Fiscal Crisis of the State*, St Martin's, New York, U.S.A.

Offe, C. 1972, 'Advanced Capitalism and the Welfare State', *Politics and Society*, vol. 2, pp. 479–488.

Olick, J. & Robbins, J. 1998, 'Social memory studies: from "collective memory" to the historical sociology of mnemonic practices', *Annual Review of Sociology*, vol. 24, pp. 105–140.

Oreskes, N. & Conway, E.M. 2010, *Merchants of Doubt: How a Handful of Scientists Obscured the Truth on Issues from Tobacco Smoke to Global Warming*, Bloomsbury Press, New York, U.S.A.

Ostrom, E. 2010, 'Polycentric systems for coping with collective action and global environmental change', *Global Environmental Change*, vol. 20, pp. 550–557.

Pearse, G. 2007, *High and Dry: John Howard, Climate Change and the Selling of Australia's Future*, Penguin, Cambelwood, Victoria, Australia.

Peters, G.P., Andrew, R.M., Boden, T., Canadell, J.G., Ciais, P. et al. 2013, 'The challenge to keep global warming below 2°C', *Nature Climate Change*, vol. 3, pp. 4–6.

Piketty, T. 2014, *Capital in the Twenty-First Century*, A. Goldhammer (trans.), Belknap Press of the Harvard University Press, Cambridge, Massachusetts, U.S.A.

Pierre, J. 2000, *Debating Governance: Authority, Steering and Democracy*, Oxford University Press, Oxford, U.K.

Pierson, P. 1996, 'The New Politics of the Welfare State', *World Politics*, vol. 48, pp. 143–179.

Polanyi, K. 1944, *The Great Transformation: The Political and Economic Origins of our Time*, Beacon Press, Boston, Massachusetts, U.S.A.

Ralston, B. & Wilson, I. 2006, *Scenario Planning Handbook: Developing Strategies in Uncertain Times*, Thompson South-Western, U.S.A.

Read, P. & Lermit, J. 2005 'Bio-energy with carbon storage (BECS): a sequential decision approach to the threat of abrupt climate change', *Energy*, vol. 30, pp. 2654–2671.

Reicher, S. & Hopkins, N. 2001, *Self and Nation*, Sage, London, U.K.

Rhodes, R. 1994, 'The hallowing out of the State', *Political Quarterly*, vol. 65, pp. 138–151.

Rip, A. & Kemp, R. 1998, 'Technological change', in S. Rayner & E.L. Malone (eds), *Human Choices and Climate Change*, Battelle Press, Columbus, Ohio, U.S.A.

Robinson, J. 1982, 'Energy backcasting: a proposed method of policy analysis', *Energy Policy*, vol. 10, pp. 337–344.

Rockström, J., Steffen, W., Noone, K., Persson, Å., Chapin, F.S. et al. 2009, 'Planetary boundaries: exploring the safe operating space for humanity', *Ecology and Society*, vol. 14, pp. 32f.

Romm, J. 2009, 'Advice to a young climate blogger: always use WWII metaphors', *Think Progress*, 11 March, http://bit.ly/1j6M31n.

Rose, N. & Miller, P. 1992, 'Political power beyond the state: problematics of government', *The British Journal of Sociology*, vol. 43, pp. 173–205.

Rostow, W.W. 1990 [1960], *The Stages of Economic Growth: A Non-Communist Manifesto*, 3rd edn, Cambridge University Press, Cambridge, U.K.

Rotmans, J., Hulme, M. & Downing, T.E. 1994, 'Climate change implications for Europe: an application of the escape model', *Global Environmental Change*, vol. 4, pp. 97–124.

Sands, P. & Peel, J. 2012, *Principles of International Environmental Law*, 3rd edn, Cambridge University Press, Cambridge, U.K.

Santer, B.D., Painter, J.F., Mears, C.A., Doutriaux, C., Caldwell, P. et al. 2013, 'Identifying human influences on atmospheric temperature', *PNAS*, vol. 110, pp. 26–33.

Schwartz, B. 1996a, 'Memory as a cultural system: Abraham Lincoln in World War II', *American Sociological Review*, vol. 61, pp. 908–927.

Schwartz, P. 1996b [1991], *The Art of the Long View: Paths to Strategic Insight for Yourself and Your Company*, Doubleday, New York, U.S.A.

Shell International 2013, *New Lens Scenarios: A Shift in Perspective for a World in Transition*, Shell International.

Skocpol, T. 1979, *States and Social Revolutions: A Comparative Analysis of France, Russia and China*, Cambridge University Press, Cambridge, U.K.

Smith, A. 2009, 'Energy governance: the challenges of sustainability', in I. Scrase & G. MacKerron (eds), *Energy for the Future: A New Agenda*, Palgrave Macmillan, Basingstoke, U.K.

Steffen, W. & Hughes, L. 2013, *The Critical Decade 2013: Climate Change Science, Risks and Responses*, The Climate Commission Secretariat, Commonwealth of Australia.

Steffen, W., Hughes, L. & Karoly, D. 2013, *The Critical Decade: Extreme Weather*, The Climate Commission Secretariat, Commonwealth of Australia.

Stern, N. 2007, *The Economics of Climate Change: The Stern Review*, Cambridge University Press, Cambridge, U.K.

Stiglitz, J. 2003, *Globalization and Its Discontents*, W.W. Norton & Company, Inc., New York, U.S.A.

Stiglitz, J. 2013, *The Prize of Inequality: How Today's Divided Society Endangers the Future*, W.W. Norton & Company, Inc., New York, U.S.A.

Stoknes, P.E. 2015, *What We Think About When We Try Not To Think About Global Warming*, Chelsea Green Publishing, White River Junction, Vermont, U.S.A.

Sunley, P. 2008, 'Relational economic geography: a partial understanding or a new paradigm?' *Economic Geography*, vol. 84, pp. 1–26.

The Climate Mobilization 2015, http://bit.ly/1iGqduV.

Tilly, C. 1984a, *Big Structures, Large Processes, Huge Comparisons*, Russell Sage Foundation, New York, U.S.A.

Tilly, C. 1984b, 'Social movements and national policies', in C. Bright & S. Harding (eds), *Statemaking and Social Movements: Essays in History and Theory*, The University of Michigan Press, Ann Arbor, Michigan, U.S.A.

Tilly, C. 1993, *European Revolutions 1492–1992*, Blackwell, Oxford, U.K.

United Nations Environment Programme 2012, *Global Environment Outlook 5: Environment for the Future We Want*, UNEP, Nairobi, Kenya.

Van Vliet, J., Van den Berg, M., Schaeffer, M., Van Vuuren, D.P., Den Elzen, M. et al. 2012, 'Copenhagen Accord Pledges imply higher costs for staying below 2°C warming', *Climatic Change*, vol. 113, pp. 551–561.

Victor, D. & Kennel, C.F. 2014, 'Ditch the 2°C warming goal', *Nature*, vol. 514, pp. 30–31.

Wagner, G. & Weitzman, M.L. 2015, *Climate Shock: the Economic Consequences of a Hotter Planet*, Princeton University Press, Princeton, New Jersey, U.S.A.

Washington, H. & Cook, J. 2011, *Climate Change Denial: Heads in the Sand*, Earthscan, London, U.K.; Washington, D.C., U.S.A.

Webster, B. & Pagnamenta, R. 2009, 'Al Gore invokes spirit of Churchill in battle against climate change', *The Times*, 8 July, http://thetim.es/1ObS3B2.

Wright, M. & Hearps, P. 2010, *Australian Sustainable Energy: Zero Carbon Australia Stationary Energy Plan*, University of Melbourne Energy Research Institute, Melbourne, Australia.

Yuan, J., Xu, Y. & Hu, Z. 2012, 'Delivering power system transition in China', *Energy Policy*, vol. 50, pp. 751–772.

1 The age of climate consequences

A global challenge, a global ambition

The principal drivers of global warming are now known with a high degree of confidence. Current mainstream scientific knowledge suggests with high certainty that the cause of increasing concentration of atmospheric greenhouse gases (GHGs) is anthropogenic. GHGs have been spewed out exceeding the natural rate that occurred before the rise of human societies, and models and scientific predictions point out the consequences of this that bring about many changes in the planet's ecology. The age of climate consequences is already upon us.

The climate agreement forged in Paris in December 2015 to address the climate challenge is the new multilateral climate response to cover the period between 2020, when the agreement should enter into force, and 2030. Within this critical decade, countries aim to bring the climate back to its safe levels through a portfolio of voluntary Intended Nationally Determined Commitments (INDCs), some of which from some high emission countries are summarised below (United Nations Framework Convention on Climate Change (UNFCCC) 2015):

- U.S.A.: an unconditional economy-wide target to reduce emissions by 26% to 28% below 2005 levels.
- China: to reduce its carbon intensity by 60% to 65% by 2030 below 2005 levels, increase the renewable energy share to 20%, expand forest stock, and peak by 2030 or earlier.
- European Union (EU): a binding, economy-wide target to reduce domestic emissions by at least 40% below 1990 levels by 2030.
- India: to lower its domestic emissions intensity by 33% to 35% by 2030 below 2005 levels, to increase the renewable energy share to 40% of installed electric power capacity by 2030, and to create an additional 2.5 to 3 $GtCO_2e$ cumulative carbon sink through additional forest cover by 2030.
- Canada: an economy-wide target to reduce emissions by 30% below 2005 levels in 2030.

- Australia: to reduce emissions by 26% to 28% from 2005 levels including land-use, land-use change and forestry (LULUCF) by 2030.
- New Zealand: to reduce emissions excluding from LULUCF by 11% below 1990 levels by 2030.
- Japan: to reduce emissions by 26% below 2013 emission levels by 2030.
- South Korea: to reduce emissions by 37% below business-as-usual (BAU) by 2030; parts of this target will be achieved through carbon credits from international market mechanisms.
- Indonesia: an unconditional 2030 GHG emissions reduction target of 29% below BAU including LULUCF emissions, and a conditional 41% reduction below BAU by 2030 with sufficient international support.
- South Africa: to reduce emissions levels to between 398 and 614 MtCO$_2$e in 2025 to 2030.
- Brazil: to reduce emissions by 37% in 2025 below 2005 levels, to increase renewable energy share to 45% in the total energy mix by 2030.
- Mexico: an unconditional 22% emissions reduction target below baseline in 2030, starting to decrease emissions in 2026; offers to reduce up to 36% below baseline with international support.

Are the aggregated voluntary Paris targets enough to meet the ambition to maintain global mean temperature below +2°C warming?

The short answer is no. Even though the 'national contributions' serve as necessary first steps toward a commitment among nations to curb global emissions, these targets may be too short or too late.

A consortium of research groups including the Potsdam Institute for Climate Impact Research, Climate Analytics, New Climate Institute, and Ecofys released a report stating that the collective targets submitted by governments could hold warming beyond +2°C (Jeffery et al. 2015). The consortium reports that only the Ethiopian and Moroccan submissions are in line with +2°C warming, while those from high emission states of Australia, Canada, Japan, New Zealand, Singapore, South Korea and Russia are 'not considered to be fair contribution...from almost any perspective' (Jeffery et al. 2015: 2). The consortium also notes that submitted commitments from China, EU, Mexico, Norway, Switzerland, and the U.S.A. are 'within the upper and least ambitious end of what could be considered as fair and if all countries put forward a similar level of ambition, warming would exceed 2°C' (Jeffery et al. 2015: 2). The consortium projects that, if government pledges in Paris are implemented, warming will most likely be around +2.7°C (Climate Action Tracker 2015).

Earlier on, climate scientists Kevin Anderson and Alice Bows (2012: 639) from the Tyndall Centre for Climate Change Research, noted that end-point targets have no scientific basis, arguing: 'what governs future global temperatures and other adverse climate impacts are the emissions from yesterday, today and those released in the next few years.' Thus, although climate mitigation targets may look good to some, because they purport to bring some certainty and reduce ambiguities, what matters in addressing the climate challenge is for emissions to peak soon and steeply decline. The International Panel on Climate Change (IPCC 2014), itself, has already moved away from using rates of reduction over time in its Fifth Assessment Report (AR5), and instead has adopted what is called a 'global cumulative carbon budget.'

The 'budget' quantifies, for the first time in IPCC's publication history, the view of some climate scientists and activists who have been warning that continued fossil fuel combustion destabilises the climate (e.g. Hansen, Sato and Ruedy 2012; Meinshausen et al. 2009; German Advisory Council for Global Change (WBGU) 2009; Global Energy Assessment 2012; McKibben 2012). The carbon budget language says that burning a trillion tonnes of carbon, between 1750 and 2500 equates to a warming of more than +2°C (Allen et al. 2009). Yet by 2011, more than half of this budget – 0.531 trillion tonnes – had already been emitted. The World Resources Institute estimated that, with unabated emissions, the budget would be used up in 30 years (Levin 2013).

Despite the use of 'carbon budget' as a concept by some scientists, it is essential to note that there are some in the climate scientific community who do not accept the idea arguing that the message could be interpreted to mean there is enough of the budget left to spend – in other words, we can still continue burning carbon – when there is actually no carbon budget left to burn. Climate scientist Ken Caldeira, for instance, worries about the use of the concept for two reasons:

> There are no such things as 'allowable CO_2 emissions.' There are only 'damaging CO_2 emissions' or 'dangerous CO_2 emissions.' Every CO_2 emission causes additional damage and creates additional risk... If you look at how our politicians operate, if you tell them you have a budget of XYZ, they will spend XYZ.
>
> (Caldeira's email to Romm 2013)

Caldeira's argument makes sense. As long as the 'budget' is left unspent, the 'allowance' only gives emitters a reason to continue with their fossil burning business when emissions should have already peaked and declined.

Indeed, data shows that emissions continue to rise. The Global Carbon Atlas (2015) reveals that between 1990 and 2013 emissions rose at an average of 2.2% per year, and that between 2012 and 2013 emissions had increased by 2.3%. In absolute terms and emissions measured in $MtCO_2$, Table 1.1 presents a list of the top 20 high emission countries in 1990, 2000, and 2013.

The table reveals how countries have remained with fossil-fuelled development despite more than three decades of scientific warning on climate change and more than two decades after nations forged an international agreement to curb emissions. Since 1751 – the dawn of the Industrial Revolution, approximately 356 billion MtC have been released into the atmosphere from fossil fuel consumption with half of these emissions spewed during the last

Table 1.1 Top 20 high-emission states in 1990, 2000 and 2013, in MtCO$_2$

	1990	2000	2013
1	**U.S.A.**: 4,764	**U.S.A.**: 5,709	*China*: 9,977
2	*China*: 2,459	*China*: 3,402	**U.S.A.**: 5,233
3	*Russian Federation*: 2,355	*Russian Federation*: 1,557	*India*: 2,407
4	**Japan**: 1,094	*Japan*: 1,219	*Russian Federation*: 1,812
5	**Germany**: 1,013	*India*: 1,186	**Japan**: 1,246
6	Ukraine: 706	**Germany**: 829	**Germany**: 759
7	*India*: 690	**United Kingdom**: 543	**South Korea**: 616
8	**United Kingdom**: 571	**Canada**: 534	Iran: 611
9	**Canada**: 450	**Italy**: 451	Saudi Arabia: 519
10	**Italy**: 417	**South Korea**: 447	**Canada**: 503
11	**France**: 399	Mexico: 381	Indonesia: 494
12	**Poland**: 367	Iran: 372	*Brazil*: 482
13	*South Africa*: 333	*South Africa*: 368	Mexico: 466
14	Mexico: 314	**France**: 365	**United Kingdom**: 462
15	Kazakhstan: 288	**Australia**: 329	*South Africa*: 448
16	**Australia**: 287	*Brazil*: 328	**Italy**: 353
17	**South Korea**: 247	Ukraine: 321	**France**: 344
18	North Korea: 245	**Poland**: 301	**Australia**: 341
19	**Spain**: 219	Saudi Arabia: 297	Thailand: 327
20	Saudi Arabia: 218	**Spain**: 294	Turkey: 325

Author's construction from the Global Carbon Atlas (2015)

Note: Countries in bold are advanced economies (International Monetary Fund (IMF) 2015: 171); those in italics are emerging transitional economies in the BRICS group; the rest are developing countries (IMF 2015: 174).

thirty years (Boden, Marland and Andres 2012). The Paris agreement, despite its good intentions to curb emissions, appears to be an ineffective mechanism for ensuring that emissions level are contained to keep temperature rise within 'safe' levels.

What comprises 'safe' levels? For a long time, scientific, economic, and political circles have grappled with this question. James Hansen, once a team leader at the National Aeronautics and Space Administration (NASA), was among the scientists warning the world about global warming decades ago (Hansen et al. 1981). Hansen has suggested that atmospheric carbon concentrations – measured in parts per million (ppm) of carbon dioxide – should be used as a benchmark demarcating 'safe' from 'dangerous'. For Hansen and his team, atmospheric carbon concentrations must be reduced to the range of

300 ppm to 325 ppm, and climate mitigation policy should be benchmarked around these numbers (Hansen et al. 2013, 2008). In 2008, Hansen et al. (2008) suggested that 350 ppm *may* represent the safe level.

The Paris talks were supposed to produce a new climate treaty to ensure that warming stays below +2°C relative to pre-industrial levels – a politically understood threshold, which is based on the warmest temperature on Earth in the past 800,000 years (Jouzel et al. 2007). The +2°C target, however, has its genesis in 1977 when Yale economist William Nordhaus, in his paper 'Strategies for the control of carbon dioxide', proposed:

> As a first approximation, it seems reasonable to argue that the climatic effects of carbon dioxide should be kept within the normal range of long-term climate variation. According to most sources the range of variation between distinct climatic regimes is in the order of ±5°C, and at the present time the global climate is at the high end of this range. If there were global temperatures more than 2 or 3°C above the current average temperature, this would take the climate outside of the range of observations which have been made over the last several hundred thousand years. Within a stable climatic regime, such as the current interglacial, a range of variation of 2°C is the normal variation.
>
> (Nordhaus 1977: 39–40)

Internationally, +2°C warming as a target entered the climate lexicon during the first Conference of Parties (COP1) of the UNFCCC in Berlin in 1995. At the Conference, the German Advisory Council on Global Change (WBGU 1995) released a statement convincing COP1 chair, Angela Merkel, then Germany's environment minister, to adopt +2°C as a target. WBGU (1995: 7) suggested that climate policy should be set regarding a tolerable 'temperature window', which they calculated to be 15.3°C, the mean global temperature in 1995. WBGU calculations also showed that this tolerable maximum temperature increase is equivalent to the +2°C warming.

In 1996, a year after COP1, the European Union acknowledged +2°C as the threshold at which average temperature on Earth may warm and adopted the target as the official climate policy standard. Thus: 'Given the serious risk of such an increase and particularly the very high rate of change, the Council believes that global average temperatures should not exceed 2°C above pre-industrial level' (European Union Council 1996, item no. 6).

The political processes in Berlin and in Europe triggered an international political process leading to the global visibility of the +2°C target. It remained, until the Paris climate summit in 2015, the threshold at which global mean temperature *may* be allowed to increase to avoid catastrophic climate change and has become a focal point of climate debate at almost all levels of governance.

On various occasions, the prominence of the +2°C target was reaffirmed internationally. For example, governments from the Group of Eight (2009, item 65) issued a Statement in 2009 '[recognising] the broad scientific view that the increase in global average temperature above pre-industrial levels ought not to exceed 2°C.' During the COP at Copenhagen, also that year, the Parties embedded this target in the text of the Copenhagen Accord, thus:

> We [the Parties] agree that deep cuts in global emissions are required according to science, and as documented by the IPCC Fourth Assessment Report with a view to reduce global emissions so as to hold the increase in global temperature below 2 degrees Celsius, and take this action to meet this objective consistent with science and on the basis of equity.
> (Copenhagen Accord 2009)

The +2°C target may have a practical basis. The assumption is that policy-makers and the public need a simple target to work with, ideally a single, round number, which the +2°C figure precisely provides (Lenton 2011). The political consensus on the +2°C target, at which many governments and the UNFCCC benchmark climate policy, however, is contested.

First, it remains uncertain what constitutes a 'safe' threshold, partly because the climate system is sensitive in many unknown ways, including uncertainties in the carbon cycle and climate response. Second, scientific assessments suggest that we are quite likely to go beyond +2°C warming by 2100 (Meinshausen et al. 2009). International organisations have also said that, without effective mitigation, the global mean temperature can be expected to go beyond +2°C warming (World Bank 2012; International Energy Agency (IEA) 2013). Even with Paris commitments implemented, warming is still projected to go beyond +2°C (Jeffery et al. 2015). Third, the +2°C target neither necessarily represents a 'safe' and stabilisation threshold nor constitutes 'dangerous' climate change (Hansen et al. 2013) given the already occurring dangerous climate change impacts at a temperature rise below +2°C warming (Mann 2009; Smith et al. 2009).

Relative to the average temperature in 1880, the beginning of the industrial age, the Earth has warmed, on average, by +0.8°C in 2010 (National Research Council 2011; cf. Mann 2009; cf. Smith et al. 2009). This warming, Hansen et al. (2013) report, has already devastated many lives, livelihoods, properties, and ecosystems as a result of the following changes in natural environments.

- Shrinkage of area and thickness of the Arctic sea ice.
- Accelerated reduction of Greenland and Antarctic ice sheets.
- Rapid recession of mountain glaciers.
- Expansion of hot dry subtropical climate belts.
- Decrease in reef-building corals.
- Significant changes in the habitats of more than half of all wild species.
- Mega heat waves.

With impacts already occurring at less than +2°C warming, Anderson and Bows (2011: 23) remark: 'it is reasonable to assume, *ceteris paribus*, that 2°C now represents a threshold, not between acceptable and dangerous climate change, but between dangerous and "extremely dangerous" climate change.'

'Extremely dangerous' warming

On 30 November 2015, Day 1 of the Paris climate talks, the daily measurement at Mauna Loa observatory registered 402.37 ppm (National Oceanic and Atmospheric Administration 2015). Never in the last million years have concentrations been so high. Breaching 400 ppm has brought human beings into a new, never before explored ecosystem and it is an 'extremely dangerous' warming. One thing is certain now; without rapid mitigation such warming becomes inevitable.

In 2012, the World Bank released an alarming report warning that the world is on track for at least 4°C warming in 2100. Analysts from the auditing firm PricewaterhouseCoopers (2012) argued to start preparing for 4°C or even 6°C warming this century. A year later, the conservative International Energy Agency (IEA 2013) pointed out that the world is geared to experience an average increase in temperature of 3.6°C to 5.3°C. A year before the agency released this report, its Chief Economist Fatih Birol, in an interview with *Reuters*, remarked that the trend 'is perfectly in line with a temperature increase of 6 degrees Celsius towards the end of this century' (Rose 2012).

Science validates the concerns of international organisations. The latest scientific assessments suggest that with continued GHG-based industrialisation the Earth is quite likely to warm beyond +2°C by 2100 (Peters et al. 2013; Meinshausen et al. 2009). In AR5, the IPCC (2014: 18) note that 'without additional mitigation efforts...warming is *more likely than not* to exceed 4°C above preindustrial levels by 2100.' Missing the +2°C target, given present efforts and even with full implementation of the Paris commitments, remains a distinct possibility.

Crossing the +4°C line could jeopardise life on Earth (Hansen et al. 2013, 2008). The IPCC (2014: 18), with *high confidence*, states that '[the] risks associated with temperatures at or above +4°C include substantial species extinction, global and regional food insecurity, consequential constraints on common human activities and limited potential for adaptation in some cases.' Climate scientist Kevin Anderson has said about the consequences of a +4°C warming:

> For humanity it's a matter of life or death... we will not make all human beings extinct, as a few people with the right sort of resources may put themselves in the right parts of the world and survive. But I think it's extremely unlikely that we wouldn't have mass death at 4 degrees. If you have got a population of 9 billion by 2050 and you hit 4 degrees, 5 degrees or 6 degrees, you might have half a billion people surviving.
>
> (quoted in Manning 2011)

Clear evidence exists that ineffective mitigation is already damaging our environment, health, infrastructure, and economy, as demonstrated in impacts with less than +1°C warming. In this age of climate consequences, we are living in a highly vulnerable time and space where climate extremes become the norm. A review of the literature on these consequences reveals that interrelated climate impacts can likely reduce the availability of potable water, food, clothing and shelter; and increase droughts, floods, heat waves, wildfires and destructive storms. These consequences affect resource availability, the use of the commons, and socio-political architectures.

Climate zones have started shifting as atmospheric circulation changes courses. The poles are warming faster than other parts of the Earth. The shift, which results in quite pleasant conditions in northern countries such as Canada, poses potential disasters for populations in equatorial countries such as Bangladesh or Somalia. Most negative consequences are now, indeed, felt in the Earth's mid-latitudes, which already are the world's poorest locations and where secondary effects such as economic disruption, disease, famine, and war are most acutely experienced. Although it remains uncertain when the impacts of the northern latitude's warming will manifest, other parts of the world are now being subjected to extreme impacts to human health, weather, and biodiversity.

Direct climate change impacts upon human health include risks from heat waves, floods, and air pollution; risks to biophysical changes including alterations in food yields leading to under-nutrition, changes in potable water quality, seasonal variations, and range of infectious diseases; and impacts because of socioeconomic disruptions such as health disorders, depression and other health consequences of tensions arising from declining resources (IPCC 2014: 8, 10, 62, 69, 74–76; National Climate Assessment 2014; Dennekamp and Abramson 2011; Spracklen et al. 2007).

Should emission trends continue to rise locking in warming, a Stanford study predicts that the 2003 European heat wave that killed more than 30,000 persons could likely happen every other year by 2040 (Diffenbaugh and Ashfaq 2010; cf. Cullen 2011). Heat waves have already occurred many times alongside droughts in the U.S. Midwest in 2012 and Texas in 2011 (Duffy and Tebaldi 2012; Christidis, Stott and Brown 2011). On 7 February 2009, the Australian state of Victoria experienced an emergency following a bushfire that killed 173, the highest number of bushfire-related deaths in the country (ABC News 2009). As the IPCC (2014: 62) reports: 'It is very likely that heat waves will occur with a higher frequency and longer duration.' Deaths from heat waves because of heat strokes and cardiovascular diseases have already occurred in the U.S. cities of Chicago, Philadelphia, and St Louis (Ye et al. 2012; Åström, Bertil and Joacim 2011; Huang et al. 2011).

Epidemics that spread infectious disease, which often occurred relative to briefer episodes of temperature shifts and food shortages, are another likely impact. Our present society's interconnectedness, where populations tend to live close to each other in denser spaces, increases our vulnerability to epidemics. Our modern social arrangements put lives at risk to health, from climatic influences on mosquito populations, for example. In the Australian state of Queensland, weather variability has been associated with dengue transmission (Hu et al. 2010). In Africa and Arabia, mosquito vectors have spread Rift Valley fever because of the changing climate (El Vilaly et al. 2013).

With warm temperatures, the water cycle is also disturbed, and water extremes are expected to intensify. A warmer atmosphere holds more moisture, meaning precipitation can be heavier and more frequent. This can cause more flooding, especially in arid and semi-arid locations, in most mid-latitude landmasses and over wet tropical regions (IPCC 2014: 12; Min et al. 2011; Santer et al. 2007; Willett et al. 2008; Dai 2012, 2006).

Although other parts of the world will likely receive heavy precipitations, many other locations will have to cope with low to zero precipitation. Societies living in these places face droughts, which would likely diminish agricultural harvests and biodiversity (World Bank 2012; Dai 2012; New et al. 2011). In 2010, the U.S. National Center for Atmospheric Research forecasted increasingly severe drought conditions by 2030 over much of the world because of climate change, including the western two-thirds of the U.S.A., much of Latin America, Southeast Asia including China, and most of Australia and Africa (Zabarenko 2010). In the U.S.A., many locations in Oklahoma and Texas have already experienced more than 100 days of record-breaking over 40°C temperatures which resulted in more than US$10 billion in direct losses to agriculture (National Climate Assessment 2014).

The Arabian Peninsula, which experienced active variability in dust activity between 2007 and 2013 (Notaro, Yu and Kalashnikova 2015), is a modern conflict site. Beginning with the Arab Spring in 2010 and persisting in the Syrian civil war, the Arabian conflicts were triggered by devastating droughts in the greater Fertile Crescent following variable dust activity, which served as 'threat multipliers' to an already politically and socially stressed region. The drought followed after precipitation changes linked to rising sea-level pressure and long-term warming trends in Eastern Mediterranean (Kelley et al. 2015). The Syrian civil war, which started as a civil uprising in 2011, resulted in more than 300,000 deaths and brought about the largest exodus of 4,013,000 refugees from a single conflict in a generation (Jones and Shaheen 2015).

Warming oceans (IPCC 2014: 2, 5, 10, 12) are also suitable environments for developing stronger typhoons (Camargo, Ting and Kushnir 2013; Coumou and Rahmstorf 2012; Ramsay and Sobel 2011; Vecchi, Clement and Soden 2008; Vecchi and Soden 2007). Thermodynamics teaches us that warmed water surface leads to water cycle extremes such as larger and intensified typhoons (Knutson et al. 2010). Australian scientist Will Steffen says of the 2013 supertyphoon Haiyan that hit central Philippines: 'We know sea-surface temperatures are warming pretty much around the planet, so that's a pretty direct influence of climate change on the nature of the storm' (Hannam 2013). Although their frequency is difficult to predict, typhoons are expected to become more intense with climate change as validated by scientific research (Emanuel 2013; cf. Knutson et al. 2010). Experiences with supertyphoon Haiyan illustrate how extreme weather events contribute to the alterations of the structure and function of ecosystems and transform thousands of lives. Social and resource stresses occurring after such events include: potable water, food, clothing, and shelter shortages; security problems; conflict; collapsed social and physical infrastructure; and failed governments.

The natural environment is also in danger. At +4°C warming, more than 80% of the Amazon forests could be destroyed by 2100 (Barley et al. 2009). Temperature changes would also expand the space burned by wildfires in the western U.S.A. by 200% to 400%, contributing to species decline (Hoag 2010; Westerling et al. 2011). With warming, the frequency and intensity of Australian bushfires are also projected to increase in the future (Lucas et al. 2007; Russell-Smith et al. 2007; Pitman, Narisma and McAneney 2007). Although trees are static, animals must shift habitats to adapt to changing temperatures, thus affecting ecosystem balance.

An example of species on the move is the mountain pine beetle (*Dendroctonus ponderosae*), a native insect of the temperate forests in western U.S.A. and Canada. A favourable climate in the northwest has opened forests for these beetles, with devastating impact. Their populations periodically explode into large-scale outbreaks leading to the death of many forests (Safranyik et al. 2010). As forests die, carbon uptake is reduced, and emissions increase as the trees decay and/or burn. A report by *The New York Times* in 2007 showed how the beetles infiltrated greater Yellowstone and infested certain pine species (Petit 2007). These pines are a vital resource for birds and squirrels which eat their nuts, and grizzly bears which feed on their seeds. As the beetles adapt to warming temperatures, the Rockies and the Cascades of Oregon and Washington in the U.S.A., and the Canadian Rockies and Columbia Mountains of Canada provide new frontiers. The Canadian Forest Service estimated that 270 MtC could be released into the atmosphere from beetle outbreaks between 2000 and 2020 in British Columbia's south-central region alone (Kurz et al. 2008), which includes approximately 374 thousand square kilometres of pristine pine and spruce forests.

Species failing to move locations or adapt to change will simply perish (IPCC 2014). Estimates vary, but additional warming of +1.5°C to +2.5°C will likely put 20% to 30% of species at increased extinction risk (IPCC 2007: 11; Rosenthal 2011).

In the seas, coral reefs will be highly vulnerable to the combined warming and ocean acidification effects (IPCC 2014: 71). Since the ocean pH level is now lower than what it has been for 20 million years (Kerr 2010: 1501), ocean acidification is already possibly decimating organisms that build calcium carbonate shells or skeletons. The iconic Great Barrier Reef off Australia's eastern coast, the Coral Sea, and the Caribbean Sea will also most likely be impacted by mass coral bleaching, diseases, and deaths, as ocean temperature increases (Hoegh-Guldberg et al. 2007). These ecosystem losses bring huge implications for more than 500 million persons depending on these ecosystems for their livelihoods. As marine ecosystems collapse, they will most likely be forced to migrate (The Economics of Ecosystems & Biodiversity 2010).

Of the many expected physical changes that climate change brings, sea level rise is often cited because it entails major destruction to lives, livelihoods, and properties. Coastal environments, home to many populations in many less economically developed communities in mid-latitudes and low-lying islands, are the most impacted locations. As sea level rises, hundreds of millions of people will potentially be affected by events such as coastal flooding, well waves, storm surges, and erosion. The number of climate refugees will also rise leading to the likelihood of security, migration, territorial, and international conflicts.

From 2003 to 2010, NASA satellites measured the Earth's melting land ice and found the melting had added approximately 4.3 trillion tonnes of water to the oceans (Jacob et al. 2012). The worrisome news is that Greenland is melting, and its glaciers are moving much faster than predicted (Rignot et al. 2011). In the South Pole, the West Antarctic Ice Sheet (WAIS) is already disintegrating. As the Earth warms to +4°C, both Greenland and WAIS could lose their ice covers quickly (Nicholls et al. 2011; Rignot et al. 2011), leading to a five to six-metre sea level rise (Guillerminet and Tol 2008). It is estimated that a two-metre rise could displace 182 million persons, result in a loss of 1.8 million km^2 of land, and cost around US$270 billion per year (Nicholls et al. 2011). Sea level rise of +2 metres, therefore, is tantamount to a catastrophe (Guillerminet and Tol 2008).

The present and future impacts of unmitigated and ineffectively mitigated climate change illustrate large-scale, dramatic, and expensive social and natural changes (cf. IPCC 2014: 7). More worrisome are the linkages between historical short-term climatic changes, the food shortages, consequent hunger, and diseases following these changes, and the eventual destabilisation and collapse of civilisations.

Climate change as 'threat multiplier' of large-scale societal crises

History provides a preview of what could happen with limited and ineffective climate mitigation. A corpus of rigorous research across multiple disciplines suggests that, partly because of short-term climatic changes, some past human civilisations underwent periods of societal crises, with some resulting in collapse (e.g. Hsiang, Burke and Miguel 2013; McMichael 2012; Zhang et al. 2011; Diamond 2005). These studies demonstrate that changes in global average temperature contributed to ecological, social, demographic, economic, and security stresses. Revisiting these histories provides a preview of what could happen with lacklustre and slow climate action.

David Zhang and his colleagues (Zhang et al. 2011), for example, show strong temporal correlations between societal crises and climate change in their exploration of agro-ecological, socioeconomic, and demographic variables to climate fluctuations between sixteenth- and nineteenth-century Europe. According to the study, the European cooling that lasted from 1560 to 1660 caused catastrophic changes in agriculture, demography, and the social and economic order of the time. Most recognisable during this period are mid-seventeenth-century European revolutions, which historian Hugh Trevor-Roper referred to as *The General Crisis* to describe widespread conflict and instability:

> The middle of the seventeenth century was a period of revolutions in Europe. These revolutions differed from place to place, and if studied separately, seem to rise out of particular, local causes; but if we look at them together they have so many common features that they appear almost as a general revolution. There is the Puritan Revolution in England which fills the twenty years between 1640 and 1660, but whose crisis was between 1648 and 1653. In those years of its crisis there was also the series of revolts known as the Frondes in France, and in 1649 there was a *coup d'état* or palace revolution, which created a new form of government in the United Provinces of the Netherlands. Contemporary with the troubles of England were those of the Spanish empire. In 1640 there was the revolt of Catalonia, which failed, and the revolt of Portugal, which succeeded: in 1641 there was nearly a revolt of Andalusia too; in 1647 there was the revolt of Naples, the revolt of Masaniello. To contemporary observers it seemed that society itself was in crisis, and that this crisis was general in Europe.
>
> (Trevor-Roper 1967: 43)

Using temperature data and climate-driven economic variables, Zhang et al. (2011) simulated the 'golden' and 'dark' ages in Europe and came out with findings that point to climate change as the ultimate cause and driver of large-scale human crises in preindustrial Europe, including *The General Crisis*.

Causality studies between climate change and population health vulnerabilities in medium and long-term climate changes have joined this corpus. Anthony McMichael (2012) describes how temperature shifts led to the destabilisation of civilisations through food shortages, and consequent hunger, disease and unrest, while brief temperature shift episodes, impoverishment and food shortages led to infectious epidemics. A historical example that McMichael points out is the 'Black Death', a pandemic of bubonic plague that spread through Europe between 1347 and 1353 (Büntgen et al. 2012). McMichael argues that the plague can be traced to climatic influences in eastern Kazakhstan and the Chinese border's Himalayan foothills. In these locations, mild climate resulted in abundant food supply allowing wild rodents to flourish for several decades. As the temperature dropped from 1310 to 1330, food supply declined, resulting in widespread rodent displacements. Also in 1330, many people in central China drowned in disastrous floods, while conflicts between the Mongols and the Chinese also flared up. These three events, McMichael (2012) theorises, spread the contact between wild rodents and humans; hence, the plague. The plague then moved westward to Europe via the Silk Road, where it killed approximately half of the European population.

The collapse of some civilisations has also been partly attributed to climate change. Eleven scientists compared the subannual climate record for the past two millennia in a cave in Belize with records of historical events compiled from well-dated stone monuments of the Mayan civilisation in Central America (Kennett et al. 2012). From this comparison, the scientists suggest that unprecedented population expansion, along with anomalous high rainfall followed by an extended drought lasting an estimated 80 years, contributed to increased warfare and the eventual collapse of the Mayan civilisation.

Another scientific team also found strong causality between climatic events and human conflict across all major world regions (Hsiang, Burke and Miguel 2013). The team examined various human conflict types – interpersonal violence and crime, intergroup violence, political instability, institutional breakdown, and collapse of human civilisations – from 10,000 BCE to 2013. Their conclusion suggests the variable influence of temperature change to social conflicts at almost all organisational levels and scales.

Although climate influence has been detected in the mid-seventeenth-century large-scale European social changes (Zhang et al. 2011), in the chain of events leading to the Black Death (McMichael 2012), and in increased conflict risks in East Africa, Sub-Saharan Africa and the tropics (Hsiang, Burke and Miguel 2013), climate change was but a contributor to already complex environments in these events and locations. In short, climate change has become a 'threat multiplier'.

With such dire consequences, the question, therefore, is: Can we still limit warming and, therefore, reduce the likelihood of climate change acting as a 'threat multiplier' to large-scale crises?

Possibly yes, with rapid mitigation.

Towards rapid mitigation

To increase the likelihood of successful climate mitigation, time remains our most important resource. The rate at which anthropogenic GHG emissions accumulate in the atmosphere should be reduced rapidly and dramatically, meaning emissions must peak as soon as possible and decline steeply thereafter.

To illustrate how this could proceed and the stringency of the required timeframe, scientists examined and compared two temperature change projections by 2100: (1) unmitigated climate change, which leads to more than +2°C warming, and (2) mitigation that could meet the +2°C international target (IPCC 2013: 21; cf. Peters et al. 2013: 5; cf. Le Quéré 2013). The first scenario indicates a projection for temperature change where the current

GHG emissions pathway continues unabated. The second scenario corresponds to a projection in what the IPCC calls a 'stringent mitigation scenario' that may keep warming likely below +2°C.

The scenarios are named after Representative Concentration Pathways (RCPs), which are used for climate modelling to describe possible climate futures. RCPs are possible ranges of radiative forcing values in 2100 relative to 1.75 W/m^2 pre-industrial value (IPCC 2007). Radiative forcing, in climate science, is the difference between the total amount of solar radiation energy absorbed by the Earth and energy radiated back to space. Positive forcing means warming; negative forcing means cooling.

The first scenario, called RCP8.5, projects CO_2 equivalent concentrations greater than 1000 ppm (IPCC 2014) and a warming to be likely in the +2.6°C to +4.8°C range (IPCC 2013: 23). Tyndall Centre's Corinne Le Quéré (2013) estimates the temperature range in this scenario to be between +3.2°C and +5.4°C. Kevin Anderson (2013) places it between +4°C and +6°C. Peters et al. (2013) suggest warming between +3.5°C and +6.2°C.

The second scenario, called RCP2.6 (Van Vuuren et al. 2006, 2007), projects CO_2 equivalent concentrations between 430 to 480 ppm (IPCC 2014) to stay within a +2°C target warming. Note that this carbon concentration is still high relative to the 350 ppm threshold posited by Hansen et al. (2008, 2013). This scenario involves the stabilisation of radiative forcing (Meinshausen et al. 2006) or 'peaking' at 3 W/m2 by 2050 followed by a decline, hence its other name, RCP3-PD, where PD stands for peak-and-decline. In RCP2.6, the IPCC (2014) estimates a warming between +0.3°C and +1.7°C. Scientists from the Global Carbon Project forecast warming within the +1.3°C to +1.9°C range (Peters et al. 2013). Le Quéré (2013) projects between +0.9°C and +2.3°C. In RCP2.6, global average surface temperatures are stabilised beyond 2100, but this 'does not imply stabilisation for all aspects of the climate system' (IPCC 2014: 16). Since RCP2.6 provides a pathway to stay the course within +2°C warming, climate policy and strategies could be aligned, constructed, and implemented around this scenario.

How much anthropogenic emissions reduction is needed to follow RCP2.6, and when should reduction start?

The IPCC provides some indicators in its Fifth Assessment Report (AR5): emissions should peak before 2030, decline sharply thereafter, reach zero by around 2070, and register negative values by 2100. WBGU (2009: Figure 3.2-1) suggests early peaking by 2020 and falling to zero levels by 2040. Anderson and Bows (2011) are more stringent, noting that emissions must peak from 2016 to 2022 followed by rapid reductions to near zero by 2050. Scientists from the Global Carbon Project note that this ambition requires early action and sustained mitigation from the largest emitters (Peters et al. 2013).

The required reductions (IPCC 2014; Peters et al. 2013; Le Quéré 2013; Anderson 2013; WBGU 2009; Anderson and Bows 2011) emphasise the importance of time and rate of mitigation. If the peak occurs beyond 2020 Anderson and Bows (2011) warn that the maximum reduction rate must exceed 9% per year, and that incremental adjustments to economic incentives such as voluntary agreements, carbon taxes and emissions trading alone would no longer be sufficient (Anderson and Bows 2012). The IPCC (2014: 25) also notes:

> Delaying additional mitigation to 2030 will substantially increase the challenges associated with limiting warming over the 21st century to below 2°C relative to pre-industrial levels. It will require substantially higher rates of emissions reductions from 2030 to 2050: a much more rapid scale-up of low-carbon energy over this period...and higher transitional and long-term economic impacts.

These timescales correspond to reductions that could keep warming below +2°C – which as discussed is 'unsafe'. With the global average temperature now heading towards +4°C to +6°C in 2100, and +2.7°C with full implementation of the Paris commitments – not +2°C – rapid climate mitigation becomes increasingly challenging.

Challenging, yet doable.

We are in a critical decade, where emissions reduction to avoid catastrophic warming means urgent, dramatic, large-scale, aggressive, and transformative changes. It should also be clear by now that the longer we peak our emissions, the steeper the decline must be in the following years. It could even come to a point when climate mitigation will be highly unlikely without shutting the global economy.

References

ABC News 2009, 'Black Saturday', http://ab.co/1Mb9HjX.

Allen, M.R., Frame, D.J., Huntingford, C., Jones, C.D., Lowe, J.A. et al. 2009, 'Warming caused by cumulative carbon emissions toward the trillionth tonne', *Nature*, vol. 458, pp. 1163–1166.

Anderson, K. 2013, 'Avoiding dangerous climate change', The Radical Emissions Reduction Conference, 10–11 December, The Royal Society, London, U.K., http://bit.ly/1bvfVsj.

Anderson, K. & Bows, A. 2011, 'Beyond "dangerous" climate change: emission scenarios for a new world', *Philosophical Transactions of The Royal Society A*, vol. 369, pp. 20–44.

Anderson, K. & Bows, A. 2012, 'A new paradigm for climate change', *Nature Climate Change*, vol. 2, pp. 639–640.

Åström, D.O., Bertil, F. & Joacim, R. 2011, 'Heat wave impact on morbidity and mortality in the elderly population: a review of recent studies', *Maturitas*, vol. 69, pp. 99–105.

Barley, S., Hawtin, N., Brahic, C. & Simonite, T. 2009, 'No rainforest, no monsoon: get ready for a warmer world', *New Scientist*, 30 September, http://bit.ly/18ZrMlQ.

Boden, T.A., Marland, G. & Andres, R.J. 2012, *Global, Regional, and National Fossil-Fuel CO₂ Emissions*, Carbon Dioxide Information Analysis Center, Oak Ridge National Laboratory, U.S. Department of Energy, Oak Ridge, Tennessee, U.S.A. doi: 10.3334/CDIAC/00001_V2012.

Büntgen, U., Ginzler, C., Esper, J., Tegel, W. & McMichael, A.J. 2012, 'Digitizing historical plague', *Clinical Infectious Diseases*, vol. 55, pp. 1586–1588.

Camargo, S.J., Ting, M. & Kushnir, Y. 2013, 'Influence of local and remote SST on North Atlantic tropical cyclone potential intensity', *Climate Dynamics*, vol. 40, pp. 1515–1529.

Christidis, N., Stott, P.A. & Brown, S.J. 2011, 'The role of human activity in the recent warming of extremely warm daytime temperatures', *Journal of Climate*, vol. 24, pp. 1922–1930.

Climate Action Tracker 2015, 'INDCs lower projected warming to 2.7°C: significant progress but still above 2°C', 1 October, http://bit.ly/1N48EIq.

Copenhagen Accord 2009, Decision 2/CP.15, in *Report of the Conference of Parties on its fifteenth session, held in Copenhagen from 7 to 19 December 2009*, UNFCCC, FCCC/CP/2009/11/Add.1.

Coumou, D. & Rahmstorf, S. 2012, 'A decade of weather extremes', *Nature Climate Change*, vol. 2, pp. 491–496.

Cullen, H. 2011, 'Sizzle factor for a restless climate', *The New York Times*, 19 July, http://bit.ly/18ZrMlQ.

Dai, A. 2006, 'Recent climatology, variability, and trends in global surface humidity', *Journal of Climate*, vol. 19, pp. 3589–3606.

Dai, A. 2012, 'Increasing drought under global warming in observations and models', *Nature Climate Change*, vol. 3, pp. 52–58.

Dennekamp, M. & Abramson, M.J. 2011, 'The effects of bushfire smoke on respiratory health', *Respirology*, vol. 16, pp. 198–209.

Diamond, J. 2005, *Collapse: How Societies Choose to Fail or Survive*, Penguin Books, New York, U.S.A.

Diffenbaugh, N.S. & Ashfaq, M. 2010, 'Intensification of hot extremes in the United States', *Geophysical Research Letters*, vol. 37, L15701. doi: 10.1029/2010GL043888.

Duffy, P.B. & Tebaldi, C. 2012, 'Increasing prevalence of extreme summer temperatures in the U.S.', *Climatic Change*, vol. 111, pp. 487–495.

El Vilaly, A.E., Arora, M., Butterworth, M.K., El Vilaly, M.A.M., Jarnagin, W. & Comrie, A.C. 2013, 'Climate, environment and disease the case of Rift Valley fever', *Progress in Physical Geography*, vol. 37, pp. 259–269.

Emanuel, K.A. 2013, 'Downscaling CMIP5 climate models shows increased tropical cyclone activity over the 21st century', *PNAS*, doi: 10.1073/pnas.1301293110.

European Union Council 1996, *Community Strategy on Climate Change – Council Conclusions*, in 1939th Council Meeting Environment, Document No. 8518/96.

Global Carbon Atlas 2015, *Emissions*, The Global Carbon Project, http://bit.ly/1JCXDMC.

Global Energy Assessment 2012, *Global Energy Assessment: Toward a Sustainable Future*, Cambridge University Press and International Institute for Applied Systems Analysis, Laxenburg, Austria.

Group of Eight 2009, *G8 Leaders Declaration: Responsible Leadership for a Sustainable Future*, L'Aquila, Italy, http://bit.ly/1mJMpes.

Guillerminet, M.-L. & Tol, R.S.J. 2008, 'Decision making under catastrophic risk and learning: the case of the possible collapse of the West Antarctic Ice Sheet', *Climatic Change*, vol. 91, pp. 193–209.

Hannam, P. 2013, 'Typhoon Haiyan influenced by climate change, scientists say', *The Sydney Morning Herald*, 11 November, http://bit.ly/1RqWs3f.

Hansen, J., Johnson, D., Lacis, A., Lebedeff, S., Lee, P. et al. 1981, 'Climate impact of increasing carbon dioxide', *Science*, vol. 213, pp. 957–966.

Hansen, J., Kharecha, P., Sato, M., Masson-Delmotte, V., Ackerman, F. et al. 2013, 'Assessing "Dangerous Climate Change": required reduction of carbon emissions to protect young people, future generations and nature', *PLOS One*, vol. 8, pp. e81648.

Hansen, J., Sato, M. & Ruedy, R. 2012, 'The new climate dice: public perception of climate change', National Aeronautics and Space Administration, Goddard Institute for Space Studies, August 2012, go.nasa.gov/2041ZIV.

Hansen, J., Sato, M., Kharecha, P., Beerling, D., Masson-Delmotte, V. 2008, 'Target atmospheric CO2: Where should humanity aim?' http://bit.ly/1eVM0em.

Hoag, H. 2010, 'Report maps perils of warming', *Nature*, vol. 466, p. 425.

Hoegh-Guldberg, I., Mumby, P.J., Hooten, A.J., Steneck, R.S., Greenfield, P. et al. 2007, 'Coral reefs under rapid climate change and ocean acidification', *Science*, vol. 318, pp. 1737–1742.

Hsiang, S.M., Burke, M. & Miguel, E. 2013, 'Quantifying the influence of climate on human conflict', *Science*, vol. 341, doi: 10.1126/science.1235367.

Hu, W., Clements, A., Williams, G. & Tong, S. 2010, 'Dengue fever and El Nino/Southern Oscillation in Queensland, Australia: a time series predictive model', *Journal of Occupational and Environmental Medicine*, vol. 67, pp. 307–311.

Huang, C., Gerard Barnett, A., Wang, X., Vaneckova, P., FitzGerald, G. & Tong, S. 2011, 'Projecting future heat-related mortality under climate change scenarios: a systematic review', *Environmental Health Perspectives*, vol. 119, pp. 1681–1690.

International Energy Agency (IEA) 2013, *Redrawing the Energy-Climate Map: World Energy Outlook Special Report*, IEA/OECD, Paris, France.

International Monetary Fund (IMF) 2015, *World Economic Outlook: Uneven Growth*, April, IMF, Washington, D.C., U.S.A., http://bit.ly/1huGQil.

IPCC (Intergovernmental Panel on Climate Change) 2007, 'Summary for Policymakers', in M.L. Parry, O.F. Canziani, J.P. Palutikof, P.J. van der Linden & C.E. Hanson (eds), *Climate Change 2007: Impacts, Adaptation and Vulnerability. Contribution of Working Group II to the Fourth Assessment Report of the IPCC*, Cambridge University Press, Cambridge, U.K.; New York, U.S.A., pp. 7–22.

IPCC 2013, 'Summary for Policymakers', in T.F. Stocker, G.D. Qin, G.-K. Plattner, M. Tignor, S.K. Allen, J. Boschung et al. (eds), *Climate Change 2013: The Physical Science Basis. Contribution of Working Group I to the Fifth Assessment Report of the IPCC*, Cambridge University Press, Cambridge, U.K.; New York, U.S.A., pp. 3–29.

IPCC 2014, *Climate Change 2014: Synthesis Report of the Fifth Assessment Report of the IPCC*, The Core Writing Team, R.K. Pachauri & L. Meyer (eds), IPCC, http://bit.ly/1umDnCQ.

Jacob, T., Wahr, J., Pfeffer, W.T. & Swenson, S. 2012, 'Recent contributions of glaciers and ice caps to sea level rise', *Nature*, vol. 482, pp. 514–518.

Jeffery, L., Alexander, R., Hare, B., Rocha, M., Schaeffer et al. 2015, *How Close are INDCs to 2°C and 1.5°C Pathways?* Potsdam Institute for Climate Impact Research, Climate Analytics, NewClimate Institute, & Ecofys, 1 September, http://bit.ly/1W54K3t.

Jones, S. & Shaheen, K. 2015, 'Syrian refugees: four million people forced to flee as crisis deepens', *The Guardian*, 9 July, http://bit.ly/1JQOPmn.

Jouzel, J., Masson-Delmotte, V., Cattani, O., Dreyfus, G., Falourd, S. et al. 2007, 'Orbital and millennial Antarctic climate variability over the past 800,000 years', *Science*, vol. 317, pp. 793–796.

Kelley, C.P., Mohtadi, S., Cane, M.A., Seager, R. & Kushnir, Y. 2015, 'Climate change in the Fertile Crescent and implications of the recent Syrian drought', *PNAS*, vol. 112, pp. 3241–3246.

Kennett, D.J., Breitenbach, S.F.M., Aquino, V.V., Asmerom, Y., Awe, J. et al. 2012, 'Development and disintegration of Maya political systems in response to climate change', *Science*, vol. 338, pp. 788–791.

Kerr, R.A. 2010, 'Ocean acidification unprecedented, unsettling', *Science*, vol. 328, pp. 1500–1501.

Knutson, T.R., McBride, J.L., Chan, J., Emanuel, K., Holland, G. et al. 2010, 'Tropical cyclones and climate change', *Nature Geoscience*, vol. 3, pp. 157–163.

Kurz, W.A., Dymond, C.C., Stinson, G., Rampley, G.J., Neilson, A.L. et al. 2008, 'Mountain pine beetle and forest carbon feedback to climate change', *Nature*, vol. 452, pp. 987–990.

Le Quéré, C. 2013, 'The scientific case for radical emissions reductions', The Radical Emissions Reduction Conference, 10–11 December, The Royal Society, London, U.K., http://bit.ly/1HNx7JY.

Lenton, T.M. 2011, 'Beyond 2°C: redefining dangerous climate change for physical systems', *Wiley Interdisciplinary Reviews: Climate Change*, vol. 2, pp. 451–461.

Levin, K. 2013, 'World's carbon budget to be spent in three decades', *World Resources Institute*, 27 September, http://bit.ly/1CfWok7.

Lucas, C., Hennessy, K., Mills, G. & Bathols, J. 2007, *Bushfire Weather in Southeast Australia: Recent Trends and Projected Climate Change Impacts*, The Climate Institute, Sydney, Australia.

Mann, M.E. 2009, 'Defining dangerous anthropogenic interference', *PNAS*, vol. 106, pp. 4065–4066.

Manning, P. 2011, 'Too hot to handle: can we afford a 4-degree rise?' *The Sydney Morning Herald*, 9 July, http://bit.ly/1wXUrko.

McKibben, B. 2012, 'Global warming's terrifying new math', *RollingStone*, 19 July, http://rol.st/LuRoru.

McMichael, A.J. 2012, 'Insights from past millennia into climatic impacts on human health and survival', *PNAS*, vol. 109, pp. 4730–4737.

Meinshausen, M., Hare, B., Wigley, T.M.L., Van Vuuren, D., Den Elzen, M.G.J. et al. 2006, 'Multi-gas emissions pathways to meet climate targets', *Climate Change*, vol. 75, pp. 151–194.

Meinshausen, M., Meinshausen, N., Hare, W., Raper, S.C.B., Frieler, K. et al. 2009, 'Greenhouse-gas emission targets for limiting global warming to 2°C', *Nature*, vol. 458, pp. 1158–1162.

Min, S.-K., Zhang, X., Zwiers, F.W. & Hegerl, G.C. 2011, 'Human contribution to more-intense precipitation extremes', *Nature*, vol. 470, pp. 378–381.

National Climate Assessment 2014, *National Climate Assessment*, U.S. Global Change Research Program, Washington, D.C., U.S.A.

National Oceanic and Atmospheric Administration (NOAA) 2015, *Recent Monthly Average Mauna Loa CO$_2$*, NOAA Earth System Research Laboratory, http://1.usa.gov/1jKojfI.

National Research Council 2011, *Climate Stabilization Targets: Emissions, Concentrations, and Impacts over Decades to Millennia*, The National Academies Press, Washington, D.C., U.S.A.

New, M., Liverman, D., Schroder, H. & Anderson, K. (eds) 2011, 'Four degrees and beyond: the potential for a global temperature increase of four degrees and its implications', *Philosophical Transactions of the Royal Society A*, vol. 369, no. 1934.

Nicholls, R., Marinova, N., Lowe, J., Brown, S., Vellinga, P. et al. 2011, 'Sea-level rise and its possible impacts given a "beyond 4°C world" in the twenty-first century', *Philosophical Transactions of the Royal Society A*, vol. 369, pp. 161–181.

Nordhaus, W.D. 1977, 'Strategies for the control of carbon dioxide', Cowles Foundation Discussion Paper No. 443, Cowles Foundation for Research in Economics at Yale University, New Haven, Connecticut, U.S.A.

Notaro, M., Yu, Y. & Kalashnikova, O.V. 2015, 'Regime shift in Arabian dust activity, triggered by persistent Fertile Crescent drought', *Journal of Geophysical Research: Atmospheres*, doi: 10.1002/2015JD023855.

Peters, G.P., Andrew, R.M., Boden, T., Canadell, J.G., Ciais, P. et al. 2013, 'The challenge to keep global warming below 2°C', *Nature Climate Change*, vol. 3, pp. 4–6.

Petit, C. 2007, 'In the Rockies, pines die and bears feel it', *The New York Times*, 30 January, http://nyti.ms/1Nh0sEO.

Pitman, A.J., Narisma, G.T. & McAneney, J. 2007, 'The impact of climate change on the risk of forest and grassland fires in Australia', *Climatic Change*, vol. 84, pp. 383–401.

PricewaterhouseCoopers (PwC) 2012, *Too Late for Two Degrees? Low Carbon Economy Index 2012*, PwC, London, U.K.

Ramsay, H.A. & Sobel, A.H. 2011, 'Effects of relative and absolute sea surface temperature on tropical cyclone potential intensity using a single-column model', *Journal of Climate*, vol. 24, pp. 183–193.

Rignot, E., Velicogna, I., Van den Brooke, M.R., Monaghan, A. & Lenaerts, J 2011, 'Acceleration of the contribution of the Greenland and Antarctic ice sheets to sea level rise', *Geophysical Research Letters*, vol. 38, L05503.

Romm, J. 2013, 'The real budget crisis: 'The CO_2 emissions budget framing is a recipe for delaying concrete action now', *Climate Progress*, 30 September, http://bit.ly/1isbbfK.

Rose, M. 2012, 'Corrected-Update 2 – Global CO_2 emissions hit record in 2011 led by China – IEA', *Reuters*, 30 May, http://reut.rs/1JP31X0.

Rosenthal, E. 2011, 'For many species, no escape as temperature rises', *The New York Times*, 21 January, http://nyti.ms/1hwXQSK.

Russell-Smith, J., Yates, C.P., Whitehead, P.J., Smith, R., Craig, R. et al. 2007, 'Bushfires "down under": patterns and implications of contemporary Australian landscape burning', *International Journal of Wildland Fire*, vol. 16, pp. 361–377.

Safranyik, L., Carroll, A.L., Regniere, J., Langor, D.W., Riel, W.G. et al. 2010, 'Potential for range expansion of mountain pine beetle into the boreal forest of North America', *The Canadian Entomologist*, vol. 142, pp. 415–442.

Santer, B.D., Mears, C., Wentz, F.J., Taylor, K.E., Gleckler, P.J. et al. 2007, 'Identification of human-induced changes in atmospheric moisture content', *PNAS*, vol. 104, pp. 15248–15253.

Smith, J.B., Schneider, S.H., Oppenheimer, M., Yohe, G.W., Hare, W. et al. 2009, 'Assessing dangerous climate change through an update of the Intergovernmental Panel on Climate Change (IPCC) "reasons for concern"', *PNAS*, vol. 106, pp. 4133–4137.

Spracklen, D.V., Logan, J.A., Mickley, L.J., Park, R.J., Yevich, R. et al. 2007, 'Wildfires drive interannual variability of organic carbon aerosol in the western US in summer', *Geophysical Research Letters*, vol. 34, pp. L16816.

TEEB (The Economics of Ecosystems & Biodiversity) 2010, *Mainstreaming the Economics of Nature: A Synthesis of the Approach, Conclusions and Recommendations of TEEB*, http://bit.ly/1gD9TLq.

Trevor-Roper, H. 1967, *The Crisis of the Seventeenth Century: Religion, The Reformation, and Social Change*, Liberty Fund, Indianapolis, Indiana, U.S.A.

UNFCCC 2015, *INDCs as Communicated by Parties*, accessed 6 November, http://bit.ly/1AAyvjS.

Van Vuuren, D.P., den Elzen, M.G.J., Lucas, P.L., Eickhout, B., Strengers, B.J., et al. 2007, 'Stabilizing greenhouse gas concentrations at low levels: an assessment of reduction strategies and costs', *Climatic Change*, vol. 81, pp. 119–159.

Van Vuuren, D.P., Eickhout, B, Lucas, P.L. & den Elzen, M.G.J. 2006, 'Long-term multi-gas scenarios to stabilise radiative forcings – exploring costs and benefits within an integrated assessment framework', *The Energy Journal*, vol. 27, pp. 201–233.

Vecchi, G.A. & Soden, B.J. 2007, 'Effect of remote sea surface temperature change on tropical cyclone potential intensity', *Nature*, vol. 450, pp. 1066–1070.

Vecchi, G.A., Clement, A. & Soden, B.J. 2008, 'Examining the tropical Pacific's response to global warming', *Eos, Transactions, American Geophysical Union*, vol. 89, pp. 81–83.

WBGU (German Advisory Council on Global Change) 1995, *Scenario for the Derivation of Global CO_2 Reduction Targets and Implementation Strategies*, Statement on the occasion of the First Conference of the Parties to the Framework Convention on Climate Change in Berlin, March 1995, WBGU, Bremerhaven, Germany.

WBGU (German Advisory Council on Global Change) 2009, *Solving the Climate Dilemma: The Budget Approach*, Special Report, WBGU, Berlin, Germany.

Westerling, A.L., Turner, M.G., Smithwick, E.A.H., Romme, W.H. & Ryan, M.G. 2011, 'Continued warming could transform Greater Yellowstone fire regimes by mid-21st century', *PNAS*, vol. 108, pp. 13165–13170.

Willett, K.M., Jones, P.D., Gillett, N.P. & Thorne, P.W. 2008, 'Recent changes in surface humidity: Development of the HadCRUH dataset', *Journal of Climate*, vol. 21, pp. 5364–5383.

World Bank 2012, *Turn Down the Heat: Why a 4°C Warmer World must be Avoided*, World Bank, Washington, D.C., U.S.A.

Ye, X., Wolff, R., Weiwei, Y., Vaneckova, P., Pan, X. & Tong, S. 2012, 'Ambient temperature and morbidity: a review of epidemiological evidence', *Environmental Health Perspectives*, vol. 120, pp. 19–28.

Zabarenko, D. 2010, 'Drought could hit world's most populous areas: study', *Reuters*, 19 October, http://reut.rs/1Oggo8R.

Zhang, D.D., Lee, H.F., Wang, C., Li, B., Pei, Q. et al. 2011, 'The causality analysis of climate change and large-scale human crisis', *PNAS*, vol. 108, pp. 17296–17301.

2   A rapid mitigation project

Focus on sustainable energy transitions

In 2013, we emitted 36,131 $MtCO_2$ globally, an average of five tonnes per person (Global Carbon Atlas 2015). The vast majority of these emissions remain largely from energy use. Energy is used in three forms: electricity, transport, and heat. At present, most electricity supply is from combustion of coal, most transport is from oil, and most heat is from gas or coal. In 2012, fossil fuel combustions for electricity and heat constituted 47% of CO_2 emissions, 23% for transport, and 20% for manufacturing and construction (Global Carbon Atlas 2015). Under current policies, including from Paris targets, emissions from this sector are projected to increase. The Intergovernmental Panel on Climate Change (IPCC) Fifth Assessment Report (AR5) suggests global emissions could double or even triple by mid-century (IPCC 2014). Curtailing emissions from the energy sector, thus, remains core in climate mitigation (IPCC 2014: 29, 31), and can happen more rapidly than in others IPCC (2013: 20).

Thus far, the only demonstrated and verified option for substantial decarbonisation in the energy sector is a staged, systematic, and structured retirement of fossil-based electricity generation and replacement with renewable energy technologies. This approach needs to be complemented by energy efficiency and conservation, and by avoiding electricity consumption whenever possible. Activities to achieve this transition can be scaled up using commercially available sustainable energy technologies, and intensified research and development of key, yet immature, infrastructure such as smart grids and storage technology. In the long-term, renewable electricity will also supply most transport and heat demand, with exceptions for air transport and long-distance rural transport that cannot yet be powered directly by electricity.

Sustainable energy transition is not a new concept. It was central in discussions to address the 1970s and 1980s energy crisis and the global overreliance on oil supply. It also gained salience as a key strategy for addressing greenhouse gas emissions. Yale economist William Nordhaus (1977: 23), for instance, suggests 'substituting non-carbon-based fuels for carbon-based fuels' in his paper 'Strategies for the control of carbon dioxide'. Scientists advocated for the transition as early as 1981 with NASA's James Hansen and colleagues (1981: 966) writing in *Science* that '[an] appropriate strategy may be to encourage energy conservation and develop alternative energy sources' to using fossil fuels.

Calls to shift towards sustainable energy sources as a core climate strategy, however, became mainstream following Al Gore's Powerpoint presentations in 2008. In 2009, the Academies of Science of the Group of Eight Industrialised Nations and of China and India highlighted the importance of the transition urging world leaders to 'show leadership in developing and deploying clean energy technologies and approaches to energy efficiency' (National Academies of Science of the Group of Eight, India, and China 2009). Many others have joined the global call to replace fossil fuels with sustainable sources as a vital climate strategy. The International Energy Agency (IEA 2013: 13) – an agency created by the world's richest countries during the 1970s oil crisis – argues that 'the growth in global energy-related CO_2 emissions must halt and start to reverse within the current decade.' The World Bank joins this call recommending that decarbonising the energy sector through early action is vital for prudential and cost reasons (Fay et al. 2015: 4). The politics of climate, therefore, is also the politics of energy.

Sustainable energy refers to the form of energy obtained from non-exhaustible resources emitting the lowest GHGs in its life cycle, and appears as bioenergy, geothermal, ocean, solar, hydro, and wind energy. Bioenergy sources from biomass and biogas provide electricity, heating and cooling services; while bioethanol sources provide energy in the transport sector. Geothermal power can be obtained through conventional or enhanced geothermal sources for electricity, and ground source heat pumps for heating. Ocean power sources are derived from wave, tidal, thermal, and osmotic processes, which can be used to produce electricity. Solar power produces electricity through photovoltaic (PV) – either in rooftops or utility scale, and concentrated solar power (CSP). Solar thermal can also be tapped to provide heating. Hydropower generates electricity from either small (<10MW), mostly run-of-the-river, or large (>10MW), usually dam, installations. Wind energy provides electricity from onshore and offshore locations. The technologies used to harness these sources and convert them to energy services are collectively called sustainable energy technologies, which also include technologies for energy conservation and energy efficiency in utilities, buildings, appliances, and equipment.

Despite the relative commercial availability of most of these technologies, the pace of transition towards higher penetration of sustainable energy technologies at the global level has been generally slow. Strategies to diffuse them also remain ineffective. This has climate repercussions since energy and climate policy are deeply intertwined.

Many governments, especially in countries with large emission footprints, are still lagging far behind in diffusing these technologies. Although some

states have adopted sustainable energy transition as a national priority –
remarkably, the Governments of Denmark (2011; cf. Richardson et al. 2011),
Germany (Palzer and Henning 2014; Morris and Pehnt 2014; see energy-
transition.de), and Scotland (Government of Scotland 2011) – the global
penetration of renewable energy technology remains low. By 2014, only
3.8% of wind, water, and sunlight energy generation capacity for a full-scale
renewable energy world in 2050 had been installed globally (Jacobson et al.
2015). The furthest five countries on the sustainable energy transition
pathway – Portugal (26%), Tajikistan (34%), Iceland (39%), Paraguay (54%),
and Norway (67%) – interestingly do not include the earlier mentioned
three countries.

The reasons for the generally slow pace of transition – and in effect, action
on climate change – are complex. Internationally, however, the lack of
incentives to rapidly diffuse sustainable energy technologies can be traced to
a free-riding problem (Nordhaus 2015; Wagner and Weitzman 2015). Free-
riding occurs when a party receives the same benefits of public goods without paying or contributing to the costs. The free market orientation of many
high emission states, where economic growth at the expense of the environment is the core objective, also precludes many states from adopting policy
allowing aggressive changes in energy production and consumption (cf. Klein
2014). The clout that big businesses – from high emission sectors including
mining, electricity, construction, manufacturing, shipping, and aviation –
have on governments, at the state, national and international levels, is also
largely responsible for the transition's slow speed (Diesendorf 2009). Instead
of supporting the transition and effective climate action, many governments
continue to provide structural and institutional support for GHG-based
industrialisation (Dunlap and McCright 2011; Washington and Cook 2011).
This is despite a sound technical and economic rationale for the transition.

The technical and economic feasibility of sustainable energy

Many scholarly investigations, including simulations beyond the operation
of renewable electricity, show the possibility of a transition to safe and ecologically sustainable energy systems. The motivations vary, but can be generally
attributed to addressing energy sector emissions, increased recognition of
other environmental issues including air and water pollution, and concerns
for security of energy supply.

For electricity generation, many simulation models demonstrate that
renewable energy technologies, when scaled up, could reliably supply 80% to
100% of the entire electricity demand in many states, countries, and regions,
and even the entire planet. Most of the technologies, according to these
studies, are safe, and are commercially available either on a utility-scale or in
limited mass production. The wide availability of renewable sources waiting
to be tapped, and the affordability of the economic cost of the transition are
also pointed out in some of these studies.

Physicist Bent Sørensen (1975), as early as 1975, suggested that all energy needs in society could be derived from renewable sources. In 2000, Sørensen and Peter Meibom provided a global renewable energy scenario using a geographical information system to show the spatial match between renewable energy supply and demand (Sørensen and Meibom 2000). In 2011, Mark Jacobson and Mark Delucchi, in a two-part article in *Energy Policy*, produced analyses of the feasibility of providing worldwide energy for electric power, transport, heating, cooling and other forms of energy services from wind, water, and sunlight (Jacobson and Delucchi 2011; Delucchi and Jacobson 2011). They suggest it is possible to produce all new energy to satisfy all end uses worldwide with renewable sources by 2030 – approximately 17 TW according to the U.S. Energy Information Administration (EIA 2008) projections – and fully replace existing fossil energy sources by 2050. In their simulation, they estimate that energy cost would be similar to the 2011 cost of energy production and distribution. Jacobson and colleagues (2015) update their scenario to show the technical possibility of an 80% conversion to 100% wind, water and sunlight power by 2030, and full conversion by 2050. Although they arrive at similar conclusions, the 2015 study strengthens their position by providing detailed estimates and scenarios for 139 countries and territories (see https://100.org/wp-addons/maps/). Other writers corroborate, in many ways, the global vision of high renewable energy penetration, including Connolly and Mathiesen (2014); Teske, Muth and Sawyer (2012); World Wide Fund for Nature, Ecofys, and Office for Metropolitan Architecture (2011); Mathiesen, Lund and Karlsson (2011); Krajačić et al. (2011); Glasnovic and Margeta (2011); Schwartzman and Schwartzman (2011); and Greenpeace International and European Renewable Energy Council (2010). These studies show, in unison, that a 100% renewable energy-fuelled world by some future date, typically by 2050, is a technical possibility.

The preponderance of scenarios suggesting high sustainable energy technology penetrations extends to more location-specific studies for some of the world regions, nations, and states. Scientists from the U.S. National Renewable Energy Laboratory (NREL) and the U.S. Department of Energy, for instance, developed scenarios demonstrating the long-term visions for an 80% renewable electricity for the U.S.A. by 2050 (Mai et al. 2014; cf. Bazilian et al. 2014). This vision suggests the transition could result in 69% to 82% lower 2050 CO_2 emissions with CO_2 intensity dropping from 0.53 tonnes/MWh in 2010 to between 0.07 and 0.11 tonnes/MWh in 2050 (Mai et al. 2014: 383). Jacobson et al. (2015) are more ambitious in their vision as they demonstrate the possibility of a fully renewable-powered U.S.A. by 2050. This can be achieved, according to their plan, by using 50% onshore and offshore wind; 45% utility-scale solar PV, CST and rooftop PV; 3% hydro; 1.25% geothermal; and 0.51% wave and tidal energy. The plan would save the U.S.A. some $3.3 trillion per year in 2050 global warming costs to the world due to U.S. emissions.

Jacobson's team also produced more detailed scenarios at the level of U.S. states (Jacobson et al. 2015). In the state of California, for instance, the team present a roadmap for converting the state's entire energy infrastructure to 100% wind, water, and sunlight in 2050. The plan creates approximately 220,000 more 40-year jobs, while reducing California's global climate contribution by US$48 billion per annum (Jacobson et al. 2014a). They analysed the potential and consequences of a similar transition in the state of Washington (Jacobson et al. 2016), where they found that a 100% renewable energy by 2050 requires only 0.08% of the state's land and could reduce global climate costs by an estimated US$4,200 per person per year. The team also produced another state-specific long-term scenario for future high renewable penetration in the State of New York (Jacobson et al. 2013). Other transition studies for U.S. states include a transition scenario for the western half of the country (Nelson et al. 2012), and all or parts of the states of Illinois, Indiana, Delaware, New Jersey, Kentucky, Maryland, Michigan, North Carolina, Ohio, Pennsylvania, Tennessee, Virginia, West Virginia, and the District of Columbia (Budishaka et al. 2013).

China, the largest emitting country in the world today, can also transition its energy system to a full-scale renewable energy penetration, according to a study from Tsinghua University and Aalborg University (Liu et al. 2011). The study proposes a 100% renewable energy in China, considering the country's substantial renewable energy resource potential, which includes hydropower, wind, photovoltaic, tidal energy, wave, solar thermal, geothermal, and biomass.

Australia, another high emission state, has also been found to have huge potential for powering its National Electricity Market (NEM) with renewable sources from wind, solar, hydro, and biomass sources (Elliston, Diesendorf and McGill 2012). The NEM, at 5,000 km, is one of the world's longest interconnected power systems linking the states of Queensland, New South Wales, Victoria, South Australia, Tasmania, and the Australian Capital Territory (AEMO (Australian Energy Market Operator) 2012). Since the network produces around one-third of the total Australian GHG emissions (Garnaut 2011; Ison et al. 2011), transitioning it towards sustainable energy provides substantial emission cuts for the country. A University of New South Wales (UNSW) Australia study demonstrates that the transition for NEM is possible and meets reliability standards (Elliston, Diesendorf and McGill 2012; Elliston, McGill and Diesendorf 2013, 2014). The 100% renewable energy (RE) mix for this simulation involves 28% biomass (24 GW), 27% wind (23.2 GW), 18% CSP with thermal storage (15.6 GW), 17% PV (14.6 GW), 6% hydro (4.9 GW), and 2% pumped hydro energy storage (2.2 GW). The simulation also shows that conventional base-load power plants are no longer necessary, even in winter evenings when demand can be high. Compared with a business-as-usual scenario to elicit the transition's cross-sectoral impacts across the Australian biophysical economy, the RE scenario appears to have significantly lower industrial water use, somewhat higher materials use, slightly lower unemployment, lower net foreign debt relative to a GDP proxy and, reduced oil imports as a result of growing use of electric vehicles

(Turner, Elliston and Diesendorf 2013). Other writers have also studied the feasibility of shifting towards 100% renewable energy systems in Australia, including Jacobson et al. (2015), AEMO (2013), WWF-Australia and Climate Risk (2012), and Wright and Hearps (2010), albeit with varying technology choices and implementation approaches. Jacobson et al. (2015; Jacobson, personal communication 2015), for instance, show that their plan for Australia – by contrast to UNSW Australia's study – requires zero biofuel.

Other national level simulations, studies and models have been produced for Germany (Palzer and Henning 2014; Eikenjager and Breitner 2012; German Advisory Council on the Environment 2011), Denmark (Lund and Mathiesen 2009; Richardson et al. 2011), The Netherlands (Kern and Smith 2008), Ireland (Connolly and Mathiesen 2014; Chiodi et al. 2013; Connolly et al. 2011), United Kingdom (Allen et al. 2013; Kemp and Wexler 2010; Parsons-Brinkerhoff 2009), New Zealand (Mason, Page and Williamson 2010, 2013; Sovacool and Watts 2009), Japan (Lehmann 2003), and Portugal (Fernandes and Ferreira 2014; Kraja, Dui and Carvalho 2011). Jacobson's team have also produced plans of 100% water, wind, and sunlight power for almost all countries (Jacobson 2015; see https://100.org/wp-addons/maps/). Scenarios were also developed for islands in Japan (Blechinger et al. 2014; Sakaguchi and Tabata 2015) and in the Mediterranean (Sanseverino et al. 2014). These studies echo the same conclusion: that an 80% to 100% renewable energy penetration is technically plausible using current technologies.

Regional transition is also possible. The European Renewable Energy Council (EREC 2010), the umbrella organisation of major European renewable energy industry, trade and research associations, for instance, suggests that the European Union (EU) could tap 96% of its energy from renewable sources by 2050. To achieve the transition, EREC (2010) assumes annual growth in renewable power capacity by 14% for 13 years. The transition will account for 1,200 $MtCO_2$ reductions by 2020, 2,000 $MtCO_2$ in 2030, and 3,800 $MtCO_2$ in 2050. With staged and programmed transition, EREC projects that the EU could reduce its energy sector emissions by more than 90% against 1990 levels by 2050. Other Europe-wide transition studies echoing similar conclusions and recommendations include those by Steinke, Wolfrum and Hoffmann 2013; Rasmussen, Andresen and Greiner (2012); Van De Putte et al. (2011); and Boot and Van Bree (2010).

Despite this optimism, renewable energy endowments and supply are obviously varied across locations, which leads to intermittency in some areas. In Siemens' Europe-wide 100% renewable energy vision (Steinke, Wolfrum and Hoffmann 2013), for instance, backup generation – roughly 40% of the total continental demand – will be required in locations where wind and sun cannot fully meet electricity demand. Some national-level plans also recognise this limitation. The UNSW Australia scenario, for instance, is cognizant of this supply lacuna, and proposes biomass combustion using crop residues to address it (Elliston, Diesendorf and McGill 2012). The EREC (2010) plan for Europe also suggests biofuels could provide 10% of total energy. While bioenergy may fill in intermittency, some areas have inadequate biomass supply (Delucchi 2010), and, in areas where biomass is not harvested from crop residues, this may compete with land and water-use (Jacobson 2009). Biomass combustion also emits greenhouse gases (Cherubini et al. 2011). Bioenergy issues highlight the importance of intensified research and development (R&D) on other technologies, particularly on renewable energy storage and smart grids to enable efficient energy transmission and trade at the trans-country, trans-national or regional level.

Bent Sørensen (2008), for instance, suggests that the northern European countries of Germany, Denmark, Sweden, Norway, and Finland can trade renewable energy – Iceland was excluded from the plan since it has no grid connections to the five countries – through hydrogen technology for energy storage and dual cell applications for stationary energy use. Siemens' Europe-wide 100% renewable energy vision (Steinke, Wolfrum and Hoffmann 2013) also invokes Sørensen's (2008) hydrogen option.

Addressing the technical question, however, is only one part of the equation; providing a sound economic basis for the transition is another essential aspect in making the most optimistic argument for rapid sustainable energy transition. A review by Fouquet (2010) of 14 historical energy transitions validates this point: energy transitions generally succeed and also bring a rapidly decreasing cost of producing alternative energy.

Some technical scenarios described above also offer approximations of power generation costs from renewable sources and, thus, elaborate the economic argument for the transition. Delucchi and Jacobson's (2011; Jacobson, personal communication 2015) global scenario, for instance, indicates that offshore wind, hydroelectric, and geothermal technologies already cost less than fossil and nuclear generation. According to their study, onshore wind power is also expected to cost less than any other utility-scale, centralised power generation. By 2030, Delucchi and Jacobson (2011) project that the cost for all renewable generation will be less than conventional fossil fuel generation. The annualised generation and transmission cost for fossil generation in the U.S., for instance, will be around US$0.08 plus social cost of US$0.14 or US$0.22 per kWh delivered, in contrast to onshore wind, which will be delivered at a cost below US$0.04 (Delucchi and Jacobson 2011: Table 1, 1175). Although solar costs were expensive in 2011 – greater than US$0.20 per kWh delivered – the authors predict that solar power will be cost-competitive by as early as 2020 at US$0.10 per kWh or less. These estimates include costs for the grid, over present-day distances. When renewable energy installations are located in long distances, the authors calculated additional cost for land-based transmission to be between US$0.003 and US$0.032 per kWh delivered, and between US$0.012 and US$0.014 per kWh delivered through 'supergrids' involving voltage transmission undersea (Delucchi and Jacobson 2011: 1182, 1185).

The 80% renewable electricity scenario for the U.S.A. produced by Mai et al. (2014) suggests a transition with 3% to 30% incremental electricity price increases, in real terms, during the next 40 years. Retiring fossil fuel infrastructure leads to a US$24/MWh electricity price increase from 2010 to 2050 and increases to US$34/MWh as greater demand growth raises investment needs (Mai et al. 2014: 381). Additional capital investments consist in expenditures on additional renewable capacity, expanded transmission – which includes making grids smart – and new storage and demand-side technologies. The authors, nonetheless, show that future electricity price increases can be reduced through demand side management.

The World Wide Fund for Nature in Australia and Climate Risk (2012) demonstrate that the transition to a 100% renewable energy supply for the country could be achieved as early as 2037 if a carbon price enables the prices of renewable technologies to converge with conventional sources. The UNSW Australia scenario also shows that 100% renewable electricity is economically feasible for the NEM as demonstrated in the cost evaluation of a generation plant in 2030 to meet a load given the 2010 demand profile for the NEM (Elliston, Diesendorf and McGill 2012). Using conservative projections of 2030 prices of renewable energy technologies by the Australian Bureau of Resources and Energy Economics, the UNSW Australia team concludes in a follow-up study that the full transition is likely to be economically competitive with gas-fired electricity and with coal- and gas-fired electricity with carbon capture and storage (CCS) (Elliston, McGill and Diesendorf 2014). Depending on the choice of discount rate and with a carbon price ranging between AU$50 and AU$60, the same study suggests that the Australian 100% renewable energy system can be cheaper on an annualised basis (Elliston, MacGill and Diesendorf 2013).

The declining cost of electricity generated from wind and solar sources in real time strengthens the economic argument for the transition. In 2013, global financial advisor and asset manager firm Lazard Freres & Co. reported that the levelised cost of electricity (LCOE) for wind and solar sources in the U.S.A. fell by more than half in six years (Lazard 2013). LCOE, used to compare electricity costs, is the quotient derived from calculating a system's expected lifetime costs over the system's lifetime expected energy output. In September 2014, Lazard reported that the LCOE per MWh in wind sources ranges from US$37 to US$81, and solar PV costs between US$72 and US$86. By contrast, LCOE for coal, which excluded health and climate-impact costs, was between US$66 and US$151 (Lazard 2014). The International Renewable Energy Agency (IRENA 2013) also reported declining costs for wind, solar, and some biomass technologies. Bloomberg New Energy Finance reports similar cost reductions (Chase 2012), as do Consulting firm McKinsey (Hastings-Simon, Pinner and Stuchtey 2014) and global financial services company UBS (Parkinson 2014).

As costs drop, solar power penetration has been doubling every two years for the last 30 years (Pourreza et al. 2014). At this rate and with appropriate policy support, solar energy can meet 100% of today's energy needs before 2030 (Wadhwa 2014), which is highly probable since residential-scale solar production has already reached grid parity in some parts of Germany,

Portugal, Spain, Australia, and the Southwest U.S.A. (UBA 2012). Grid parity occurs when generating power at an LCOE is equal to or less than the price of purchasing power from the electricity grid. In the last five years, prices of solar panels have fallen 75%, and will most likely fall as technologies to produce them improve and the scale of production increases. Other sustainable energy technologies are also advancing at a rapid rate including wind, biomass, geothermal, wave, and tide. All over the world many are working to improve their efficiency, which would bring costs – and consequently electricity prices – further down.

The economic argument for adopting energy efficiency measures, often called the 'low-hanging fruit' in climate mitigation, has also been studied to be of big potential. While powerplants produce megawatts, energy efficiency strategies produce 'negawatts', meaning reductions in energy use, ergo reductions in emissions. A McKinsey report in 2009, for instance, indicates that the U.S.A. could reduce its annual energy consumption by 23% by 2020 with efficiency measures alone representing savings in monetary terms, not just emissions reduction (Granade et al. 2009). As energy efficiency is captured at its full potential, the reduction translates into approximately 1.1 $GtCO_2e$ carbon savings per year in 2020 with 40% saved from the industrial sector, 35% from the residential sector, and 25% from the commercial sector (Granade et al. 2009).

The technological portfolio for rapid climate mitigation

Although the preponderance of scenarios and studies neither specify a transition path nor share common methodology in their analyses, they remain valuable in showing the plausibility of bold, aggressive, large-scale reduction in fossil fuel use based on source availability, technological readiness, and economic costs. The scenarios, both technical and economic, provide bases for envisioning future sustainable energy systems as a key component for rapid climate mitigation, or, what this book calls, the *Rapid Mitigation Project*.

The technologies chosen in the many scenarios mentioned above vary depending on natural endowments of the location under study and its existing technical, social, and institutional capacity. In general, these technologies, except for storage, are already commercially available. In sum, these technologies rank the highest among the proposed options for addressing climate change. Based on scenario studies and simulations, the following technologies could be adopted to diffuse sustainable energy reliably, quickly, and safely enough to reduce large emissions from the energy sector.

For electricity generation, conventional fossil-based power plants should be retired and replaced with sustainable energy systems, in a staged, structured, and systematic manner. Depending on location and capacity, the primary technologies to accomplish the transition include commercially available on-shore and offshore wind turbines, solar PV modules, CSP, hydroelectric, geothermal, and tidal power. Reduction in demand through energy efficiency and behavioural changes complements these technologies. In summary, the technologies work as follows.

- Wind turbines convert the wind's mechanical energy to electricity in a generator, and appear as assemblages of on-shore and offshore wind turbines in wind farms, and as small turbines in homes or buildings.
- Solar PVs are arrays of cells containing material, such as silicon, converting solar radiation to electricity and are used to generate residential or utility-scale power.
- CSP uses mirrors or reflective lenses to focus sunlight on a fluid or salt to heat it to high temperature, which then flows from the collector to a heat engine where a portion of the heat is converted to electricity.
- Hydroelectricity is produced when water drops by gravity, driving a turbine and generator in dams or in run-of-the-river schemes.
- Geothermal power provides heat for buildings, industrial processes, and domestic water, and generates electricity through steam that drive turbines.
- Tidal power is produced similar to wind energy using rotors mounted on the sea floor that turn because of their interaction with the tide's ebb and flow.

In some locations, where wind, solar, and water sources are below demand, anaerobic digestion and biomass gasification and combustion, preferably with CCS, may have roles in the energy mix. They are, however, replaced as storage technologies become more available, as grids become smarter, and the above technologies become more efficient.

Before proceeding, it is essential to pay attention to competing technologies, which have emerged in the discourse and gained salience in scientific, political, and social domains. These are fossil energy with CCS, fossil gas, nuclear energy, and geoengineering.

An end-to-end CCS aims to capture GHGs from large stationary point sources such as fossil-fuelled power plants, refineries, and steel mills, transport and inject the compressed gas into a suitable deep geologic structure, typically more than 800m below the surface, and then apply a suite of measurement, monitoring and verification technologies to ensure the safety, efficacy, and permanence of the captured gas's isolation from the atmosphere (Herzog 2011; IPCC 2005). Although CCS can reduce emissions from the stacks of coal-fired power plants by 85% to 90% or more (IPCC 2014), it has minimal mitigation impact since coal mining and transport still accrue emissions. Because CCS requires 25% more energy (IPCC 2005), impacts from coal mining, transport, and processing will increase emissions and air pollutants per unit of net delivered power and result in more ecological, land-use, and air and water pollution. The technology is also beyond commercial diffusion, a key criterion for the Rapid Mitigation Project.

Another competing technology, fossil gas – natural gas, coal seam methane, or shale gas – has gained national and international attention as a possible 'bridge fuel' between coal and renewable energy systems based upon the idea that renewable energy technologies must be scaled up first and, before they are ready for diffusion, some kind of transition fuel will be needed (Bruckner et al. 2014; Alvarez et al. 2012; Myhrvold and Caldeira 2012; Pickens 2009; Pacala and Socolow 2004). The decline in U.S. emissions between 2007 and 2013 has been attributed to the shift from the use of coal to natural gas. However, the factors leading to the decline were not critically examined. A 2015 study published in *Nature Communications* sets the record straight by demonstrating that the shift to fossil gas does not cause the drop, but the decline in consumption levels during the 2008 Global Financial Crisis (Feng et al. 2015). Simply replacing coal with gas in base-load power generation and motor vehicles, therefore, would not achieve sufficient emissions reduction (Grattan Institute 2012).

Fossil gas extraction is also concerning. Drilling fossil gas emits large volumes of methane, a more potent GHG than CO_2, due to widespread leaks as well as purposeful gas venting (Caulton et al. 2014; Howarth 2014). Other valid concerns include water and land-use resource competition and social impacts to communities. In the short-term, there might be some limited role for gas including small, efficient contributions to energy supply such as cogeneration, trigeneration, peak-load gas turbines for the grid, and backing-up or boosting for solar heating and solar thermal electricity. Its use in fuel motor vehicles or base-load power generation, however, needs to be capped. In the long-term, fossil gas is eliminated in the energy mix through demand-response measures, smart grid technology, storage technology, and increases in solar and wind capacities.

Nuclear energy is another technology competitor. In November 2013, James Hansen, Ken Caldeira, Kerry Emanuel, and Tom Wigley published a joint statement in favour of supporting safe nuclear power given 'the need to sharply reduce [GHG] emissions' (see text at Revkin 2013). During the Paris climate talks, they reiterated this position suggesting that it is the 'only viable path forward' (Hansen et al. 2015). Earlier suggestions to include the nuclear option in the mix came from the IEA (2010), Pacala and Socolow (2004), James Lovelock (2004) and U.K. government's former chief scientist Sir David King (see Harvey 2011). The nuclear option, however, cannot be part of the technology portfolio for rapid climate mitigation since it is high-risk, water intensive, slow to construct, and expensive (Koplow 2011; Jacobson 2009; Koomey and Hultman 2007; Schneider and Froggatt 2014). When some countries, such as Germany, are already phasing out nuclear power in favour of renewable energy technologies, the fissile option is but a costly diversion.

There is for the moment no consensus on the risks of the nuclear option. In 2011, the Union of Concerned Scientists released a report stating nuclear power should be excluded in mitigation plans since 'nuclear plants are unique in their potential to cause catastrophic damage due to accidents, sabotage, or terrorism; to produce very long-lived radioactive wastes; and to exacerbate nuclear proliferation' (Koplow 2011: 112). Over the years, some of these risks have been aptly demonstrated at Three Mile Island, Chernobyl, and Fukushima. Although new performance records for new reactor designs have emerged, with some touting their safety records (cf. Piera 2010), the public is still divided in its interpretation of the risks associated with nuclear energy.

In addition, the same problems attached to nuclear weapons are also attached to nuclear energy. The technology could fall into the wrong hands. The threat of a nuclear war, moreover, can only divide attention to rapid climate mitigation. A large-scale global increase in nuclear energy only exacerbates the ability of some states, and to some extent, of terror groups to obtain or enrich uranium for nuclear weapons, putting the world at greater risk of a nuclear war or catastrophic terror attacks (Miller and Sagan 2009; Harding 2007). Moreover, the radioactive wastes produced by nuclear reactors must be stored for thousands of years, which has technical and long-term cost implications (Adamantiades and Kessides 2009).

For rapid mitigation, the nuclear option could not meet its speed requirement. Nuclear power has long construction and deployment times – a median of nine years plus the time required for planning and siting (Koomey and Hultman 2007). In his computations, Mark Jacobson (2009) showed that the overall time between planning and operation of a nuclear power plant ranges between 10–19 years. Globally, trends show that nuclear power plant construction times are increasing. Between 2004 and 2014, for instance, average construction time was ten years, with some facilities constructed at 36.3 years (Schneider and Froggatt 2014). By contrast, utility-scale wind, solar, and geothermal installations can be accomplished within two to five years (Jacobson 2009). Wind farms take one to three years in the development stage – that is, the time required to identify a site, purchase or lease a land, monitor winds, install transmission, negotiate a power-purchase agreement, and obtain permits – and between one and two years to construct. CSPs have a similar construction and deployment timeline as a wind farm. A geothermal power plant takes between two and three years in the development stage and two to three years to build (Jacobson 2009). The sustainable energy technology portfolio, therefore, fits well with the Project's speed and time requirements.

There are other downsides of nuclear energy that need elaboration. The longer time required for siting, permissions, and constructions of nuclear reactors only contribute to rise in emissions. In the long-term, as high-grade uranium ore becomes scarce, and low-grade ore also becomes the major fuel, conventional nuclear plants become significant emitters on a life-cycle basis, 9–25 times more than wind energy (Lenzen 2008; Sovacool 2008; Hondo 2005). Although fast breeder reactors have much lower life-cycle emissions, they are still commercially unavailable and may not become so for decades if ever. Moreover, emissions from nuclear power plants accrue from the greater loss of soil carbon because of greater loss in vegetation resulting from land-use for nuclear power plants relative to wind turbine towers, which require minimal space (Jacobson and Delucchi 2011).

Another nuclear option disadvantage is its water intensive property. With climate change already altering the water cycle and putting stress on water supply, the viability of nuclear power for rapid climate mitigation becomes more questionable. Public perception, key in designing a country's energy portfolio (Goodfellow, Williams and Azapagic 2011), still revolves around the hazards of nuclear power (Sovacool 2011; cf. Slovic 1987; cf. Fischhoff et al. 1978). At a time when rapid climate mitigation is required, options that present fewer risks to society should be given priority in decision-making.

In addition to fossil fuel with CCS, fossil gas, and nuclear power, geoengineering, which received some attention in the mitigation narrative (e.g. Keith 2013; Hamilton 2013; Schellnhuber 2011; Royal Society 2009; Lenton and Vaughan 2009; Rasch et al. 2008; Schneider 2008; Carlin 2007; Crutzen 2006; Angel 2006), is and can be a key technology competitor to sustainable energy technologies. Geoengineering is a combined term for climate-altering technologies. Prominent among these are those that promise to remove CO_2 from the atmosphere, and those that aim to place an atmospheric 'protective cloud' through intentional emission of sulphate aerosols, an approach known as solar radiation management (SRM).

SRM has gained particular prominence and salience within the modeling community (see Vaughan and Lenton 2011), and has even been described as being effective and affordable by some (e.g. Keith 2013; Royal Society 2009). The technology tries to replicate the artificial mechanism of temporary global cooling that occurred after the 1991 eruption of Mount Pinatubo in the Philippines. The volcanic eruption blasted 20 million tonnes of sulphur dioxide into the stratosphere resulting in global mean temperatures falling by 0.5°C as the particles reflected the sunlight back into space.

David Keith is among the most vocal advocates of serious research into geoengineering, which he calls 'cheap and technically easy' (Keith 2013: ix). Keith proposes to use a fleet of 20 Gulfstream G650 jets to inject tonnes of sulphuric acid vapour into the stratosphere in a growing volume year by year: 25,000 tonnes in the first year, then 50,000 in the next, then 250,000 after a decade, then a million after a half century. Keith estimates this will cost less than US$6 billion for a decade, which is less than US$300 billion per year spent on sustainable energy technologies. The result, according to Keith's simulations, would warm the Earth by 1°C. He, however, does not suggest we let geoengineering take care of climate mitigation, and still advocates for the decarbonisation of the energy system.

Despite their potential for climate mitigation, geoengineering technologies are not yet widely demonstrated, primarily because of the huge associated risks of interfering with the climate (Hamilton 2013; Robock, Oman and Stenchikov 2008). Studies demonstrate that SRM, for instance, could reduce summer monsoon precipitation over China and India (Robock, Oman and

Stenchikov 2008), drought in Asia and Africa, ozone depletion, rapid warming, human error, commercial control, and military use of technology (Robock 2011: 384). Even Keith (2013) acknowledges the potential repercussions of putting a million tonnes of sulphur into the stratosphere, which could result in thousands of air pollution deaths a year. SRM, Keith (2013: 8–11) also notes, does nothing to stop ocean acidification. SRM could also result in system failure, ushering in abrupt climate change (Fleming 2010). Matthews and Caldeira (2007) estimate that abrupt failure or future deliberate termination of geoengineering projects could weaken climate sinks and climate-carbon cycle feedbacks and likely accelerate emissions leading to extremely high rates of temperature rise between +2°C and +4°C per decade.

The risks are further increased since adequate scientific backing and governance framework for geoengineering technologies remain conspicuously absent (Davies 2010). Should these many negative consequences occur, causality and liability will be impossible to attribute (Hulme, O'Neill and Dessai 2011; Hulme 2010), and can likely result in international conflicts and strains in international relations (Szerszynski et al. 2013). As with nuclear waste, the technological shelf life of geoengineering technologies also far exceeds the intent of its contemporary engineers, and this has long-term consequences about how it should and could be monitored, managed, and administered.

Fossil fuel with CCS, fossil gas, nuclear energy, and geoengineering, although they promise to quickly reverse warming, may only result in fatal consequences. These options are risky, temporary, band-aid approaches, failing to address the root causes of anthropogenic climate change. At a time when limited resources must be efficiently spent, these three options, which can have expensive consequences, only reduce and crowd out available resources that can be better spent towards the diffusion of proven and demonstrated sustainable energy technologies. These policy competitors, therefore, have zero role in the Rapid Mitigation Project. By contrast, sustainable energy systems address the causes of warming and achieve what these competing techniques cannot, that is, a safe and sustainable global energy supply system that can exist forever (Schellnhuber 2011).

Technical strategies for the Rapid Mitigation Project

Renewable resource potential for some high emission countries far exceeds any projected electricity demand. Globally, the potential surpasses current energy demand. To tap this potential, renewable electricity generation demands new power generator installations, including wind turbines, rooftop solar PV, utility-scale solar (solar PV plants and CSP), hydroelectric plants, geothermal plants, wave devices, and tidal turbines. In the context of the Project, these diffusions have to be rapid.

The volume of required devices to be installed has land-use implications, since space is needed for replacing current energy infrastructure with renewables. Along this line, Vaclav Smil (2015) raises concerns on the constraints imposed by low power densities, or power capacity per unit of area, to wind and solar. He has omitted, however, to note the compatibility of wind farms with agricultural land, as they only occupy 1% to 2% of land spanned (this is approximately 1.6% of U.S. land, according to Jacobson et al. 2016), and a large fraction of solar PV can be installed on existing rooftops or on elevated canopies above highways, parking lots, and other structures (Jacobson et al. 2016; Denholm et al. 2009). Additionally, Sørensen and Meibom (2000) have demonstrated by means of a global information system study that a global 100% renewable energy is possible without coming into conflict with food production if international trade in renewable energy takes place.

Since renewable electricity technologies have unique location dependent characteristics, land-use implications are largely dependent on the natural endowments of the locality, state, or country. For the state of Washington, for example, the scenario developed by Jacobson et al. (2016) proposes no CSP since the state does not have much direct solar radiation exposure. Instead, the plan for Washington State is to have wind play a larger role, with 48% of electricity to be provided by this source. Hydropower will provide 35.42% of the total energy; solar, mostly through solar PVs will supply the 15.3% remaining demand (Jacobson et al. 2016). In the plan for Washington, a spacing area estimated at 2% of the state's total land will be used for onshore wind turbines, which, according to the authors, is relatively small and can be used for growing agricultural crops, grazing, or open space.

Globally, a 100% renewable energy scenario needs approximately 0.652% of new land area, which will mostly be located in deserts and barren lands (Jacobson et al. 2015). Indeed, the regions with the best solar potential, specifically for CSP, also have the largest non-agricultural land with little vegetation: Australia, northwest China, the Middle East, northwest India, North Africa and southwest U.S.A. Jacobson and Delucchi (2011: 1160) suggest that the total footprint on the ground for the 3.8 million wind turbines' tubular tower and base that could provide 50% of the global power demand in 2030 is approximately 48 km^2, smaller than the island of Manhattan by 11.5 km^2.

To power the entire U.S.A. with wind, water, and sunlight, Jacobson et al. (2015) estimate that approximately 0.42% of U.S. land area, mostly for solar PV power plants, is required. NREL and Carnegie Institution show that sites for renewable energy installations in the country can take an estimated 11% of the U.S. mainland, which can be located in approximately 11% of marginalised U.S. land area. These marginalised locations are disadvantaged by natural and/or artificial forces and are generally underused, difficult to cultivate, and have low economic value, yet are suitable for renewable energy development. On these lands, approximately 4.5 PWh of electricity could be produced from utility-scale PV, 4 PWh from CSP, 2.7 PWh from wind,

1.9 PWh from biomass, 11 TWh from mini-hydropower plants, 8.8 TWh from hydrothermal and geothermal, and 7.3 TWh from landfill gas (Milbrandt et al. 2014). If utilised to their full potentials, these are even beyond the projected requirements of power global energy end use in 2050.

The Project requires renewable electricity system deployments according to natural endowments availability, capacity, end-use, and service locations, which could be centralised or decentralised/distributed; on-grid or off-grid; small or utility-scale. In choosing what technologies to deploy, decision makers take into account the contingent impacts on social, natural and physical environments. The emissions contribution of these technologies and systems as they occur across the value chain are also accounted for in decision-making. For instance, new installations of large hydroelectric dams should be kept to a minimum considering their methane emissions (Beaulieu et al. 2014; Li and Lu 2012) and their social, political and cultural implications (Tilt, Braun and He 2009).

Delivery of energy service to end-users is made as efficient as possible, conserving all possible energy along the way. For centralised, on-grid infrastructure, grids are improved through an accelerated development of new transmission lines that link renewable energy generation regions with end-users. Existing grids are refurbished to reduce losses from aging grids. Smart technologies are integrated to enable greater system demand response.

Storage technologies are key for addressing intermittency – and, therefore, are an important component of the transition. Storage technologies in various forms and capacities are connected to the grid where it balances power delivery from renewable energy generators (Mathiesen et al. 2015). They are tapped to provide other energy services including load levelling, peak shaving/valley filling, load following, spinning reserve, power quality, investment deferral, end-use applications, demand side management, loss reduction, and contingency service (Lopes Ferreira et al. 2013). Since most of these technologies are not yet fully developed to their commercial potential, support is provided to accelerate research and development (R&D) for their efficiency and for reducing their costs.

Storage technologies for large-scale applications comprise mechanical, electrical, electro-chemical, and chemical options (Soloveichik 2011). Of these four, the electrochemical option is popular because of its pollution free operation, high round-trip efficiency, low maintenance, and long lifecycle. Electro-chemical storage also has essential energy characteristics for sustainable energy transition, such as quick response to meet grid functions (Winter and Brodd 2004). For integrating renewable sources, batteries represent excellent energy storage technology, while fuel cells and super capacitors are appropriate media for electric energy with high power or energy density (Simon and Gogotsi 2008).

As electricity demand is met by renewable energy supply, strategies for reducing emissions from the transport and mobility sector are also envisaged. Fossil fuel-based passenger transport is phased out and replaced with improved public transport, such as trains and buses fuelled by renewable electricity and low-carbon private cars. Increased use of active transport such as cycling and walking, and other means of demand reduction of private car use are also encouraged and supported by policy. In addition, electric vehicles whose batteries are charged with renewable electricity, electric vehicles and hydrogen fuel cells for urban use and biofuelled vehicles for rural road and air travel are extensively deployed. Battery electric vehicles with fast charging or battery swapping are used in long-distance, light-duty ground travel. Battery electric-hydrogen fuel cell hybrid vehicles dominate heavy-duty ground travel and long-distance water-borne shipping. Aircrafts are powered by electrolytic cryogenic hydrogen, combined with batteries used for idling, taxiing, and internal power. Similar with storage technologies for renewable electricity, R&D for battery technologies for transport will also be aggressively supported.

For efficient mobility, complementary transport sector strategies are necessary. These include: improving transport infrastructure; integrating urban and transport planning; improving route capacity, connectivity, and service frequency of existing public transport; creating more cycling and pedestrian walkways; instituting moratoria on new urban highway construction; and installing renewable energy-powered recharging and battery swapping stations for electric vehicles.

Fossil fuel-based sea and air travel and freight transport are phased out, and replaced with greater rail use for long-distance transport, electric urban delivery vehicles, biofuelled truck transport in rural areas. Shipping route efficiencies and fuel consumption reduction are also improved. Moratoria on the construction of new cargo and airport terminals are also necessary to reduce transport sector emissions. Moratoria on new airport construction are also key as carbon-intensive airplanes are phased out in favour of more efficient planes and rail alternatives to on-shore air trips. Air travel is also limited, while R&D on less carbon-intensive, ecologically sustainable jet fuels, including advanced biofuel blends, is aggressively pursued.

For heating and cooling, heat pumps powered by renewable electricity are widely used. Solar hot water preheating and/or heat pumps with electric resistance elements are used to generate hot water. Cogeneration, trigeneration, air-source, and ground-source heat pumps, solar space heating and cooling, and solar hot water in appropriate regions are expanded. High-temperature industrial heat from coal and gas combustion are phased out and replaced where possible with renewable electricity and solar heat. Where available, geothermal energy is also tapped for heating purposes.

Strategies for the sustainable energy transition also adopt energy efficiency measures in lighting, appliances, industrial equipment, buildings, and the built environment. Where possible, demand-side monitoring technologies such as smart meters that can track electricity consumption and reduce unnecessary use are deployed.

Minimum energy performance standards (MEPS) are implemented for all energy-using appliance, lighting, and electrical equipment. Efficiency measures are introduced through: LED lighting; optimised air conditioning; water-cooled heat exchangers; improved air flow management; and advanced lighting controls. MEPS play a crucial role in the transition from less efficient to more efficient products since standards stimulate the market penetration of energy efficient items by generating large unit cost reductions.

Existing buildings are monitored for their energy use. Energy audits are performed to determine wasteful processes and energy waste discovery. Building codes for renovation of existing buildings as new technologies become available are regularly revised to maximise building efficiency potential. Existing buildings falling below efficiency standards are retrofitted whenever possible. A comprehensive programme to increase energy efficiency of all inhabited buildings is implemented. The programme includes insulation and upgrading of existing technologies to reduce heating losses by: sealing leaks in windows, doors, and fireplaces; converting to double-paned windows; and using more passive solar heating. For new construction, only highly efficient and sustainable buildings are allowed. Less carbon intensive construction materials and techniques are used. MEPS for new buildings, stricter than those for retrofits, are also implemented.

Most emissions reduction from managed energy demand is behavioural. In pushing for the adoption of these behaviours, some forms of social architecture are developed. Richard Thaler and Cass Sunstein (2008: 6) call this design of social architecture 'nudges', which they describe as

> any aspect of the choice architecture that alters people's behavior in a predictable way without forbidding any options or significantly changing their economic incentives. To count as a mere nudge, the intervention must be easy and cheap to avoid. Nudges are not mandates.

An example of a social nudge that can produce significant emissions reductions through demand management is emissions information disclosures for significant emitters, vehicles, and buildings. By having information about their current emissions widely publicised, top emitters can be nudged to significantly reduce their emissions. Using the U.S. Toxic Release Inventory as example, Thaler and Sunstein (2008: 190–191) show how companies can be nudged to adopt stronger measures by being threatened with 'environmental blacklists'.

Voluntary labelling is another form of nudge (Li, Molodtsov and Delina 2010). Since cost is a key reason for reducing energy use for most consumers, labels on appliances and buildings that show the dollar amount of savings in electricity bills can nudge end users to opt for emission-reducing products and activities. Efficiency in transport can also be achieved by labelling vehicles with their emissions and monetary savings potential. This can nudge carmakers and consumers towards producing and purchasing highly efficient and low-carbon vehicles. Making public transport accessible and efficient to everyone, and providing cycling and walking pathways are other ways to nudge the public to opt for low-carbon choices.

A sustainable energy transition – the locus of and mode for the Rapid Mitigation Project – requires dramatic diffusion of new energy technologies. The Project, however, is not merely a technical pursuit; it is also about rethinking the way we order our societies and arrange our institutions. These processes require the coupling of technical change with wide-ranging changes in the ways we, and our institutions, behave. Since these are much more challenging to address than the technical transition itself, further elaborations on the ways we think are required.

References

Adamantiades, A. & Kessides, I. 2009, 'Nuclear power for sustainable development: current status and future prospects', *Energy Policy*, vol. 37, pp. 5149–5166.

AEMO (Australian Energy Market Operator) 2012, '*Fact sheet: the National Electricity Market*', Australia, http://bit.ly/1VV7m7g.

AEMO 2013, *100 Per Cent Renewables Study – Modeling Outcomes*, Australia, http://bit.ly/1eTEST7.

Allen, P., Blake, L., Harper, P., Hooker-Stroud, A., James, P. & Kellner, T. 2013, *Zero Carbon Britain: Rethinking the Future*, Centre for Alternative Technology, Powys, U.K.

Alvarez, R.A., Pacala, S.W., Winebrake, J.J., Chameides, W.L., Hamburg, S.P. 2012, 'Greater focus needed on methane leakage from natural gas infrastructure', *PNAS*, vol. 109, pp. 6435–6644.

Angel, R. 2006, 'Feasibility of cooling the Earth with a cloud of small spacecraft near the inner Lagrange point (L1)', *PNAS*, vol. 103, pp. 17184–17189.

Bazilian, M., Mai, T., Baldwin, S., Arent, A., Miller, M. & Logan, J. 2014, 'Decision-making for high renewable electricity futures in the United States', *Energy Strategy Reviews*, vol. 2, pp. 326–328.

Beaulieu, J.J., Smolenski, R.L., Nietch, C.T., Townsend-Small, A., Elovitz, M.S. 2014, 'High methane emissions from a midlatitudes reservoir draining an agricultural watershed', *Environmental Science and Technology*, vol. 48, pp. 11100–11108.

Blechinger, P., Seguin, R., Cader, C., Bertheau, P. & Breyer, C. 2014, 'Assessment of the global potential for renewable energy storage systems on small islands', *Energy Procedia*, vol. 46, pp. 294–300.

Boot, P.A. & Van Bree, B. 2010, *A Zero-carbon European Power System in 2050: Proposals for a Policy Package*, Energy Research Centre of the Netherlands, Amsterdam, The Netherlands.

Bruckner, T., Bashmakov, I.A., Mulugetta, Y., Chum, H., Navarro, A. et al. 2014, 'Energy Systems', in O. Edenhofer, R. Pichs-Madruga, Y. Sokona, E. Farahani, S. Kadner et al. (eds), *Climate Change 2014: Mitigation of Climate Change, Contribution of Working Group III to the Fifth Assessment Report of the Intergovernmental Panel on Climate Change*, Cambridge University Press, Cambridge, U.K; New York, U.S.A., pp. 511–597.

Budishaka, C., Sewell, D., Thomson, H., Mach, L., Veron, D.E. & Kempton, V. 2013, 'Cost-minimised combinations of wind power, solar power and electrochemical storage, powering the grid up to 99.9% of the time', *Journal of Power Sources*, vol. 225, pp. 60–74.

Carlin, A. 2007, 'Global climate change control: is there a better strategy than reducing greenhouse gas emissions?' *University of Pennsylvania Law Review*, vol. 155, pp. 1401–1492.

Caulton, D.R., Shepson, P.B., Santoro, R.L., Sparks, J.P., Howarth, R.W. et al. 2014. 'Toward a better understanding and quantification of methane emissions from shale gas development', *PNAS*, vol. 111, pp. 6237–6242.

Chase, J. 2012, 'Breakthroughs in solar power: It's not just about technology any more', Presentation at the Bloomberg New Energy Finance Summit, 5 April, http://bit.ly/1eCy39c.

Cherubini, F., Peters, G.P., Bernstein, T., Stromman, A.H. & Hertwich, E. 2011, 'CO2 emissions from biomass combustion for bioenergy: atmospheric decay and contribution to global warming', *Global Change Biology: Bionenergy*, vol. 3, pp. 413–426.

Chiodi, A., Gargiulo, M., Rogan, F., Deane, J.P., Lavigne, D. et al. 2013, 'Modeling the impacts of challenging 2050 European climate mitigation targets on Ireland's energy system', *Energy Policy*, vol. 53, pp. 169–189.

Connolly, D. & Mathiesen, B.V. 2014, 'A technical and economic analysis of one potential pathway to a 100% renewable energy system', *International Journal of Sustainable Energy Planning and Management'*, vol. 1, pp. 7–27.

Connolly, D., Lund, H., Mathiesen, B.V. & Leahy, M. 2011, 'The first step towards a 100% renewable energy-system for Ireland', *Applied Energy*, vol. 88, pp. 502–507.

Crutzen, P. 2006, 'Albedo enhancement by stratospheric sulfur injections: A contribution to resolve a policy dilemma?' *Climatic Change*, vol. 77, pp. 211–219.

Davies, G. 2010, 'Geoengineering: a critique', *Climate Law*, vol. 1, pp. 429–441.

Delucchi, M. 2010, 'Impacts of biofuels on climate, land, and water', *Annals of the New York Academy of Sciences*, vol. 1195, pp. 28–45.

Delucchi, M. & Jacobson, M. 2011, 'Providing all global energy with wind, water, and solar power, part II: reliability, system and transmission costs, and policies', *Energy Policy*, vol. 39, pp. 1170–1190.

Denholm, P., Hand, M., Jackson, M. & Ong, S. 2009, *Land-Use Requirements of Modern Wind Power Plants in the United States*, Technical report NREL/TP-6A2-45834, National Renewable Energy Laboratory, Golden, Colorado, U.S.A.

Diesendorf, M. 2009, *Climate Action: A Campaign Manual for Greenhouse Solutions*, University of New South Wales Press, Sydney, Australia.

Dunlap, R.E. & McCright, A.M., 2011, 'Organized climate change denial', in J.S. Dryzek, R.B. Norgaard and D. Schlossberg (eds), *The Oxford Handbook of Climate Change and Society*, Oxford University Press, Oxford, U.K., pp. 144–160.

Eikenjager, M.-I. & Breitner, M.H. 2012, '100% renewable fuel in Germany 2050: a quantitative scenario analysis', in S. Helber et al. (eds), *Operations Research Proceedings 2012*, Springer, Switzerland, pp. 327–332.

Elliston, B., Diesendorf, M. & McGill, I. 2012, 'Simulation of scenarios with 100% renewable electricity in the Australian National Electricity Market', *Energy Policy*, vol. 45, pp. 606–613.

Elliston, B., MacGill, I. & Diesendorf, M. 2013, 'Least cost 100% renewable electricity scenarios in the Australian National Electricity Market', *Energy Policy*, vol. 59, pp. 270–282.

Elliston, B., MacGill, I. & Diesendorf, M. 2014, 'Comparing least cost scenarios for 100% renewable electricity with low emission fossil fuel scenarios in the Australian National Electricity Market', *Renewable Energy*, vol. 66, pp. 196–204.

Energy Information Administration (EIA) 2008, *International Energy Outlook 2008*, U.S. Department of Energy, Washington, D.C., U.S.A.

European Renewable Energy Council (EREC) 2010, *Rethinking 2050: A 100% Renewable Energy Vision for the European Union*, EREC, http://www.erec.org.

Fay, M., Hallegatte, S., Vogt-Schiilb, A., Rozenberg, J., Narloch, U. & Kerr, T. 2015, *Decarbonizing Development: Three Steps to a Zero-Carbon Future*, The World Bank, Washington, D.C., U.S.A.

Feng, K., Davis, S.J., Sun, L. & Hubacek, K. 2015, 'Drivers of the US CO_2 emissions 1997–2013', *Nature Communications*, doi: 10.1038/ncomms8714.

Fernandes, L. & Ferreira, P. 2014, 'Renewable energy scenarios in the Portuguese electricity system', *Energy*, vol. 69, p. 51–57.

Fischhoff, B., Slovic, P., Lichtenstein, S., Read, S. & Combs, B. 1978, 'How safe is safe enough? A psychometric study of attitudes towards technological risks and benefit', *Policy Sciences*, vol. 9, pp. 127–152.

Fleming, J.R. 2010, *Fixing the Sky: The Checkered History of Weather and Climate Control*, Columbia University Press, New York, U.S.A.

Fouquet, R. 2010, 'The slow search for solutions: lessons from historical energy transitions by sector and service', *Energy Policy*, vol. 38, pp. 6586–6596.

Garnaut, R. 2011, *The Garnaut Review 2011: Australia in the Global Response to Climate Change*, Cambridge University Press, Melbourne, Australia; New York, U.S.A.

German Advisory Council on the Environment (SRU) 2011, *Pathways Towards a 100% Renewable Electricity System*, SRU, Berlin, Germany.

Glasnovic, Z. & Margeta, J. 2011, 'Vision of total renewable electricity scenario', *Renewable and Sustainable Energy Reviews*, vol. 15, pp. 1873–1884.

Global Carbon Atlas 2015, *Emissions*, The Global Carbon Project, http://bit.ly/1JCXDMC.

Goodfellow, M.J., Williams, H.R. & Azapagic 2011, 'Nuclear renaissance, public perception and design criteria: an exploratory review', *Energy Policy*, vol. 39, pp. 6199–6210.

Government of Denmark 2011, *Our Future Energy*, Copenhagen, Denmark, http://bit.ly/1dcC1XD.

Government of Scotland 2011, *2020 Routemap for Renewable Energy in Scotland*, http://bit.ly/184zcXF.

Granade, H.C., Creyts, J., Derkach, A., Farese, P., Nyquist, S. & Ostrowski, K. 2009, *Unlocking Energy Efficiency in the U.S. Economy*, McKinsey & Company.

Grattan Institute 2012, *No Easy Choices: Which Way to Australia's Energy Future?*Grattan Institute, http://bit.ly/19EXRwp.

Greenpeace International & European Renewable Energy Council (EREC) 2010, *Energy [R]evolution: A Sustainable World Energy Outlook*, Greenpeace International and EREC, Amsterdam, The Netherlands.

Hamilton, C. 2013, *Earth Masters: Playing God with the Climate*, Allen & Unwin, Crows Nest, New South Wales, Australia.

Hansen, J., Emanuel, K., Caldeira, K. & Wigley, T. 2015, 'Nuclear power paves the only viable path forward on climate change', *The Guardian*, 3 December, http://bit.ly/1lZEU4j.

Hansen, J., Johnson, D., Lacis, A., Lebedeff, S., Lee, P. et al. 1981, 'Climate impact of increasing carbon dioxide', *Science*, vol. 213, pp. 957–966.

Harding, J. 2007, *Economics of New Nuclear Power and Proliferation Risks in a Carbon-Constrained World*, Nonproliferation Policy Education Center, Washington, D.C., U.S.A., http://bit.ly/1Oui00D.

Harvey, F. 2011, 'Nuclear is the safest form of power, says top UK scientist', *The Guardian*, 30 March, http://bit.ly/1ay3fYf.

Hastings-Simon, S., Pinner, D. & Stuchtey, M. 2014, 'Myths and realities of clean technologies', *Insights*, McKinsey & Co., http://bit.ly/1t5yjnW.

Herzog, H. 2011, 'Scaling up carbon dioxide capture and storage: From megatons to gigatons', *Energy Economics*, vol. 33, pp. 597–604

Hondo, H. 2005, 'Life cycle GHG emission analysis of power generation systems: Japanese case', *Energy*, vol. 30, pp. 2042–2056.

Howarth, R. 2014, 'A bridge to nowhere: Methane emissions and the greenhouse gas footprint of natural gas', *Energy Science and Engineering*, vol. 22, pp. 47–60.

Hulme, H. 2010, 'Climate intervention schemes could be undone by geopolitics', *Yale Environment 360*, http://bit.ly/1fdZ431.

Hulme, H., O'Neill, S.J. & Dessai, S. 2011, 'Is weather event attribution necessary for adaptation funding?' *Science*, vol. 334, pp. 764–765.

IEA (International Energy Agency) 2010, *Energy Technology Perspectives 2010*, IEA/OECD, Paris, France.

IEA 2013, *Redrawing the Energy-Climate Map: World Energy Outlook Special Report*, IEA/OECD, Paris, France.

IPCC (Intergovernmental Panel on Climate Change) 2005, *IPCC special report on carbon dioxide capture and storage*, prepared by Working Group III of the Intergovernmental Panel on Climate Change [B. Metz, O. Davidson, H.C. de Coninck, M. Loos & L.A. Meyer (eds)], Cambridge University Press, Cambridge, U.K; New York, NY, USA.

IPCC 2013, 'Summary for Policymakers', in T.F. Stocker, G.D. Qin, G.-K. Plattner, M. Tignor, S.K. Allen, J. Boschung et al. (eds), *Climate Change 2013: The Physical Science Basis. Contribution of Working Group I to the Fifth Assessment Report of the IPCC*, Cambridge University Press, Cambridge, U.K.; New York, U.S.A., pp. 3–29.

IPCC 2014, *Climate Change 2014: Synthesis Report of the Fifth Assessment Report of the IPCC*, The Core Writing Team, R.K. Pachauri & L. Meyer (eds), IPCC, http://bit.ly/1umDnCQ.

International Renewable Energy Agency (IRENA) 2013, *Renewable Power Generation Costs in 2012: An Overview*, IRENA, Abu Dhabi, U.A.E.

Ison, N., Usher, J., Cantley-Smith, R., Harris, S. & Dunstan, C. 2011, *The NEM Report Card: How well does the National Electricity Market serve Australia?* Institute for Sustainable Futures (ISF) Technical Report, ISF, University of Technology Sydney, Sydney, Australia.

Jacobson, M. 2009, 'Review of solutions to global warming, air pollution, and energy security', *Energy and Environmental Science*, vol. 2, pp. 148–173.

Jacobson, M. 2015, personal communication to the author, email, 29 November. Cited with permission.

Jacobson, M. & Delucchi, M. 2011, 'Providing all global energy with wind, water, and solar power, Part I: Technologies, energy resources, quantities and areas of infrastructure, and materials', *Energy Policy*, vol. 39, pp. 1170–1190.

Jacobson, M., Delucchi, M., Bazouin, G., Bauer, Z.A.F., Heavey, C.C. et al. 2015, '100% clean and renewable wind, water, sunlight (WWS) all-sector energy roadmaps for the 50 United States', *Energy & Environmental Science*, vol. 8, pp. 2093–2117.

Jacobson, M., Delucchi, M., Bazouin, G., Dvorak, M.J., Arghandeh, R. et al. 2016, 'A 100% wind, water, sunlight (WWS) all-sector energy plan for Washington State', *Renewable Energy*, vol. 86, pp. 75–88.

Jacobson, M., Delucchi, M., Bauer, Z.A.F., Goodman, S.C., Chapman, W.E. et al. 2014, '100% clean and renewable wind, water, and sunlight (WWS) all-sector energy roadmaps for 139 countries of the world', 27 November 2015, http://stanford.io/1lvUaVS, accessed 30 November 2015.

Jacobson, M., Delucchi, M., Ingraffea, A.R., Howarth, R.W., Bazouin, G., et al. 2014, 'A roadmap for repowering California for all purposes with wind, water, and sunlight', *Energy*, vol. 73, pp. 875–889.

Jacobson, M., Howarth, R.W., Delucchi, M., Scobies, S.R., Barth, J.M. et al. 2013, 'Examining the feasibility of converting New York State's all-purpose energy infrastructure to one using wind, water, and sunlight', *Energy Policy*, vol. 57, pp. 585–601.

Keith, D. 2013, *A Case for Climate Engineering*, The MIT Press, Cambridge, Massachusetts, U.S.A.

Kemp, M. & Wexler, J. (eds) 2010, *Zero Carbon Britain 2030: A New Strategy*, Centre for Alternative Technology (CAT), CAT Publications, Wales, U.K.

Kern, F. & Smith, A. 2008, 'Restructuring energy systems for sustainability? Energy transition policy in the Netherlands', *Energy Policy*, vol. 36, pp. 4093–4103.

Klein, N. 2014, *This Changes Everything: Capitalism vs. The Climate*, Simon & Schuster, New York, U.S.A.

Koomey, J. & Hultman, N.E. 2007, 'A reactor-level analysis of bus bar costs for US nuclear plants, 1970–2005', *Energy Policy*, vol. 35, pp. 5630–5642.

Koplow, D. 2011, *Nuclear Power: Still Not Viable without Subsidies*, Union of Concerned Scientists Publications, Cambridge, Massachusetts, U.S.A., http://bit.ly/1jYqn3o.

Kraja, G., Dui, N. & Carvalho, M. 2011, 'How to achieve a 100% RES electricity supply for Portugal?' *Applied Energy*, vol. 88, pp. 508–517.

Krajacić, G, Duic, N, Zmijarevic, Z, Mathiesen, B.V., Vucinic, A.A. & Carvalho, M. 2011, 'Planning for a 100% independent energy system based on smart energy storage for integration of renewables and CO2 emissions reduction', *Applied Thermal Engineering*, vol. 31, pp. 2073–2083.

Lazard 2013, *Lazard's Levelized Cost of Energy Analysis – Version 7.0*, http://bit.ly/1a lI6On.

Lazard 2014, *Lazard's Levelized Cost of Energy Analysis – Version 8.0*, http://bit.ly/1m ixlEH.

Lehmann, H. 2003, *Energy Rich Japan, Technical Report*, Institute for Sustainable Solutions and Innovations, http://bit.ly/1EKqhFE.

Lenton, T.M. & Vaughan, N.E. 2009, 'The radiative forcing potential of different climate geoengineering options', *Atmospheric Chemistry and Physics*, vol. 9, pp. 5539–5561.

Lenzen, M. 2008, 'Life cycle energy and greenhouse gas emissions of nuclear energy: a review', *Energy Conversion and Management*, vol. 49, pp. 2178–2199.

Li, S. & Lu, X.X. 2012, 'Uncertainties of carbon emission from hydroelectric reservoirs', *Natural Hazards*, vol. 62, pp. 1343–1345.

Li, T., Molodtsov, S. & Delina, L.L. 2010, *Assessment Report of Energy Efficiency Institutional Arrangements in Asia and the Pacific*, United Nations, Bangkok, Thailand.

Liu, W., Lund, H., Mathiesen, B.V. & Zhang, X. 2011, 'Potential of renewable energy systems in China', *Applied Energy*, vol. 88, pp. 518–525.

Lopes Ferrera, H., Garde, R., Fulli, G., Kling, W. & Pecas Lopes, J. 2013, 'Characterisation of electrical energy storage technologies', *Energy*, vol. 53, pp. 288–298.

Lovelock, J. 2004, 'James Lovelock: nuclear power is the only green solution', *The Independent*, 24 May, http://ind.pn/1hL92sq.

Lund, H. & Mathiesen, B.V. 2009, 'Energy system analysis of 100% renewable energy systems – the case of Denmark in years 2030 and 2050', *Energy*, vol. 34, pp. 524–531.

Mai, T., Mulcahy, D., Hand, M.M. & Baldwin, S.F. 2014, 'Envisioning a renewable electricity future for the United States', *Energy*, vol. 65, pp. 374–386.

Mason, I.G., Page, S.C. & Williamson, A.G. 2010, 'A 100% renewable electricity generation system for New Zealand utilising hydro, wind, geothermal and biomass resources', *Energy Policy*, vol. 38, pp. 3973–3984.

Mason, I.G., Page, S.C. & Williamson, A.G. 2013, 'Security of supply, energy spillage control and peaking options within a 100% renewable electricity system for New Zealand', *Energy Policy*, vol. 60, pp. 324–333.

Mathiesen, B.V., Lund, H. & Karlsson, K. 2011, '100% Renewable energy systems, climate mitigation and economic growth', *Applied Energy*, vol. 88, pp. 488–501.

Mathiesen, B.V., Lund, H., Connolly, D., Wenzel, H., Ostergaard, P.A. et al. 2015, 'Smart Energy Systems for coherent 100% renewable energy and transport solutions', *Applied Energy*, vol. 145, pp. 139–154.

Matthews, H.D. & Caldeira, K. 2007, 'Transient climate-carbon simulations of planetary geoengineering', *PNAS*, vol. 104, pp. 9949–9954.

Milbrandt, A.R., Heimiller, D.M., Perry, A.D. & Field, C.B. 2014, 'Renewable energy potential on marginal lands in the United States', *Renewable and Sustainable Energy Reviews*, vol. 29, pp. 473–481.

Miller, S. & Sagan, S. 2009, 'Nuclear power without proliferation?' *Daedalus*, Fall, pp. 7–18.

Morris, C. & Pehnt, M. 2014, *Energy Transition: The German Energiewende*, Heinrich Böll Stiftung, Berlin, Germany.

Myhrvold, N.P. & Caldeira, K. 2012, 'Greenhouse gases, climate change and the transition from coal to low-carbon electricity', *Environmental Research Letters*, vol. 7, 014019.

National Academies of Science of the Group of Eight, India, and China 2009, *Joint Science Academies' Statement: Global Response to Climate Change*, http://bit.ly/1xRTPOi.

Nelson, J., Johnston, J., Mileva, A., Fripp, M., Hoffman, I. et al. 2012, 'High resolution modeling of the western North American power system demonstrates low-cost and low-carbon futures', *Energy Policy*, vol. 43, pp. 436–447.

Nordhaus, W.D. 1977, *Strategies for the control of carbon dioxide*, Cowles Foundation Discussion Paper No. 443, Cowles Foundation for Research in Economics at Yale University, New Haven, Connecticut, U.S.A.

Nordhaus, W.D. 2015, 'Climate clubs: Overcoming free-riding in international climate policy', *American Economic Review*, vol. 105, pp. 1339–1970.

Pacala, S. & Socolow, R. 2004, 'Stabilization wedges: solving the climate problem for the next 50 years with current technologies', *Science*, vol. 305, pp. 968–972.

Palzer, A. & Henning, H.-M. 2014, 'A comprehensive model for the German electricity and heat sector in a future energy system with a dominant contribution from renewable energy technologies – Part II: Results', *Renewable and Sustainable Energy Reviews*, vol. 30, pp. 1019–1034.

Parkinson, G. 2014, 'UBS: Australian households could go off-grid by 2018', *RenewEconomy*, 9 May, http://bit.ly/1mMH3uo.

Parsons-Brinkerhoff 2009, *Powering the Future: Mapping our Low-carbon Path to 2050*, December, http://bit.ly/1OuhBex.

Pickens, T.B. 2009, *Pickens Plan*, http://bit.ly/1L8hotF.

Piera, M. 2010, 'Sustainability issues in the development of nuclear fission energy', *Energy Conversion and Management*, vol. 51, pp. 938–946.

Pourreza, S., Levine, R., Karp, S.K., Rudovic, M., Channell, J. et al. 2014, 'Evolving economics of power and alternative energy', *Citi Research*, 23 March, http://citi.us/1GEDYG0.

Rasch, P.J., Tilmes, S., Turco, R.P., Robock, A., Oman, L. et al. 2008, 'An overview of geoengineering of climate using stratospheric sulphate aerosols', *Philosophical Transactions of the Royal Society A*, vol. 366, pp. 4007–4037.

Rasmussen, M.G., Andresen, G.B. & Greiner, M. 2012, 'Storage and balancing synergies in a fully or highly renewable pan-European power system', *Energy Policy*, vol. 51, pp. 642–651.

Revkin, A.C. 2013, 'To those influencing environmental policy but opposed to nuclear power', *The New York Times*, 3 November, http://nyti.ms/1gHUU5I.

Richardson, K., Dahl-Jensen, D., Elmeskov, J., Hagem, C., Henningsen, J. et al. 2011, 'Denmark's roadmap for fossil fuel independence', *Solutions*, vol. 2, pp. 46–55.

Robock, A. 2011, 'Bubble, bubble, toil and trouble', *Climatic Change*, vol. 105, pp. 383–385.

Robock, A., Oman, L. & Stenchikov, G.L. 2008, 'Regional climate responses to geoengineering with tropical and Arctic SO2 injection', *Journal of Geophysical Research*, vol. 113, D16101.

Royal Society 2009, *Geoengineering the Climate: Science, Governance and Uncertainty*, The Royal Society, London, U.K.

Sakaguchi, T. & Tabata, T. 2015, '100% electric power potential of PV, wind power, and biomass energy in Awaji island Japan', *Renewable and Sustainable Energy Reviews*, vol. 51, pp. 1156–1165.

Sanseverino, E.R., Sanseverino, R.R., Favuzza, S., & Vacaro, V. 2014, 'Near zero energy islands in the Mediterranean: supporting policies and local obstacles', *Energy Policy*, vol. 66, pp. 592–602.

Schellnhuber, H.J. 2011, 'Geoengineering: the good, the MAD, and the sensible', *PNAS*, vol. 108, pp. 20277–20278.

Schneider, M. & Froggatt, A. 2014, *The World Nuclear Industry Status Report 2014*, Mycle Schneider Consulting, Paris, France.

Schneider, S. 2008, 'Geoengineering: could we or should we make it work?' *Philosophical Transactions of the Royal Society A*, vol. 366, pp. 3843–3862.

Schwartzman, P.D. & Schwartzman, D.W. 2011, *A Solar Transition is Possible*, Institute for Policy Research & Development, London, U.K.

Simon, P. & Gogotsi, Y. 2008, 'Materials for electrochemical capacitors', *Nature Materials*, vol. 7, p. 845–854.

Slovic, P. 1987, 'Perception of risk', *Science*, vol. 236, pp. 280–285.

Smil, V. 2015, *Power Density: A Key to Understanding Energy Sources and Uses*, The MIT Press, Cambridge, Massachusetts, U.S.A.

Soloveichik, G.L. 2011, 'Battery technologies for large-scale stationary energy storage', *Annual Review of Chemical and Biomolecular Engineering*, vol. 2, p. 503–527.

Sørensen, B. 1975, 'Energy and resources', *Science*, vol. 189, pp. 255–260.

Sørensen, B. 2008, 'A renewable energy and hydrogen scenario for northern Europe', *International Journal of Energy Research*, vol. 32, pp. 471–500.

Sørensen, B. & Meibom, P. 2000, 'A global renewable energy scenario', *International Journal of Global Energy Issues*, vol. 13, pp. 196–276.

Sovacool, B.K. 2008, 'Valuing the greenhouse gas emissions from nuclear power: A critical survey', *Energy Policy*, vol. 36, pp. 2950–2963.

Sovacool, B.K. 2011, *Contesting the Future of Nuclear Power: A Critical Global Assessment of Atomic Energy*, World Scientific, Singapore.

Sovacool, B.K. & Watts, C. 2009, 'Going completely renewable: is it possible (let alone desirable)?' *The Electricity Journal*, vol. 22, pp. 95–111.

Steinke, F., Wolfrum, P. & Hoffmann, C. 2013, 'Grid vs. storage in a 100% renewable Europe', *Renewable Energy*, vol. 50, pp. 826–832.

Szerszynski, B., Kearnes, M., Macnaghten, P., Owen, R. & Stilgoe, J. 2013, 'Why solar radiation management geoengineering and democracy won't mix', *Environment and Planning A*, vol. 45, pp. 2809–2816.

Teske, S., Muth, J. & Sawyer, S. 2012, *Energy [r]evolution: A Sustainable World Energy Outlook*, Greenpeace International, European Renewable Energy Council, Global Wind Energy Council, Hamburg, Germany.

Thaler, R.H. & Sunstein, C.R. 2008, *Nudge: Improving Decisions About Health, Wealth, and Happiness*, Yale University Press, New Haven, Connecticut, U.S.A.; London, U.K.

Tilt, B., Braun, Y. & He, D. 2009, 'Social impacts of large dam projects: a comparison of international case studies and implications for best practice', *Journal of Environmental Management*, vol. 90, pp. S249–S257.

Turner, G.M., Elliston, B. & Diesendorf, M. 2013, 'Impacts on the biophysical economy and environment of a transition to 100% renewable electricity in Australia', *Energy Policy*, vol. 54, pp. 288–299.

UBA 2012, *Nachhaltige Stromversorgung der Zukunft. Kosten und Nutzen einer Transformation hin zu 100% erneuerbaren Energien*, Dessau-Roßlau, http://bit.ly/1K4ShDY.

Van De Putte, J., Short, R., Beranek, J., Thies, F. & Teske, S. 2011, *Battle of the Grids Report 2011: How Europe can go 100% Renewable and Phase Out Dirty Energy*, Greenpeace, Amsterdam, The Netherlands.

Vaughan, N. & Lenton, T. 2011, 'A review of climate geoengineering proposals', *Climatic Change*, vol. 109, pp. 791–825.

Wadhwa, V. 2014, 'The coming era of unlimited – and free – clean energy', *The Washington Post*, 19 September, http://wapo.st/1G9V187.

Wagner, G. & Weitzman, M.L. 2015, *Climate Shock: the Economic Consequences of a Hotter Planet*, Princeton University Press, Princeton, New Jersey, U.S.A.

Washington, H. & Cook, J. 2011, *Climate Change Denial: Heads in the Sand*, Earthscan, London, U.K; Washington, D.C., U.S.A.

Winter, M. & Brodd, R.J. 2004, 'What are batteries, fuel cells, and supercapacitors', *Chemical Reviews*, vol. 104, p. 4245–4270.

World Wide Fund for Nature in Australia & Climate Risk 2012, *Our Clean Energy Future: 100% Renewables Powering Australia's Future*, WWF-Australia and Climate Risk, Sydney, Australia.

World Wide Fund for Nature, Ecofys, & Office for Metropolitan Architecture 2011, *The Energy Report: 100% Renewable Energy by 2050*, WWF International, Gland, Switzerland.

Wright, M. & Hearps, P. 2010, *Australian Sustainable Energy: Zero Carbon Australia Stationary Energy Plan*, University of Melbourne Energy Research Institute, Melbourne, Australia.

3 Scale, speed, scope

A Rapid Mitigation Agreement

With large carbon emissions, deep cuts can be realised by rapid, aggressive, and scalable actions that present large-scale opportunities for having resilient infrastructure, reaping the benefits and co-benefits of transition to health, economy and society, and reducing the burdens of climate change. Moving fast enough on a grand scale requires quick decision-making that is currently out of reach in many contemporary neoliberal-oriented democratic governments. Using a *Gedankenexperiment*, I offer a scenario – undoubtedly highly idealised and even utopian – for executing what this book calls 'the Rapid Mitigation Project'.

The scenario postulates an international agreement on the accelerated approach to climate mitigation, called the *Rapid Mitigation Agreement*, or henceforth the Agreement, which is different in structure and content from the Paris Agreement and its Kyoto predecessor. Its focus on the benefits that can be harvested from aggressive actions overshadows the burden-framing characteristics of previous and current climate agreements.

The Agreement sets the stage for achieving deep national emission cuts and auditing national achievements. Under the aegis of the Agreement, governments of developed and rapidly developing countries, whose emissions are the highest, both historically and currently, agree to accomplish a global target of close to zero emission from the energy sector within 30 years, but not later than 2035. Least developed countries, meanwhile, implement the Project within 40 years, but not later than 2050. This ensures that by mid-century, global emissions have peaked and will be declining steeply.

The Agreement differs from previous climate agreements since it addresses free-riding – one of the reasons cited for non-cooperative, ineffective, and general lack of progress on climate mitigation to date (Wagner and Weitzman 2015; Nordhaus 2015). Free-riding has, for long, been tempting, and inarguably driving, countries to push policies towards minimal abatements. The Paris agreement, which remain essentially voluntary similar to its Kyoto predecessor, reflect this condition; thus, it has a minimal prospect for ensuring deeper and rapid cuts on emission.

The Project focuses on the energy sector based on high confidence in sustainable energy transition's contribution to rapid mitigation. The scenario envisages countries with substantial excess renewable energy capacity providing international exports, either by transmission line or by modified liquefied natural gas tanker ships carrying hydrogen or a hydrogen compound produced by renewable energy. As renewable energy technologies are deployed and scaled, demand reductions through energy efficiency technologies and energy conservation spread swiftly across the world. At some stages, programmes to peak anthropogenic GHG emissions from other sectors, such as agriculture and forestry, are included in the Project. Options for addressing population and economic growth – two other conceptual drivers of anthropogenic emissions – are also aggressively adopted.

A body, on a par with the United Nations (UN) Security Council, called the *UN Council for Climate Mitigation* is established by the new accord as a formal expression of the normative and cooperative need to address the anthropogenic root causes of climate change. Until a separate secretariat of the UN Council for Climate Mitigation is established to serve as a clearinghouse and secretariat for monitoring, reporting, evaluating, and auditing country commitments towards accelerated approach to mitigation, a transitional secretariat called the *Rapid Mitigation Secretariat* is created within the Office of the UN Secretary General.

The Project's international aspect is essential since rapid mitigation necessitates an international collective response (cf. Peters et al. 2013). Collective action from all countries – in following the key principles of the 1992 UNFCCC – specifies the varying degrees of climate mitigation targets and mitigation contributions depending on historical and present emissions, development stages, natural resources, and mobilisation capacities. Through the Agreement, nations undertake sustainable energy transitions to decarbonise all economies that would ensure negative emissions by 2100, while pursuing substantial emissions reductions in other key sectors. The Project proceeds under the following schedule:

- Group 1: Countries in the top 20 high emission list from high income, highly industrialised, and emerging economies. From Table 1.1, these are China, U.S.A., India, the Russian Federation, Japan, Germany, South Korea, Canada, Brazil, Poland, U.K., South Africa, Italy, Spain, France, and Australia. They are required to provide Group 3 and 4 countries with technical, financial and other resources for mitigation. Decarbonisation timeframe: 15 years at most.
- Group 2: Other highly industrialised and emerging economies (IMF 2015: 171): the Netherlands, Belgium, Austria, Greece, Portugal, Ireland, Finland, Slovak Republic, Lithuania, Slovenia, Luxembourg, Latvia,

Estonia, Cyprus, Malta, Taiwan Province of China, Switzerland, Sweden, Singapore, Hong Kong SAR, Norway, Czech Republic, Israel, Denmark, New Zealand, Iceland, and San Marino. They are also required to provide developing countries with preferential technical, financial, and other resources for mitigation. This group also includes developing countries with substantial renewable energy resources such as the geothermal energy-rich countries located in the Pacific ring of fire, hydro-energy rich countries in the tropics, and solar-rich regions in the Middle East, Northern Africa, and elsewhere. Decarbonisation timeframe: 20 years at most.

- Group 3: Developing countries in the list of top 20 high-emission countries in Table 1.1, which include Ukraine, Mexico, Kazakhstan, North Korea, Saudi Arabia, Iran, Indonesia, Thailand, and Turkey. Decarbonisation timeframe: 25 years at most.
- Group 4: Other developing countries. Decarbonisation timeframe: 35–40 years.

National targets, which are expectedly more intense than those committed to in the Paris Agreement closely resemble the 'stringent mitigation scenario' proposed in IPCC's (2014) RCP2.6 scenario. The submitted INDCs are strengthened, and following a methodology, amended to ensure that national emission reductions are commensurate with the global target: net zero emissions by 2050. The proposal also calls to make 100% sustainable energy by 2050 the benchmark, not volume of emissions reduction – which, as illustrated by the Paris targets, is subject to various country interpretations.

The proposal above means that, if work starts in 2016, Group 1 countries are fully transitioned into 100% renewable energy, at most, by 2030; Group 2 by 2035; Group 3 by 2040; and Group 4 by 2050. By mid-century, therefore, a 100% renewable energy-powered world should be possible – in line with the RCP2.6 pathway. The Agreement should strictly use the year 2050 as a reckoning year to highlight the temporal element of effective climate action.

Nonetheless, national target emissions reduction and increased renewable energy capacity should be treated as dynamic targets; meaning they are reviewed every two years, and accordingly modified – i.e. improved as they make progress – until full transition to a 100% sustainable energy system and zero level of emissions are achieved by 2050 and 2100. Some developing countries in Groups 3 and 4 may want to decarbonise their economies within 20 years – something that should be encouraged and supported; in this, case, they may want to join Group 2 countries and avail of preferential transition assistance.

Some countries listed in Groups 1 and 2 may declare that their Paris commitments are already ambitious enough. Some may say their existing mitigation pathways are sufficient for reaching close to zero emission in the energy sector and may argue that an exceptional whole-of-economy mobilisation as required by the Agreement may no longer be necessary. Germany, for example, may declare that their technological innovations and socio-political and economic capacities to deal with mitigation through *Energiewende* are already ambitious and sufficient (cf. Morris and Pehnt 2015). Similar claims may be made by Denmark since it also has a national decarbonisation programme. China may also declare similar sufficiency given its capacity to expand sustainable energy technology diffusion within tight timeframes (cf. Mathews and Tan 2014). Declarations such as these will surely arise; however, these pathways must be verified against a robust and transparent measurement and verification methodology by an independent review body at the Secretariat.

Contrary to what might be claimed, these countries are still far from reaching 100% sustainable energy, according to a study by Mark Jacobson et al. (2015). The study ranks 139 countries based on energy generation installed capacity coming from wind, water, and sunlight sources by end-2014. In this list, Denmark ranks 20th at 12% of its generation installed capacity considered as renewable; Germany ranks 33rd with 6.7%; and China ranks 65th at 3.4%. Renewable energy penetrations in Groups 1 to 3 countries in end-2014 needed for a full transition by 2050, according to this methodology (Jacobson et al. 2015) are as follows.

- Group 1: China (3.4%), U.S.A. (4.2%), India (2.1%), the Russian Federation (2.8%), Japan (7.5%), Germany (6.7%), South Korea (0.82%), Canada (12%), Brazil (6.6%), Poland (2.9%), U.K. (6.1%), South Africa (0.88%), Italy (7.8%), Spain (17%), France (7.2%), Australia (5.2%).
- Group 2: The Netherlands (1.6%), Belgium (2.9%), Austria (13%), Greece (13%), Portugal (26%), Ireland (10%), Finland (3.4%), Slovak Republic (6.4%), Lithuania (4.2%), Slovenia (8.2%), Luxembourg (7.4%), Latvia (5.7%), Estonia (2.5%), Cyprus (2.3%), Malta (0.76%), Taiwan Province of China (1.7%), Switzerland (21%), Sweden (21%), Singapore (0%), Hong Kong SAR (0%), Norway (67%), Czech Republic (3.4%), Israel (1%), Denmark (12%), New Zealand (17%), Iceland (39%), San Marino (no data).
- Group 3: Ukraine (1.6%), Mexico (2.4%), Kazakhstan (0.83%), North Korea (no data), Saudi Arabia (0.01%), Iran (1.2%), Indonesia (0.7%), Thailand (0.92%), Turkey (8.7%).

Obtaining an international, legally binding, and mandatory agreement, such as is proposed here will be no easy task. It took the international community more than 20 years to tread the road from Rio to Paris, and despite the long and agonising process, the Paris agreement remains incoherent with the UNFCCC and AR5 in terms of timeframe and rate of mitigation. Therefore it is key that policymakers around the world have a shared understanding not only of the challenge – this is already apparent with almost universal submission of INDCs – but also the required scale, speed and scope of mitigation, which remains missing in current discussions on climate action.

Achieving the intended goals of climate action, however, is persistently challenged with the same and fundamental, yet asymmetric and multifarious, prisoner's dilemma. In climate negotiations, consensus is often stalled since it is in every country's self-interest to do almost nothing on climate since they can simply hitch a free ride on mitigation activities by other countries (Nordhaus 2015; Wagner and Weitzman 2015). For this proposal's highly ambitious Agreement to be feasible, thus, it has to effectively and coherently address free-riding, while highlighting the many benefits of collective action, including:

- The huge collective pay-offs for the climate, for health, for social cohesion, and for the economy following rapid and aggressive mitigation efforts.
- The possibility of side bilateral and multilateral agreements on issues other than climate change.
- Motivations, other than self-interest, including notions of national pride, responsibility, capability, and self-respect.
- The redistribution of wealth between and within nations.
- Lower volume of stranded high-carbon assets for quick and early moving countries (cf. Hepburn and Stern 2009).

Implementation and achieving rapid mitigation targets, in the required scale, speed, and scope, will be more challenging than getting countries to sign the Agreement. In this context, another key challenge relates to the design and implementation of audit mechanisms that would reduce the possibility that some nations might break off the Agreement, and to lay sanctions for countries that fail to meet their targets. Absent credible and transparent monitoring, review and verification mechanisms for incentives and disincentives, it is likely that more than one nation will fail to adhere to their obligations, with some repeating what happened with the Kyoto Protocol. Selfish countries might also be expected to continue emitting. In this context, the military alliances forged through the 1943 Casablanca Agreement between Allied Nations, which included a text on unconditional surrender by the Axis states during World War II, provides a useful model.

At the height of the war, Allied leaders met at Casablanca in then French Morocco between 14 and 24 January 1943. Key players in attendance were British Prime Minister Winston Churchill, U.S. President Franklin D. Roosevelt, Joint Chiefs of Staff, U.S. Field Marshall Dwight Eisenhower, and British Field Marshall Harold Alexander. Joseph Stalin had been invited but he was needed on home ground as the Russian Red Army was, at that time, battling to hold Stalingrad. The conference aimed to decide a common future strategy. High on the agenda was an attack against the Germans in France. Aside from tactical agreements, which included the combined bomber offensive against Germany from Britain and materialised in the Invasion of Normandy, the agreement at Casablanca holds key insights for forging the Rapid Mitigation Agreement.

On their final day at Casablanca, Roosevelt announced that he and Churchill had decided that the only way to ensure post-war peace was to adopt a policy of unconditional surrender. This policy was made to avoid a situation that followed World War I, where large segments of German society supported the position that Germany was not defeated militarily; hence the German rearmament during the interwar years, which was a clear violation of the Treaty of Versailles (British Broadcasting Corporation 2012; Wilt 1991; United States Department of State n.d.).

The least we can expect from the Rapid Mitigation Agreement is to have another Treaty of Versailles-like infraction happening post-Paris. The Agreement, therefore, should specify a policy tantamount to the policy of 'unconditional surrender' made in Casablanca.

This is not a new proposal, but only cements out the original aims of the UNFCCC: to require climate polluters to undertake deep emissions cuts, and for rich countries to provide the resources for poor countries to adapt to the changing climate and contribute to mitigation. Following the Casablanca model, these aims can be met through:

- Establishing mandatory emissions cuts that ensure a 100% sustainable energy regime and close-to-zero emissions by 2050.
- Establishing an assessed contributions approach to a multilateral fund for Rapid Climate Mitigation (see details of this proposal in Chapter 4).
- Establishing a global monitoring mechanism to periodically review mitigation pledges. The mechanism should also facilitate proper accounting of climate mitigation assistance to developing countries to avoid double counting.
- Establishing penalties for reneging, non-adherence, or for seceding from the Agreement, to deter countries from free riding.

Trade sanctions, which although are often ineffective, especially when imposed by a country against another, work well in some situations, especially multilaterally, and thus offer a possibility (Hufbauer, Schott and Elliott 1990). Nobel laureate Joseph Stiglitz (2006: 1) has been suggesting using them as mechanisms for preventing countries 'which refuse to agree or to implement emission reductions from inflicting harm on the rest of the world.' In a paper prepared for the Harvard conference on *The Timing of Climate Change Policies* in 2001, Joseph Aldy, Peter Orszag, and Joseph Stiglitz (2001: 15) explain how trade sanctions in the context of a climate agreement could be implemented.

> If one country refused to comply with that approach, the rest of the world could simply impose a compensating tax on the relevant nation's exports. Indeed, the other nations could impose a punitive carbon tax – i.e., a tax against the rogue nation's exports equal to, say, three times the carbon tax that would have had to have been paid in the first place. (Countries that failed to impose the carbon tax on the imports of commodities from the rogue country would themselves face taxes on their

exports (and similarly for countries that failed to impose taxes on those who failed to punish rogue states).) The tax could even vary with the ratio of exports to domestic production, so that the total carbon tax collections collected from the country by foreign governments would be a fixed multiple of what the country would have collected itself, had it imposed the carbon tax. (The proceeds of such fees could be contributed to a global carbon fund. It is important that the decision both to levy the carbon tax and to allocate the proceeds be international, so that the taint of hidden protectionism be avoided.)

A uniform percentage tariff on the imports of non-participants offers another approach (Nordhaus 2015). Countries must weigh the cost of participation against the potentially larger costs of reduced trade with countries in the Agreement or sanctions because of non-participation. The concept of most-favoured nation status for countries that join the World Trade Organization (WTO), and losing the status for not joining, is a kind of mechanism that can be used as a model.

Complementing trade sanctions and material losses from opting out, reneging, or seceding from the Agreement can also be pursued internationally through diplomatic sanctions and reduced foreign aid, as well as shaming in international bodies such as at the UN, WTO, and other pan-global institutions (Tingley and Tomz 2013).

Agreeing on international sanctions is another uphill battle. This, time and again, repeats itself in every climate negotiation. Indeed, it was easy for Japan, Russia, Canada, and Australia to break away from their Kyoto pledges by simply abandoning the Protocol because there was no sanction for non-participation. The Protocol was left to expire in 2012 without a successor. The Paris agreement is also bereft of sanctions and it is easy to suggest that secessions similar to Kyoto Protocol could likely occur. Without a binding and legal Agreement, effective climate action is derailed. The promise of economic pay-offs, the use of values evoking national pride and responsibility, and the threat of trade sanctions can assist in achieving a legally binding treaty-like Agreement. However, these may not be enough. A stronger climate agreement that meets the below +2°C warming target may need additional stimuli to be forged.

Psychological stimuli can hold some solutions (Wagner and Zeckhauser 2012). Following on our *Gedankenexperiment*, large-scale physical and nature-based stimuli might be needed to drive the signing of the Agreement, and in making them hold onto it. The Casablanca Agreement was, in the first place, collectively forged because world leaders were presented with a key stimulus: the prospect of being annihilated. This type of stimulus needs to be explored and critically interrogated.

Psychology and behavioural sciences suggest that the importance of an event heavily depends upon its saliency, recency, proximity, and frequency to the observer, or what has been called the 'availability heuristic' (Kahneman and Tversky 1972). The assumption that humans react best in emergency situations is based on the conjecture that humans are generally hostile to change in the absence of a perceptible driver. Human evolution has favoured this fight response, in circumstances, instances, and moments when: (1) real and immediate threats or harm are suddenly presented; (2) there is an immediate experience of fear, anger, and/or embarrassment; and (3) an alarm is sounded about a risk or a hazard (Slovic et al. 2002; Sloman 1996).

These observations make sense. During wartime, the constant threat of Axis invasion of Australia, Canada, and the U.K. stimulated rapid mobilisation in these countries. The Japanese attacks on Pearl Harbor and Manila, both U.S. territories, provided the U.S.A. with the stimuli to mobilise. It seems that similar visceral and physical manifestation of threats might drive countries to agree on the aggressive international Rapid Mitigation Agreement. Some form of climate instability manifesting itself as a dramatic event – an emergency – may hold these stimuli.

Stimuli that could psychologically drive humans to push for stronger and rapid climate mitigation can be assumed from wide-scale catastrophic events or series of surprise climate events. They are tail events in a bell-shaped probability distribution, or 'black swans', meaning they are beyond regular observations because they are highly unlikely to occur. Elmar Kriegler, Jim Hall, Hermann Held, Richard Dawson, and Hans Joachim Schellnhuber (2009) list them as follows:

- Reorganisation of the Atlantic Meridional Overturning Circulation.
- Melt of the Greenland ice sheet.
- Disintegration of the West Antarctic Ice Sheet (WAIS).
- Dieback of the Amazon rainforest.
- More persistent El Niño regime bringing about severe droughts, floods and other extreme weather patterns.

Climate risks, according to Gernot Wagner and Martin Weitzman (2015), however, have 'fat tail' distributions, meaning, in contrast to a normal bell-shaped probability curve where the tails ends fall quickly to zero where extreme outcomes are highly unlikely, there are small, yet non-negligible risks of extreme outcomes from climate impacts that could profoundly alter life on Earth. According to Kriegler et al. (2009) there is a one in six chance (17%) that at least one of their five identified tipping points will be triggered under conditions of warming between +2°C and +4°C, and a more than one in two chance (56%) for temperature change above 4°C relative to year 2000 levels. Kriegler et al. (2009: 5) concludes that, although there are large uncertainties in these findings, this does not 'necessarily imply that such events are considered remote'.

In our *Gedankenexperiment*, let us assume that WAIS collapse, a climate black swan, stimulates global climate action. In AR5, the IPCC registers high confidence that the Greenland and Antarctic ice sheets are already losing mass at a larger rate during the last two decades (Vaughan et al. 2013). If WAIS collapses (Gillis and Chang 2014; Dutton and Lambeck 2012), sea level can rise between five and 40 metres higher than at present – which may lead to conditions like those during the Pliocene (Raymo et al. 2009). With fear that more could follow the dramatic and catastrophic climate impacts brought about by sea level rise, the public collectively agree that dramatic, aggressive, and transformative climate mitigation response is needed immediately, and charge their governments to act on it.

The occurrences of climate-related tipping events, however, are not guarantees that governments will indeed enact an aggressive Agreement. Most likely, instead, governments will be choked on a crisis response mode through large-scale adaptation measures – including protecting territorial integrity through intense border patrols. Worst of all, governments may opt to proceed on a large-scale deployment of risky geoengineering techniques.

The possibility of black swans occurring, however, should highlight the need to view rapid climate mitigation as insurance for hedging against their occurrence. This rationalises and underscores the need for rapid mitigation now, where policy decisions are designed and framed around cutting off the possibility of catastrophic temperature increases, and not when black swans suddenly occur. Since the prospect for a binding Agreement on rapid mitigation is less likely to be forged without strong physical, economic, political, and social stimuli, it is only logical not to place all our bets singly on the Agreement. This, therefore, highlights the need for multiple rapid mitigation activities at various levels and scales from nation-states to regions, cities, towns and local communities (Diesendorf 2009; McKibben 2012; Delina, Diesendorf and Merson 2014).

Magnitude of mitigation

The Rapid Mitigation Project, where emissions are significantly reduced through accelerated sustainable energy transition, requires the massive diffusion of proven and demonstrated technologies, alongside intensified research and development (R&D) for increased efficiency, storage, smart grids, aviation fuels, and other technologies.

Globally, the estimates to meet the projected global 17 TW demand for energy in 2030 by 100% renewable energy systems include the installation of: 4 million 5-MW wind turbines; 2 billion 3-kW rooftop solar photovoltaic (PV); 90,000 300-MW solar PV and concentrated solar power (CSP) plants; 900 hydroelectric plants (70% of which are already in place); 5,350 geothermal plants; 720,000 wave devices; and 490,000 tidal turbines (Delucchi and Jacobson 2011: 1178; Jacobson and Delucchi 2011: Table 4, 1160). Wind and solar, in this estimate, are assumed to comprise 90% of 2030 global supply because of their relative abundance. The authors also noted the need to expand the grid to accommodate new power plants, expand the production of storage technologies, and increase R&D for aviation fuel and electric resistance heating (Delucchi and Jacobson 2011).

By 2050, Jacobson et al. (2015) project that in a global 100% renewable energy scenario demand will be 11.8 TW – with some reduction from the 2030 level due to assumed efficiency. Utility-scale solar will supply 49.8% of this demand, which require 496,700 50-MW utility-scale solar PV, 15,400 100-MW utility-scale CSP plants with storage, 653 million 5-kW residential rooftop PV systems, and 35.3 million 100-kW commercial and government rooftop systems. Wind energy will contribute 32.3% generated from 1.17 million new onshore 5-MW wind turbines and 762,000 offshore 5-MW wind turbines. Existing hydropower plants will be increased in their capacity factor to supply 4.8%. No new hydropower will be installed. Wave and tidal technologies will contribute 0.8% using 496,000 0.75-MW wave devices and 32,100 1-MW tidal turbines. Geothermal energy will provide the remaining 0.7% from 840 100-MW geothermal plants. To help stabilise the grid, another estimated 9,300 100-MW CSP plants with storage and 99,500 50-MW solar thermal collectors for heat generation and storage will be installed. In this scenario, there is zero bioenergy, nuclear, fossil gas, and CCS.

At the national level, volume projections for the required technologies are also available. To meet the full 3 TW demand in 2030 in the U.S.A., 590,000 wind turbines, 265 million rooftop solar PV, 6,200 solar PV plants, 7,600 CSP plants, 140 hydroelectric plants (with 70% of these already in place), 830 geothermal plants, 110,000 wave devices, and 7,600 tidal turbines are necessary (Jacobson and Delucchi 2011: Table 4, 1160). By 2050, a fully renewable energy-powered U.S.A., according to Jacobson et al. (2015) will require 48.4% wind, 46.8% solar, 3.9% hydro, 0.5% geothermal, and 0.4% wave energy. Note that there is no bioenergy proposed in this plan. Another simulation for the U.S.A. – an 80% renewable energy penetration by 2050 – shows that 28% to 33% of total renewable energy generation will be contributed by onshore wind, 10% to 15% by hydropower and utility-scale and rooftop PV, 5% each from biomass and CSP, and 2% to 3% from geothermal (Mai et al. 2014). By using more local PV and biomass resources, Mai et al. (2014) suggest that an 80% renewable energy penetration of the entire U.S. electricity system is possible with limited transmission expansion.

In Australia, a study suggests that the 2010 actual energy demand in the Australian National Electricity Market could be met by generating 23.2 GW from wind farms, 14.6 GW from solar PV, 2.6 GW from CSP, 2.2 GW from pumped storage hydro. 4.9 GW from hydro without pumped storage, and 24 GW from biofuelled gas turbines (Elliston, Diesendorf and MacGill 2012). The plan for Australia elaborated by Jacobson et al. (2015) requires 53.3% solar, 36.2% wind, 4.9% hydroelectric, 5% wave and 0.4% geothermal energies, and 0.1% tidal turbines. See the mix of sustainable energy technologies for other countries to meet 100% renewable energy-powered world by 2050 in http://thesolutionsproject.org/resource/139-country-100-infograp hics/.

To enable the state to achieve effective climate mitigation through a sustainable energy transition – that is, with or without a Rapid Mitigation Agreement, the production and deployment of mitigation technologies is required in a scale, speed, and scope of mobilisation that calls for large-scale changes in industrial, labour, and finance landscapes. The closely related form of global mobilisation of industrial capacity to have occurred, thus far, in human history has been the full mobilisation of national economies for World War II. During this period, major combatant countries, particularly in democracies, were presented with the major challenge to convert their capitalist economic orientations to a centrally planned war economy. Instead of producing consumer goods, workers and businesses were driven by public policy to produce munitions on a huge scale, with the primary intentions of defeating the enemy. But, just how immense was the mobilisation for the war?

Magnitude and intensity of wartime mobilisation

At the end of World War II in 1946, Raymond Goldsmith, a technocrat at the U.S. War Production Board (WPB), published an estimated balance sheet of war production. His introduction aptly captures the correlation between massive munitions production and victory. He wrote:

> Figures…may not rule the world, but they show how it is ruled. Similarly, statistics may not win wars, but they certainly show how they are won… The cold figures…probably tell the story of this war in its essentials as well as extended discussion or elaborate pictures: the initial disadvantage of the Western Allies; the surprising stand of the USSR; the rapid improvement in the United Nations position in 1943; their decisive superiority over Germany in 1944; and the rapid collapse of Japan once the [theatre] of war was restricted to the Pacific…whatever may have saved the United Nations from defeat in the earlier phases of the conflict, what won the war for them in the end, was their ability – and particularly that of the United States – to produce more, and vastly more, munitions than the Axis.
>
> (Goldsmith 1946: 69)

Between 1941 and 1945, warring countries rapidly converted their national economies to large-scale manufacture of military munitions. Munitions is the generic term used in this book to include, but not limited to, combat aircrafts, naval vessels, guns, small arms, armoured and unarmoured motor vehicles such as tanks and trucks, ammunition, and electronic and communication equipment. The conversions entailed restructurings that encompass all sectors. This chapter presents the processes occurring during these large-scale and aggressive restructurings using select mobilisation experiences from the U.S.A., U.K., Canada, Australia, Japan, Germany, and Russia. These countries were chosen broadly because they were the principal belligerents, were the locations of transformative socio-technical changes, and are richly studied foci of inquiry on wartime scholarship.

With war, governmental structures and machineries, industries and the economy restructured in a magnitude, scale, and scope that surpassed previous wartime mobilisation. Actions in many governments' war rooms were directed at a single objective: to win the war. To achieve this ambition, governments demanded the mass production of munitions in a volume and speed never before seen. In the process, wartime brought forth extraordinary capital fund expansion, increased labour productivity, new forms of industrial management, and structured governmental intervention in predominantly market-led institutions. The general outputs of wartime production and the expenditures incurred as countries restructured their economies for war were extraordinary.

At the beginning of the war, national leaders already knew that World War II would not only be a show of military force, but of industrial might. On 26 January 1941, barely 12 months before the U.S.A. officially went to war, U.K. Prime Minister Winston Churchill quipped to Harry Hopkins, then President Roosevelt's unofficial emissary to the Prime Minister: 'Modern war is waged with steel' (Colville 1985: 346). Nine months later, Joseph Stalin, the leader of the U.S.S.R., speaking before visiting American and British diplomats at a State Dinner in the Kremlin on 2 October 1941, said that the war 'would be won by industrial production' (United States Department of State 1959: 840). The perception, therefore, was that those having the most advanced technologies and industries, and the capacity to rapidly deploy them to battlefields, would likely emerge as winners. In the next three years, as the global war was waged, countries embarked on an unprecedented material, labour, and financial resource mobilisation to achieve this ultimate ambition.

The U.S. response to Japanese aggression at Pearl Harbor best illustrates the speed and magnitude of wartime industrial mobilisation. On 6 January 1942, less than a month after the attack on American soil, the U.S. President addressed Congress. In this televised speech, Roosevelt informed the world of his country's ambition to deploy munitions in quantities never produced in America or elsewhere. He reported that he

> sent a letter of directive to the appropriate departments and agencies of our Government, ordering that immediate steps be taken...to increase our production rate of airplanes so rapidly that in this year, 1942, we shall produce 60,000 planes...next year, 1943, we shall produce 125,000 airplanes...to increase our production rate of tanks so rapidly that in this year, 1942, we shall produce 45,000 tanks; and to continue that increase so that next year, 1943, we shall produce 75,000 tanks...to increase our production rate of anti-aircraft guns so rapidly that in this year, 1942, we shall produce 20,000 of them; and to continue that increase so that next year, 1943, we shall produce 35,000 anti-aircraft

guns....And...to increase our production rate of merchant ships so rapidly that in this year, 1942, we shall build 6,000,000 deadweight tons... And finally, we shall continue that increase so that next year, 1943, we shall build 10,000,000 tons of shipping.

(Roosevelt 1942)

In the following months, the engines of U.S. war production rolled at a pace never seen. The goal was to quickly, massively, and efficiently produce munitions and to deploy them to battlegrounds. To achieve this goal, the U.S. government enforced executive controls, and instituted extraordinary financial and labour strategies that affected American society. Industries were asked to limit their peacetime productions to give way to more immediately required munitions.

Wartime quantitative data survey reveals colossal economic changes not only in the U.S.A. but also in many other countries demonstrating the magnitude, scale, and scope of rapid wartime industrial production. The proportion of military outlays vis-à-vis the total size of the economy, presented in Table 3.1, provides a numerical description of the intensity of wartime expenditures and, at the same time, sketched wartime burdens on the general economy.

Defence expenditures were substantial as war intensified from 1942 to 1944. Military expenditures, however, varied across countries and across time particularly before 1942, when the U.S.A. was not yet a formal actor. In 1939, for instance, U.S. military expenditures accounted for only an estimated 1% of the country's GNP. By contrast, Germany and Japan had already allocated close to a quarter of their national incomes for rearmaments that year. The U.S. military industry continued to receive minimal government funding compared to Germany and Japan despite the country's capacity to produce more steel, oil and motor vehicles than all the other major countries together (Overy 2006: 232).

The straightforward reason for the low expenditure levels in the U.S.A. from 1939 to 1941 is that the country was still politically and geographically

Table 3.1 Military outlays as percentage (%) of national income, 1939–1944

	1939	*1940*	*1941*	*1942*	*1943*	*1944*
U.K.	15	44	53	52	55	53
U.S.A.	1	2	11	31	42	42
U.S.S.R.	-	17	28	61	61	53
Germany	23	40	52	64	70	-
Japan	22	22	27	33	43	76

Author's calculation from Harrison (1998a: 21, Table 1.8)

Figures for the U.K. are % of net national expenditures; U.S.A., % of Gross National product (GNP) at 1958 prices; U.S.S.R., % of GNP at 1937 prices; Germany, % of GNP at 1939 prices; Japan, % of Gross Domestic Product (GDP).

isolated from the war in Europe and Asia because of its non-interventionist policy. The U.S. Congress enacted neutrality legislation in 1935–1939 to limit the country's armaments trade and production and to keep the country out of the war. For this reason, American mobilisation was slow to occur despite the outbreak of war in Europe and in China. When Japan attacked the U.S.A. in 1941, things changed drastically. By 1942, the U.S.A. proved it had the capacity to arm quickly. That year, U.S. military expenditure climbed by 20% from its 1941 level; a year later military expenditures reached its peak at 42% of its GNP.

The intensity of the U.S. wartime mobilisation demonstrated by the volume of military resources became even more evident in 1942–1944. Wartime Production Board (WPB) economist R. Elberton Smith, writing in *The Army and Economic Mobilization* in 1959, reported that the U.S. defence expenditure in 1944, considered the apex year of the American wartime mobilisation, stood at US$91 billion or approximately US$1.23 trillion in its 2015 value, up from a mere US$2 billion five years earlier: a 44-fold expansion (Smith 1959: 4). In 1998, economic historian Hugh Rockoff adjusted Smith's values and arrived at US$162.4 billion (Rockoff 1998: 83), which, if adjusted for inflation, was approximately US$2.2 trillion in its 2015 value. Regardless of variations between figures by Smith and Rockoff, the rate of change exemplifies the country's capability to direct and mobilise close to half of its entire economic resources to a pressing challenge.

Other Allied countries showed similar, if not more intense, mobilisation. The U.K., for instance, used more than half of its national income to prosecute the war between 1941 and 1944. The U.S.S.R. experience is the most illuminating. Milward (1977: 93) suggests that the Soviet military expenditure soared from 39.2 billion roubles in 1939 to 137.7 billion in 1944, or a 72% increase in six years (Note: figures are in their 1939 and 1944 values). For that matter, the U.S.S.R. holds the record among the Allied countries with the highest percentage allocation for military pursuits. In 1942, 61% of its GNP, or approximately 101.4 billion roubles in its 1942 value, were allocated for its military: this was 3.6 times higher than the figures in 1940 (Harrison 1998b: 287).

The Axis states also quickly apportioned large shares of their national resources for war purposes. Mobilisation in Germany and Japan commenced as early as 1935 and 1937, during which war preparations in the U.S.A. were still mostly non-existent. In 1935, Germany started rearming itself, spending approximately 5.5 billion Reichsmark (RM) that year and increasing it to RM27 billion in 1939 (Abelshauser 1998: 134, Table 4.4; Note: figures in their 1935 and 1939 values). Four years later, Germany was allocating close to a quarter of its national income to strengthen its military. On the other side of the world, Japan similarly mobilised close to a quarter of its national income for military purposes during this time.

As World War II commenced, military expenditures in Germany and Japan increased even more rapidly. Expenditure in Japan expanded four times from 5 billion yen in 1940 to 20 billion in 1944 (Milward 1977: 85–86; Note: figures in their 1940 and 1944 values). In Germany, military expenditures received RM91 billion allotments in 1943 increasing to as much as RM112 billion in 1944 (Klein 1959: 256, Table 65; Note: figures in their 1943 and 1944 values). In 1943 and 1944, at the height of the war, when major battles were waged, military outlays in Germany and Japan attained their all-time highs, allocating 70% and 76% of their national incomes for war purposes. These figures were the highest rates of military expenditures ever carried out by any country during the war.

The belated outpourings of resources, regardless of amounts, proved insignificant. In 1943, the battles in European and Pacific theatres reached their peak. That year, clashes were fierce. The Battle of Stalingrad and the Battle of Kursk in Europe eventually signalled Germany's forthcoming defeat. During the same year, Japan experienced several battle losses in the Southeast Asian and the Pacific theatres. By 1945, Germany and Japan were defeated and their economies subsequently collapsed.

The global military expenditures translated directly into impressive munitions production outputs. Harrison (1998a: 15–17), summarising the magnitude of war production by all combatants, reported the following outputs: 'nearly 50 million rifles, automatic weapons, and machine guns, more than 2 million guns and mortars, more than 200,000 tanks, more than 400,000 combat aircraft, nearly 9,000 major naval vessels.' The American industry, between July 1940 and V-Day (Victory in Europe Day) on 8 May 1945, produced 299,300 airplanes, 86,700 tanks, more than 100,000 naval vessels, more than 20 million rifles, 2.4 million trucks and jeeps, 41 billion bullets and millions of other war items (Cardozier 1995: 157; Overy 2006; see Smith 1959: 3–31 for detailed breakdowns of U.S. munitions production).

Although other economies failed to approach the level and volume of American industrial production, they, nevertheless, exhibited similar intensity. For detailed descriptions, see Plumptre (1941a, b) for the Canadian war production; Walker (1947) for Australia; Overy (1982), Kaldor (1945–1946), and Klein (1948) for Germany; Kaldor (1945–1946) for the U.K.; and Milward (1977: 85–86, 93) for Japan and the U.S.S.R. Table 3.2 summarises

Table 3.2 Wartime production outputs between 1942 and 1944 (in thousands)

	Combat aircraft	Major naval vessels	Tanks	Rifles, carbines, machine pistols, machine guns	Mortars
U.K.	61.6	651	20.7	6,661	65.3
U.S.A.	153.1	6,755	86.0	15,202	61.6
U.S.S.R.	84.8	55	77.5	17,070	306.5
Germany	65.0	703	35.2	8,347	66.0
Japan	40.7	438	2.4	2,429	4.3

Harrison (1998a: 17, Table 1.7)

the volume of wartime production outputs select combatant countries churned out at the height of the war. The table shows how the period of an astonishing arms race produced previously unimaginable munitions' quantities that forever changed these countries' industrial landscapes.

Although the U.S.S.R. produced more rifles, carbines, pistols, guns and mortars than any other country, it never reached the volume and level of American production. Beginning in 1942, the U.S.A. became a military superpower as its domestic munitions production intensified. While other countries spent four to five years developing their sizable military industries, the U.S. spent only one (Overy 2006; cf. Rockoff 1998: 81–181; Harrison 1998a: 32; Simonson 1960: 20). By the end of the war, America showed the world that munitions – that were technically more complex than the passenger cars they customarily manufactured before the war – could be produced with comparable methods and intensity.

The scale, scope, and speed of wartime mobilisation – munitions production in particular through rapid movements in the mobilisation and direction of vital resources, technologies, and infrastructure – reveal a country's inherent capacity to respond to great threats. These threats mostly present themselves in the form of crises. The intense mobilisation for war in the U.S.A., for instance, occurred following the attack on Pearl Harbor and the Philippines in December 1941. Moreover, this came at a time when the country was just recovering from another crisis, the Great Depression, which was brought about by the stock market crash of 1929.

The series of crises coalesced to trigger the American mobilisation for war. They steered industrial production to provide employment and, at the same time, address the war's materiel requirements. The mobilisation's lasting transformative impacts not only brought about Allied victory but also launched the U.S.A. and its Allies as global hegemons. A new architecture for international understanding, the United Nations, was also created as a spin-off of the war. If there is a key lesson to be learned from this historical piece beyond the rise of U.S. hegemony and new pan-global institutions, it is about realising that it should not take another large-scale crisis to get our bearings right on climate mitigation.

Rapid climate mitigation through sustainable energy transition could limit the extent and scale of future climate-related crises. Mitigation of this scale, speed, and scope is possible by following or mimicking efforts made towards wartime mobilisation to design strategies for sustainable energy technologies' rapid diffusions (Rao 2015; The Climate Mobilization 2015; Matthew England in Cooper 2012; Delucchi and Jacobson 2011; Gilding 2011; Wright and Hearps 2010; Romm 2009; Al Gore in Webster and Pagnamenta 2009; Brown 2008). The intensified diffusion process most likely entails changes in the manufacturing and logistics support industries as equipment production for renewable power plants increases, along with the management and administration of transport and installation of these technologies (Arent et al. 2014). Considerable growth in additional renewable capacity, during the recent years, however, demonstrates the ability to scale manufacturing at speed.

The growth in the manufacturing and installation of additional wind power generators illustrates the manufacturing sector's readiness. Installed capacity for wind power has, on average, doubled every three years, with 28% average annual growth between 2001 and 2011 (Zhao et al. 2013). Globally, wind power's cumulative installed capacity grew by 19% at the end of 2012 (REN 21 2013). Supply is also available for many of renewable energy technologies' material requirements. For solar PV, another dominant technology in the sustainable energy scenario, worldwide production capacity is already sizable, with capacity quickly increasing at 35–40% per annum (Mathews and Tan 2014; Tyagi et al. 2013; European Photovoltaic Industry Association 2013). Both wind and solar technologies are ready for diffusion.

In manufacturing the equipment for renewable energy generation lessons can be learnt from wartime munitions production. Among major combatant countries producing impressive munitions volume during the war (Table 3.2), the American wartime industrial production was the most immense. Contemporary industrial production for sustainable energy technologies could learn from this experience. The story of industrial production at Willow Run illustrates one key example of the American-discovered genius for accelerated mass production.

The 'most enormous room in the history of man'

In 1942, Roosevelt asked for 60,000 planes. A year later, he asked for more than double that figure. As expected, many American industrialists met his request with general scepticism; and the consensus was that it was simply impossible to achieve. Industrialist, Henry Ford, who spent decades creating the world's largest vertically integrated manufacturing system, however, saw it as a new challenge too great to resist.

Ford was a war sceptic for several reasons: (1) his doubt over Roosevelt's interest in confronting German aggression, a stance inseparable from Ford's anti-Semitism; (2) his belief that his competitors, General Motors and the DuPont family, controlled the President; (3) his opposition over American support for the British; and (4) his disappointments with the appointment of his competitor and former subordinate, General Motors' William Knudsen, to run the American mobilisation programme (Ferguson 2005: 149). Nevertheless, Ford was determined to exploit the opportunity presented by the war and forward his own economic and technological agenda (Ferguson 2005: 153).

A year earlier, in January 1941, Consolidated Aircraft Corporation invited Ford's company to produce parts for a Liberator bomber they had built in their California plant. When Ford's general manager Charles Sorensen visited the plant, he was, however, disappointed with their production methods. On the evening of 8 January 1941, Sorensen sketched out a plan of a plant to mass-produce bombers – a plan that essentially followed the Fordist system that Ford was using in his passenger car business. That night heralded the beginning of one of America's most famous wartime projects.

The Army, however, disagreed with the plan and the government's eventual decision to invest heavily in new plants, since it would have slowed the mobilisation process; hence, their lack of enthusiasm for Sorensen and Ford's idea of a new Ford-like plant (Overy 2006: 239–241). Nonetheless, they eventually concurred. By March 1941 work commenced to build the plant.

Located in open country south of Detroit at Ypsilanti, Michigan, the lot selected to accommodate the size of Sorensen's plans was a flat, tree-covered farmland. They named the project after a rivulet called 'Willow Run' that traversed the lot. Spread in approximately four square-kilometre space (Overy 2006: 240) and supported with US$480 million investment in 1942, or approximately US$ 7 billion in 2015 (Woodford 1942: E7), the factory at Willow Run eventually housed a 1.7-kilometre assembly line in a space of more than 271,000 square meters. At the time, the factory was regarded as 'the most enormous room in the history of man' (Overy 2006: 240; Walton 1956: 305). They also built hangars with another 112,000 square metres of space. The landing field had seven runways (Woodford 1942: E7).

At Willow Run, Ford replicated the Fordist system as planned, breaking down the processes to construct aircrafts so that the components could be fed into a continuously moving assembly line. Although the Fordist production model worked well with passenger cars, it met with challenges in an aircraft production setting. To mass-produce a more complex product such as a bomber meant that mechanised production had to be pushed to its limits (Walton 1956: 306–309). The project, despite optimism from Ford, Sorensen, and the government, was so demanding that it almost failed (Overy 2006: 240–241).

The initial lack of enthusiasm in army circles tended to be justified. By 31 January 1943, 18 months after production begun, WPB complained: 'there have been many disappointments in connection with the Willow Run operation and the plant, even now, is far from peak production' (*Chicago Daily Tribune* 1943: A7). Such disappointments even reached Congress with Harry Truman, then Senator and Chair of the Senate Committee Investigating the War Effort, ordering an inquiry into the plant.

In February 1943, Truman publicly criticised the Ford plant: 'There has been so little production [at Willow Run] as to amount to virtually none' (*The New York Times* 1943b: 14). He reversed his criticism, nevertheless, after his Committee visited the factory. On the 19th of the same month, Truman himself said he was 'quite impressed with what he saw and [that] most [of the Committee members] feel this mass production plan will work out' (*The Wall Street Journal* (WSJ) 1943: 3).

The complexity of mass-producing bombers translated into production challenges. These included: (1) constant delays in the supply of tools because of inefficient coordination between the designers and those at the plant; (2) pressure from the army; (3) insufficient labour largely because of plant location (Associated Press 1943: 12; *The Wall Street Journal* 1942: 3); and (4) absence of nearby housing units for the workers (Associated Press 1943: 12; *The Wall Street Journal* 1942: 3). Together these multiple challenges held up Willow Run's promise to contribute to Roosevelt's appeals (Overy 2006: 241). In the end, nevertheless, Willow Run, for all the challenges it faced, came to symbolise the drive of American industry to mass-produce aircrafts quickly as it possibly could.

By the end of 1943, the plant delivered more than ten bombers daily. By April 1944, Willow Run was producing one of the four-engine Liberator bombers every hour (The United Press 1944: 6). The next month, May 1944, the U.S. Army and Air Forces noted: 'Willow Run is producing on schedule and will meet its May quota at the same time...' (*The Wall Street Journal* 1944: 6). At the end of 1944, more than 5,000 bombers were produced reaching a rate of one bomber every 63 minutes. By 14 March 1945, Willow Run produced its 8,000th Liberator bomber (*The New York Times* 1945a: 10). On 29 June 1945, the factory rolled out of the plant the 8,685[th] and last Liberator bomber. At its peak, Willow Run churned out approximately 18 bombers per day (*The New York Times* 1945b: 22; *The New York Times* 1944: 12; *The New York Times* 1943a: 21).

The industrial successes at Willow Run, as well as its challenges, offer lessons for meeting the technical needs for large-scale, transformative, and speedy deployment of sustainable energy technologies. Although these two projects differ economically, politically, and technically, Willow Run exemplifies the capacity to surmount the material requirements of the Rapid Mitigation Project. How can public policy be redirected to accelerate the growth of the sustainable energy industry? How can wartime mobilisation offer an analogy for the rapid diffusion of sustainable energy technologies? The next two chapters explore responses to these questions.

References

Abelshauser, W. 1998, 'Germany: guns, butter, and economic miracles', in M. Harrison (ed.), *The Economics of World War II: Six Great Powers in International Comparison*, Cambridge University Press, Cambridge, U.K., pp. 122–176.

Aldy, J.E., Orszag, P.R. & Stiglitz, J.E. 2001, 'Climate change: an agenda for global collective action', paper prepared for the conference on The Timing of Climate Change Policies, Pew Center on Global Climate Change, October, Harvard University, Cambridge, Massachusetts, U.S.A.

Arent, D., Pless, J., Mai, T., Wiser, R., Hand, M., Baldwin, S. et al. 2014, 'Implication of high renewable electricity penetration in the U.S. for water use, greenhouse gas emissions, land-use, and materials supply', *Applied Energy*, vol. 123, pp. 368–377.

Associated Press (AP) 1943, 'Manpower lack delays Ford plant', *AP*, 31 January, p.12.

British Broadcasting Corporation (BBC) 2012, 'Fact File: Casablanca Conference', http://bbc.in/1qUckyO.

Brown, L.R. 2008, *Plan B 3.0: Mobilizing to Save Civilization*, W.W. Norton & Co., New York; London, U.K.

Cardozier, V.R. 1995, *The Mobilization of the United States in World War II: How the Government, Military, and Industry Prepared for War*, McFarland & Company, Jefferson, North Carolina, U.S.A.

Chicago Daily Tribune 1943, 'WPB discloses output is slow at Willow Run', 31 January, p. A7.

Colville, J. 1985, *The Fringes of Power: 10 Downing Street Diaries, 1939–1955*, W.W. Norton & Company, New York, U.S.A.

Cooper, H. 2012, 'Transcript, 7.30 program', *Australian Broadcasting Corporation*, 3 December, http://ab.co/1fowzxZ.

Delina, L.L., Diesendorf, M. & Merson, J. 2014, 'Strengthening the climate action movement: strategies from histories', *Carbon Management*, vol. 5, pp. 397–409.

Delucchi, M. & Jacobson, M. 2011, 'Providing all global energy with wind, water, and solar power, part II: reliability, system and transmission costs, and policies', *Energy Policy*, vol. 39, pp. 1170–1190.

Diesendorf, M. 2009, *Climate Action: A Campaign Manual for Greenhouse Solutions*, University of New South Wales Press, Sydney, Australia.

Dutton, A. & Lambeck, K. 2012, 'Ice volume and sea level during the last interglacial', *Science*, vol. 337, pp. 216–219.

Elliston, B., Diesendorf, M. & McGill, I. 2012, 'Simulation of scenarios with 100% renewable electricity in the Australian National Electricity Market', *Energy Policy*, vol. 45, pp. 606–613.

European Photovoltaic Industry Association 2013, 'Global market outlook for photovoltaics 2012–2017', http://bit.ly/1Kc15rH.

Ferguson, R.G. 2005, 'One thousand planes a day: Ford, Grumman, General Motors and the Arsenal of Democracy', *History and Technology*, vol. 21, pp. 149–175.

Gilding, P. 2011, *The Great Disruption: How the Climate Crisis Will Transform the Global Economy*, Bloomsbury, London, U.K.

Gillis, J. & Chang, K. 2014, 'Scientists warn of rising oceans from polar melt', *The New York Times*, 12 May, http://nyti.ms/1mS1hTz.

Goldsmith, R.W. 1946, 'The power of victory: munitions output in World War II', *Military Affairs*, vol. 10, pp. 69–80.

Harrison, M. 1998a, 'The economics of World War II: an overview', in M. Harrison (ed.), *The Economics of World War II: Six Great Powers in International Comparison*, Cambridge University Press, Cambridge, U.K., pp. 1–42.

Harrison, M. 1998b, 'The Soviet Union: the defeated victor', in M. Harrison (ed.), *The Economics of World War II: Six Great Powers in International Comparison*, Cambridge University Press, Cambridge, U.K., pp. 268–301.

Hepburn, C. & Stern, N. 2009, 'The global deal on climate change', in D. Helm & C. Hepburn (eds), *The Economics and Politics of Climate Change*, Oxford University Press, Oxford, U.K.

Hufbauer, G.C., Schott, J.J. & Elliott, K.A. 1990, *Economic Sanctions Reconsidered*, Peterson Institute for International Economics, Washington, D.C., U.S.A.

IMF (International Monetary Fund) 2015, *World Economic Outlook: Uneven Growth*, April, IMF, Washington, D.C., U.S.A., http://bit.ly/1huGQil.

IPCC (Intergovernmental Panel on Climate Change) 2014, *Climate Change 2014: Synthesis Report of the Fifth Assessment Report of the IPCC*, The Core Writing Team, R.K. Pachauri & L. Meyer (eds), IPCC, http://bit.ly/1umDnCQ.

Jacobson, M. & Delucchi, M. 2011, 'Providing all global energy with wind, water, and solar power, Part I: Technologies, energy resources, quantities and areas of infrastructure, and materials', *Energy Policy*, vol. 39, pp. 1170–1190.

Jacobson, M., Delucchi, M., Bauer, Z.A.F., Goodman, S.C., Chapman, W.E. et al. 2015, '100% clean and renewable wind, water, and sunlight (WWS) all-sector energy roadmaps for 139 countries of the world', 27 November, http://stanford.io/1lvUaVS, accessed 30 November 2015.

Kahneman, D. & Tversky, A. 1972, 'Subjective probability: a judgment of representativeness', *Cognitive Psychology*, vol. 3, pp. 430–454.

Kaldor, N. 1945–1946, 'The German war economy', *Review of Economic Studies*, vol. 13, pp. 33–52.

Klein, B. 1948, 'Germany's preparation for war: a re-examination', *American Economic Review*, vol. 38, pp. 56–77.

Klein, B. 1959, *Germany's Economic Preparations for War*, Harvard University Press, Cambridge, Massachusetts, U.S.A.

Kriegler, E., Hall, J.W., Held, H., Dawson, R. & Schellnhuber, H.J. 2009, 'Imprecise probability assessment of tipping points in the climate system', *PNAS*, doi: 10.1073/pnas.0809117106.

Mai, T., Mulcahy, D., Hand, M.M. & Baldwin, S.F. 2014, 'Envisioning a renewable electricity future for the United States', *Energy*, vol. 65, pp. 374–386.

Mathews, J.A. & Tan, H. 2014, 'Manufacture renewables to build energy security', *Nature*, vol. 513, pp. 166–168.

McKibben, B. 2012, 'It's time to fight the status quo', *Solutions*, vol. 3, May, http://bit.ly/1Ndal3z.

Milward, A.S. 1977, *War, Economy and Society, 1939–1945*, Allen Lane, London, U.K.

Morris, C. & Pehnt, M. 2015, *Energy Transition: The German Energiewende*, Heinrich Böll Stiftung, Berlin, Germany, http://bit.ly/1LMbYIh.

Nordhaus, W.D. 2015, 'Climate clubs: Overcoming free-riding in international climate policy', *American Economic Review*, vol. 105, pp. 1339–1970.

Overy, R.J. 1982, 'Hitler's war and the German economy: a reinterpretation', *Economic History Review*, vol. 35, pp. 272–291.

Overy, R.J. 2006, *Why The Allies Won*, Pimlico, London, U.K.

Peters, G.P., Andrew, R.M., Boden, T., Canadell, J.G., Ciais, P. et al. 2013, 'The challenge to keep global warming below 2°C', *Nature Climate Change*, vol. 3, pp. 4–6.

Plumptre, A.F.W. 1941a, 'Organizing the Canadian economy for war', in J.F. Parkinson (ed.), *Canadian War Economics*, University of Toronto Press, Toronto, Canada.

Plumptre, A.F.W. 1941b, *Mobilizing Canada's Economy for War*, The MacMillan Company of Canada, Ltd., Toronto, Canada.

Rao, V. 2015, 'Why solving climate change will be like mobilizing for war', *The Atlantic*, 15 October, http://theatln.tc/1G7R6sS.

Raymo, M.E., Hearty, P., De Conto, R., O'Leary, M., Dowsett, H.J., Robinson, M.M. & Mitrovica, J.X. 2009, 'PLIOMAX: Pliocene maximum sea level project', *PAGES News*, vol. 17, pp. 58–59.

REN 21 2013, *Renewables 2013: Global Status Report*, Renewable Energy Policy Network for the 21st Century (REN 21).

Rockoff, H. 1998, 'The United States: from ploughshares to swords', in M. Harrison (ed.), *The Economics of World War 2: Six Great Powers in International Comparison*, Cambridge University Press, Cambridge, U.K., pp. 81–121.

Romm, J. 2009, 'Advice to a young climate blogger: always use WWII metaphors', *Think Progress*, 11 March, http://bit.ly/1j6M31n.

Roosevelt, F.D. 1942, *State of the Union Address*, 6 January, http://bit.ly/1eoIds0.

Simonson, G.R. 1960, 'The demand for aircraft and the aircraft industry, 1907–1958', *The Journal of Economic History*, vol. 20, pp. 361–382.

Sloman, S.A. 1996, 'The empirical case for two systems of reasoning', *Psychological Bulletin*, vol. 119, pp. 3–22.

Slovic, P., Finucane, M., Peters, E. & MacGregor, D.G. 2002, 'Rational actors or rational fools: implications of the affect heuristic for behavioral economics', *The Journal of Socio-Economics*, vol. 31, pp. 329–342.

Smith, R.E. 1959, *The Army and Economic Mobilization*, Office of the Chief of Military History, Department of the Army, Washington, D.C.

Stiglitz, J. 2006, 'A new agenda for global warming', *Economists' Voice*, vol. 3, http://bit.ly/1R9Bm8I.

The Climate Mobilization 2015, http://bit.ly/1iGqduV.

The New York Times 1943a, 'Foremen strike at Willow Run', 22 December, p. 21.

The New York Times 1943b, 'Willow Run faces inquiry by Senate', 16 February, p. 14.

The New York Times 1944, 'Ford technicians strike, seek union', 19 January, p.12.

The New York Times 1945a, 'Willow Run has 8,000th bomber', 15 March, p. 10.

The New York Times 1945b, 'Willow Run ends plane output', 28 June, p. 22.

The United Press 1944, 'Willow Run turning out a big bomber each hour', *The New York Times*, 17 April, p. 6.

The Wall Street Journal 1942, 'Supply shortage holds up bids on war housing', 20 June, p. 3.

The Wall Street Journal 1943, 'Truman Committee reverses stand on Ford bomber plant', 20 February, p. 3.

The Wall Street Journal 1944, 'Willow Run bomber plant, ahead of schedule, will close two days', 25 May, p. 6.

Tingley, D. & Tomz, M. 2013, 'Conditional cooperation and climate change', *Comparative Political Studies*, vol. 20, pp. 1–25.

Tyagi, V.V., Rahim, N.A.A., Rahim, N.A. & Selvaraj, J.A.L. 2013, 'Progress in solar PV technology: research and achievement', *Renewable and Sustainable Energy Review*, vol. 20, pp. 443–461.

United States Department of State n.d., *Milestones: 1937–1945, The Casablanca Conference, 1943*, Office of the Historian, http://1.usa.gov/1m5hfIt.

United States Department of State 1959, *Foreign Relations of the United States Diplomatic Papers, 1941. General, The Soviet Union*, Department of State, U.S. Government Printing Office, Washington, D.C., U.S.A.

Vaughan, D.G., Comiso, J.C., Allison, I., Carrasco, J., Kaser, G., et al. 2013, 'Observations: Cryosphere', in T.F. Stocker et al. (eds), *Climate Change 2013: The Physical Science Basis. Contribution of Working Group I to the Fifth Assessment Report of the Intergovernmental Panel on Climate Change*, Cambridge University Press, Cambridge, U.K.; New York, New York, U.S.A.

Wagner, G. & Zeckhauser, R.J. 2012, 'Climate policy: hard problem, soft thinking', *Climatic Change*, vol. 110, pp. 507–521.

Wagner, G. & Weitzman, M.L. 2015, *Climate Shock: the Economic Consequences of a Hotter Planet*, Princeton University Press, Princeton, New Jersey, U.S.A.

Walker, E.R. 1947, *The Australian Economy in War and Reconstruction*, Oxford University Press, New York, U.S.A.

Walton, F. 1956, *Miracle of World War II: How American Industry Made Victory Possible*, The Macmillan Company, New York, U.S.A.

Webster, B. & Pagnamenta, R. 2009, 'Al Gore invokes spirit of Churchill in battle against climate change', *The Times*, 8 July, http://thetim.es/1ObS3B2.

Wilt, A.F. 1991, 'The significance of the Casablanca decisions, January 1943', *The Journal of Military History*, vol. 55, pp. 517–529.

Woodford, F. 1942, 'Ford turning out bombers', *The New York Times*, 24 May, p. E7.

Wright, M. & Hearps, P. 2010, *Australian Sustainable Energy: Zero Carbon Australia Stationary Energy Plan*, University of Melbourne Energy Research Institute, Melbourne, Australia.

Zhao, Z-y, Yan, H., Zuo, J., Tian, Y-x & Zillante, G. 2013, 'A critical review of factors affecting the wind power generation industry in China', *Sustainable and Renewable Energy Review*, vol. 19, pp. 499–508.

4 Mobilising funding

Intensity, scale, volume

Despite high profile analyses on the economics of climate change mitigation, such as those produced in the Stern Report (Stern 2007), and integrated assessment models which 'integrate' climate science models with economic models (e.g. Van Vuuren et al. 2011; Nordhaus 2008, 1993a, 1993b), the 50-to-100 year cost of climate mitigation is unknowable (Rosen and Guenther 2015). 'Economies are highly complex non-linear systems and it is impossible to accurately predict their future evolution' (Scrieciu, Barker and Ackerman 2013: 157). Despite the many uncertainties in forecasting, rapid climate mitigation efforts still need support (Pindyck 2013). This means climate policy must be rigorously designed and vigorously implemented, given both the physical and social changes that climate change brings, and the many potential co-benefits of climate action to the economy, human health, and society.

For the Rapid Mitigation Project through sustainable energy transition to take off, current funding needs shoring up. Increased volume and access to finance is necessary for education and training new workers and re-skilling existing workers for the new sustainable energy regime. Industry also needs new finance in tooling up to mass-produce sustainable energy technologies, energy infrastructure such as transmission lines, and for research and development (R&D) on storage technologies, smart grids, and improved efficiency of renewable energy technologies. Funds too are needed in expanding opportunities for energy demand management, efficiency, and conservation. Substantial investment is also required to replace or upgrade many parts of the energy supply and transport systems.

A range of estimates spans different timescales, decarbonisation costs, and/ or how to accomplish sustainable energy transition. Although these estimates are uncertain (cf. Pindyck 2013), including 'how much' investment is required, they provide a tool for envisioning the scale, intensity, and volume of the necessary finance.

At the global level, the German Advisory Council on Global Change (2011) estimates that US$200 billion to US$1 trillion per annum will be required to decarbonise the global energy system by 2030. Lester Brown (2011) estimates that around US$200 billion per year is required to reduce global CO_2 emissions by 80% in 2020 relative to 2006 levels. Paul Gilding (2011) estimates that US$2.5 trillion per year will be required to cut global green house gas (GHG) emissions to zero over 15 years. A study by the World Wide Fund for Nature, Ecofys, and the Office for Metropolitan Architecture (2011) suggests that approximately EUR1 trillion per year is required in order to peak and decline global GHG emissions within five years and to achieve 100% renewable energy regime by 2050. Greenpeace International and the European Renewable Energy Council (2010) estimate that new sustainable energy power plants globally would cost approximately US$15 trillion. Mark Jacobson and Mark Delucchi (2011) project US$100 trillion will be required over 20 years, that is approximately US$5 trillion per annum, to switch the global energy system to 100% renewable energy. In their 2015 estimate, the US$100 trillion requirement would be between now and 2050, but decreasing to 80% by 2030 (Jacobson 2015).

At the national level, the Government of Denmark (2011) estimates that DKK5.6 billion, or approximately US$820 million in its 2015 value, will be required to convert the Danish energy supply to 100% renewable energy by 2050. Denmark, nonetheless, is already advancing on its path, which means that the cost could decline in the near future. *Zero Carbon Britain* requires approximately GBP50 billion per year, or US$78 billion in its 2015 value, to reduce the net GHG emissions in the U.K. to zero by 2030 (Kemp and Wexler 2010).

Although it is apparent that huge money investments are required, nevertheless, they will be offset by an array of benefits through avoidance of costs associated with: (1) building new fossil fuel technologies; (2) prospecting, mining and distributing the fuels they use; (3) maintaining existing and constructing new fossil-based power plants; and, most significantly, (4) the immense pollution and impacts of unmitigated climate change.

A key economic issue on which the financial policy to support the Rapid Mitigation Project focuses is how to ensure its cost-effectiveness. Using a *Gedankenexperiment* to envisage climate finance for rapid mitigation, we look at the intensity, scale, and volume of financial mobilisation for wartime industrial production to see how it reflects the Project's requirements.

The global cost of the war, including indirect costs such as property damage, pensions, and interests, was estimated at US$4 trillion, or around US$36 trillion in its 2015 value (Lumer 1954: 16). If this amount is averaged for the war's six year duration, i.e. from 1939 to 1945, this equates to an average US$6 trillion annual expenditures in its 2015 value, which, interestingly, is still less than the highest estimate for the global transition cost set by Jacobson and Delucchi (2011), which is US$5 trillion per annum. The maximum amount of money spent by the U.S.A. during the war was approximately 42% of its Gross National Product (GNP), which occurred in 1943 and 1944. This amounts to approximately US$7.30 trillion in its 2015 value – still more than the maximum available estimate to accomplish a global transition. The Manhattan Project that created the atomic weapon – the pinnacle of U.S. government-led wartime innovations – alone costed approximately US$24 billion in its 2015 value (Stine 2009: 6).

In terms of the proportion of national income, other combatant countries even spent more than what the Americans had disbursed. The highest volume of wartime expenditures in the U.K. reached 55% in 1943 (Harrison 1998), translating to around US$1.60 trillion in 2015. The USSR disbursed 61% of its GNP in 1942 and 1943 (Harrison 1998). In 2015, this translates to US$1.14 trillion. Germany spent a maximum of 70% of its GNP in 1943 (Harrison 1998), or approximately US$2.70 trillion in 2015 (currency conversion rates provided in Officer 2015). Japan, the country with the highest military outlay during the war, spent 76% of its Gross Domestic Product (GDP) in 1944 (Harrison 1998), or approximately US$3.50 trillion in its 2015 value. If wartime spending is used as barometer, its volume and level show that countries could afford to mobilise and spend substantial amounts for a large-scale endeavour.

To finance the war, governments raised as much money as they could through usual revenue sources available to them at the time: first, through taxation and, then, through borrowing, in anticipation of future tax receipts. Other fund sources included receipts of international aid, such as through the Lend-Lease agreement among Allied nations (Harrison 1988), domestic and overseas public asset liquidations (Gatrell and Harrison 1993) and, 'paid occupation costs' charges from Germany's annexation of its European neighbours (Abelshauser 1998), among others.

To date, contemporary means of capital provision for climate mitigation, particularly on sustainable energy transition appear in various forms. They can be categorised according to sources: public or private funds. Public funds include receipts from carbon taxes and financial transaction taxes; fossil fuel subsidy reductions; and auctions from carbon market instruments. Private capital, both commercial and personal funds, can be sourced from stocks and shares in sustainable energy firms, venture capital, and from savings, including deposits, which are reintroduced into the financial system in terms of bank loans to support projects and investments.

Climate finance can also be categorised according to the recipients: public agencies, households, and the non-state sector. Public agencies receive revenues from: taxation such as a carbon tax; tradable emissions permit auctions; development aid from bilateral and multilateral support; and the Kyoto mechanisms, which include the Clean Development Mechanism and Joint Implementation projects. These funds are used to support climate-related projects. Households receive rebates from their energy efficient choice of appliances through feebates, for example (Eilert et al. 2010); participate in feed-in tariffs, which are achieved through contracts to household renewable energy producers; and receive grants for making their homes more energy efficient. Businesses accumulate capital from private means such as from loans and guarantees from individual and corporate investors, commercial banks, public banks, and multilateral development banks. Other non-state actors also receive public support through grants, low-interest loans, and loan guarantees for training and retooling, small-scale micro-generation, retrofitting, and in new technology research, development, and demonstration.

In 2014, the UNFCCC's Standing Committee on Finance estimated that between 2010 and 2012, global climate finance ranged from US$340 to US $650 billion per year (UNFCCC 2014). The estimate is provided in a range because of complexities in domestic and international accounting, as well as fragmentations in public and private investments on climate. In addition, UNFCCC data includes financing for adaptation.

Despite the variety of financial mechanisms and increasing fund volume available for climate mitigation (see for instance the complex climate finance architecture in Heinrich Böll Stiftung and Overseas Development Institute 2015), studies continue to suggest capital shortages to fully support the transition (Center for International Climate and Environmental Research (CICERO) and Climate Policy Initiative 2015; Buchner et al. 2013; Olmos, Ruester and Liong 2012; Delina 2011). There will always be gaps for climate finance since most funding for these schemes is generally capped. The gap becomes more apparent when the highest value of the UNFCCC range, i.e. US$650 billion, is compared to the volume of funds required in achieving a global sustainable energy transition, estimated in one study to be US$5 trillion per annum (Jacobson and Delucchi 2011).

Considering the scale, scope, and speed of the Project and despite falling costs of renewable energy technologies, the funding gap for its implementation is most likely wider. The scale and volume of needed technology and new highly skilled workforce necessitates a strategic approach for fund mobilisation. Although private capital may provide some of the required funds, the transition cannot be fully left for non-state actors to fund. The state, therefore, must coordinate the transition by providing policy toolkits, public institutions, and new climate financial instruments (CICERO and Climate Policy Initiative 2015). Strengthened climate finance architecture at the national level through concrete policy measures is similarly required to reduce the price of and increasing the returns for sustainable energy technologies (CICERO and Climate Policy Initiative 2015; Atkinson and Ezell 2012; Shellenberger et al. 2008: 113).

Public sector balance sheets, however, are always constrained, with many public budgets, including those in rich countries often in deficit. Since public expenditures for the Project is likely to put pressure on public budgets, the state must redesign its fiscal policies, review existing fiscal arrangements, strengthen fiscal architecture, and prepare public financial institutions in the new climate finance regime.

Pricing emissions

The most discussed response to securing funds for climate mitigation to date has been market-based prices on emissions, based on the assumption that a rapidly increasing carbon price can discourage investments in high-emission industries. The market approach to emissions reduction tries to internalise environmental costs to encourage energy investments in renewable energy technologies (Nordhaus 1990; Cansier and Krumm 1997).

In economics, the externality problem is widely discussed beginning in Arthur Pigou's *The Economics of Welfare* (1920) and is viewed as a system problem in Garrett Hardin's *The Tragedy of the Commons* (1968). Both have argued that externalities in the economy result to misallocation, even to catastrophe. The age of climate consequences is perhaps the biggest evidence of externalities. William Nordhaus (1977: 19), indeed, suggests that climate change is 'a pure example of an externality'; thus, controlling emissions requires control by 'internalising the externality so that individual [emission] producers and consumers have proper incentives to implement the control strategy on an individual level' (1977: 20). As early as 1977, Nordhaus suggested 'putting a positive price on emissions of carbon' (1977: 25) – an approach that gained strong consensus and persists among international organisations, such as the World Bank (Kyte 2013), Organisation for Economic Co-operation and Development (OECD 2013), and the International Monetary Fund (IMF 2014).

Pricing emissions can be done in three main ways: carbon taxes, carbon trading, and implicit pricing via regulations and standards. Taxes and implicit pricing offer clear and simple signals for investment and decision-making. If the rates or the price are set high and wide enough, carbon taxes result in rapid emissions' reduction as firms and households are provided incentives to reduce their pollution. Getting the carbon tax level right, therefore, is key: too high and the costs will rise impacting on profits, jobs, and the consumers; too low and emission will only increase. Cap-and-trade schemes, by contrast, comprise trading of scarce permits or allowances, and could be an effective mechanism to accelerate emissions' reduction only if the quantity cap or the ceiling on the overall emissions quantity is progressively and quickly set to zero. Although a carbon price – either through tax or a cap-and-trade – is necessary, it is, by itself, insufficient considering the urgency of reducing emissions, the inertia of policymaking, and other market imperfections (Hepburn 2006). Nonetheless, this does not mean they are not necessary; instead, they should be strategically designed, employed, and complemented with other mechanisms and instruments.

Wartime experience regarding fund mobilisation for munitions' production and for the prosecution of the war itself provides some lessons for securing the necessary volume of climate mitigation finance. To ensure state coffers were filled enough for wartime requirements, governments designed new collection strategies and created enabling environments. New fiscal policies were instituted through new legislation on taxation, stricter financial and banking controls, such as for foreign currency exchange, interventions by regulations especially in banking and lending, and other capital-sourcing mechanisms such as public borrowing through war bond issues (see Chapter 6).

Taxing carbon pollution

At wartime, taxation, the primary source of state revenues, had to be modified to suit wartime requirements to ensure efficient and maximum collection. Wartime taxation was based on the basic principle of spreading the burden of war fairly, equitably and, as much as possible, evenly across segments of society. Taxation was also used to promote wider public recognition of the war's implications to the state, public life, and citizenship (Walker 1947: 234).

Although collection volume varied across the spectrum, taxes collected for the war had intensified in volume across major combatant countries. In the Allied states, for instance, wartime taxation largely supported wartime expenditures. Of the total war costs, 55% were provided by wartime tax in Canada (Milward 1977: 107), 53% in the U.K. (Walker 1947), and 45% in the U.S.A. (Kennedy 1999: 625; Lumer 1954: 20).

In addition to increases in tax collection volume, wartime also paved the way for rapid evolution of the tax system through innovative tax schemes that continue to permeate democratic societies today. The U.S.A., for example, owes much of its current federal revenue structure to its war taxation history. Universal income taxation was never heard of in the country until efforts to prepare for the probable U.S. entry into the war began. The U.S. Government started extending income taxation to all Americans through three defence tax laws increasing levies on personal income as enacted in June 1940, October 1940, and September 1941 (Vernon 1994: 859). As a result of universal income tax, the proportion of the American workforce paying taxes rose from 7% in 1940 to 64% in 1942 (Mayhew 2005: 478). By 1945, close to 43 million American taxpayers, from a total population of 140 million, were required to pay federal income taxes (Tassava 2010).

As the number of taxpayers increased, the amount of taxes Americans paid also increased. In 1944, the new mass-based taxation allowed the U.S. Federal Government to collect taxes 132% higher from the previous year's level (Rockoff 1998: 108, Table 3.15). That year, the U.S. Government collected US$45 billion worth of taxes, or approximately US$608 billion in its 2015 value – a figure dwarfing its US$8.7 billion collection in 1941 (Tassava 2010). At the peak of the war in 1945, an average American citizen paid US$313 annual tax, or approximately US$4,138 in its 2015 value – an 800% rise in only seven years (Lumer 1954: 21, Table 1). The intensity of U.S. wartime tax collection becomes more apparent when contemporary tax collections are compared to the pre-war level. In 2012, personal income tax collections represented 8.85% of the country's GNP (OECD 2014) in contrast to the pre-war level where revenues never exceeded 1.5% of GNP (Witte 1985).

Outside the U.S.A., many governments also recognised the potential of income tax collection for wartime finance such that income taxation almost became universal. In Australia, income tax was the most prominent wartime tax imposed on citizens. Before 1942, income tax rates varied across Australian states (Haig-Muir and Hay 1996: 131); following the threats of Japanese invasion, however, states agreed to a uniform income tax scheme applicable throughout the Commonwealth. As in the U.S.A., Australians saw increased tax rates levied against their personal income. By 1943, Australians were asked to pay 10% more on their usual income tax rates (Haig-Muir and Hay 1996: 124). In 2011, taxes collected on personal income stood at 10.4% of Australia's GDP (OECD 2014).

Wartime taxation also expanded its reach to include resource-competing consumer goods to discourage non-war item production and consumption. These indirect taxation methods were implemented in the U.S.A. in the form of increased excise tax rates on gasoline, gifts, capital stock, and estates (Vernon 1994: 859–862; Rockoff 1998; Cardozier 1995: 128). In Canada, indirect taxes were levied on motorcars, radios, cameras, and other 'luxuries' at the time including gasoline, alcohol, cigarettes, cosmetics, soft drinks, and movies (Plumptre 1941: 123–125, 135–137, 147–148; Gibson 1941: 39–42; cf. Bartels 2001). Indirect wartime tax collections also intensified following additional rates on entertainment tax, and customs and excise duties (Walker 1947: 237). U.S. corporations earning more than 'normal' profits were also taxed to a maximum of 90% on all profits above 'normal' (Cardozier 1995: 155; cf. Vernon 1994: 859). A 'normal' profit refers to the minimum level of profit needed for a company to remain competitive in the market as determined by tax agencies. In Australia, a similar scheme called 'excess profits tax' was also in place (Walker 1947: 231; Haig-Muir and Hay 1996: 124).

Axis countries also invigorated their wartime collection approaches. In Germany, personal and business income taxes were collected earlier than in Allied countries (Walker 1939: 128–129; Overy 1995). This included an emergency surtax called *Kriegszuschlag* (Overy 1995), which was levied as early as 1933. Early increases in tax rates, and their collections, contributed to the rapid German rearmament during the interwar years. Because of the *Kriegszuschlag* alone, the German government revenues more than doubled: from RM10.2 trillion in 1933 to RM22 trillion in 1938 (Walker 1939: 128–129). In their 2015 values, these translate to US$57 trillion and US$149 trillion. By 1943, tax receipts were still high at RM34 trillion even with Germany's defeats in major battlegrounds (Overy 1995: 271). Despite the absence of conversion rate data for the Reichsmark at the height of war, i.e. between 1942 and 1944 (see Officer 2015), it is sufficient to contend that collections were still substantially made.

Wartime tax history illuminates the relative capacity of countries to mandate wide-scale levies on incomes, profits, consumer goods, and services, to intensify collection efforts, and to provide substantial fund volume to meet wartime requirements for new funds. If this lesson is to be heeded, the state can strengthen its climate finance policy so that it can collect similarly scaled volumes of funds for the Rapid Mitigation Project.

Setting carbon price high enough, either through a tax or a cap-and-trade, so that using and patronising high-carbon goods and services becomes expensive for consumers and businesses is one key approach. To maximise the potential of a carbon price, Nobel laureate Joseph Stiglitz (Bloomberg 2015) and economist William Nordhaus (2015) suggest a universal, global price for emissions, which can be set at a rate high enough to encourage divestment from carbon-intensive industries. A uniform global rate, either as a tax rate or a ceiling price or a hybrid – although this may appear too simplistic – can address the free-riding challenge. Nordhaus (2015) suggests a universal US$50 per tonne carbon price at current income and emission levels. Since an expensive price on carbon has ramifications for consumers, particularly the poor, a portion of the collections accruing from the carbon price needs to be returned as dividends to citizens (Skocpol 2013).

Experiences from countries having carbon taxes such as Denmark, Finland, the Netherlands, Norway, Sweden, and Switzerland – some of which have had carbon taxes for nearly 20 years – demonstrate that a carbon price can deliver real emission abatements (Tietenberg 2013; Lin and Li 2011). Australia, which legislated a carbon price in 2012, although it was removed 15 months later following a change of government, provides an example.

When the Australian carbon price was operational between September 2012 and September 2013, the country was able to reduce its electricity-sector emissions by 5.5% (Australian Government, Department of the Environment 2014). During the same period, emissions from companies covered by the carbon price also fell by 7% (IGCC 2014). Revenues raised directly from pricing carbon amounted to AU$6.6 billion, approximately US$6.53 billion in its 2015 value (Heath 2014). Despite warnings from vested interests and their supporters that the Australian economy would ebb because of the carbon price, inflation during this period was safely within the target laid by the Reserve Bank of Australia (Jotzo and Burke 2014). From mid-2014 to 2015, following carbon price removal, carbon emissions from electricity generation increased, despite falling demand (Pitt and Sherry 2015).

As a carbon price swells in rates, some sectors, especially low-income earners, can be disadvantaged. Some compensation and other assistance measures must, therefore, be carefully embedded into the carbon price programme. In addition to dividend pay-out (Skocpol 2013), other forms of support can be embedded in the policy. The short-lived Australian carbon price scheme used two approaches. First, income tax for low-income earners was cut by increasing the annual income tax threshold, or the amount one can earn before paying tax, from AU$6,000 to AU$18,200. Second, pensions, allowances and family benefits for those in social security were increased by 1.7% (Simpson 2011).

Other than direct taxes on carbon polluters, the state can, as in wartime, institute profit caps and higher taxes on luxury items and competing products and technologies. To save on precious funding resources, the state can also place prohibitions on the production, sale, and consumption of some goods, especially those requiring materials relevant for sustainable energy transition. Moreover, some form of emergency surtax, such as the German *Kriegszuschlag*, may be explored as an additional revenue source.

As heavy emitters are penalised with high carbon taxes for their pollution and emissions, sectors working towards abating and reducing emissions must be supported by favourable measures. To encourage funding support for rapid mitigation, the state can initiate some tax incentives for these sectors and entities.

- *Accelerated depreciation and other tax deferrals.* Preferential tax treatment through exemptions and deferrals can encourage sustainable energy project developers to invest, as illustrated in the accelerated depreciation tax incentives for wind power projects in India, which drove 30% to 50% of annual installations in the country in 2013 (Pearson 2013; Prasad 2012).
- *Credit refunds and exemptions from income tax.* These also involve preferential tax treatment for sustainable energy project developers. The 80% discount on taxes paid for distributing solar-generated electricity in Brazil is one example (Nielsen 2012). On the demand side, some form of tax exemption can also be provided to manufacturers and buyers of highly efficient appliances and equipment
- *Relief from indirect taxes.* With most countries now using value-added taxes (VAT) alongside direct taxes to raise revenues, some form of VAT relief can be initiated for the sustainable energy industry. In China, 50% value added tax (VAT) refund is paid on wind power sales, while 100% VAT refund is paid on the sale of biodiesel oil generated by using abandoned animal fat and vegetable oil (Whitley 2013).

A review of existing tax policies is also necessary to maximise government revenues while re-assessing their social implications relative to the execution of the Project. For instance, the universal income tax, which saw its genesis during the war, may be altered in favour of a progressive tax on consumption. Although the principal aim of the progressive tax is to generate revenues, it is different from the current personal income tax since it can serve as a nudge for reducing emissions. A consumption tax also encourages savings, thrift and investment, and raises additional revenue and productivity, which, by contrast, are discouraged in the personal income tax system (Engler and Knoll 2003). Universal income tax is also unfair and unjust in its design, a sentiment shared by Warren Buffett:

> Last year [2010] my federal tax bill – the income tax I paid, as well as payroll taxes paid by me and on my behalf – was [US]$6,938,744. That sounds like a lot of money. But what I paid was only 17.4 percent of my taxable income – and that's actually a lower percentage than was paid by any of the other 20 people in our office. Their tax burdens ranged from 33 percent to 41 percent and averaged 36 percent.
>
> (Buffett 2011)

A progressive consumer tax responds to this injustice and, at the same time, promotes better values. Since a progressive tax nudges citizens to spend less, reduce consumption, and be more savings-conscious, they are led to adopt more energy-efficient behaviours, which have implications on emissions' reduction. Robert Frank illustrates how a progressive tax can work.

> Families would report their incomes and their annual savings to the [Internal Revenue Service]...Their taxable consumption would then be calculated as income minus savings minus a large standard deduction, say, [US]$30,000 for a family of four. For example, a family that earned [US]$50,000 and saved [US]$5,000 during a given tax year would have taxable consumption of [US]$50,000-$5,000-$30,000, or $15,000 total. Tax rates would start off low, say, 10 percent for the first [US]$30,000 of taxable consumption. Under the consumption tax, this family would owe [US] $1,500 about half of what it would pay under the current income tax.
>
> (Frank 2008: 22)

Taxes levied on consumption, such as the progressive tax proposal, instead of income could also improve economic equality since no painful sacrifice is required from the public, especially the poor. Moreover, a progressive universal tax on consumption is consistent with Herman Daly's (2008: 8) suggestion of: 'taxing what we want less of (depletion and pollution), and ceasing to tax what we want more of (income, value added).'

Regardless whether the state pursue a carbon tax or a progressive tax on consumption, or both, a taxation policy in a democracy needs ample time to process – making it a cumbersome proposal in the context of rapid mitigation since, customarily, it takes time to legislate, levy, and collect new taxes. The repercussions to politicians when voting for tax increases also limit the effectiveness of these traditional sources of public finance (Rockoff 1998: 109). At wartime, only when there was significant, visceral threat to security and actual evidence of foreign aggression did the public readily accept policy proposals that eventually changed tax landscapes. In the absence of similar threats, therefore, altering current taxation systems is likely to be an uphill challenge.

The technical, procedural, and political challenges, however, could be minimised if politicians are incentivised to act resolutely on rapid mitigation. Although it is difficult to ascertain these kinds of incentives, it is possible to envisage that they can be brought about by the Rapid Mitigation Agreement with strong sanctions on non-participation as discussed in Chapter 3 (Stiglitz in Bloomberg 2015; Nordhaus 2015). Psychological stimuli such as those provided by physical climate impacts (see Chapter 3) may also lead to the adoption of a new tax system. A push from a highly engaged public, acting as a collective social movement, can also drive innovations in tax policy (Delina, Diesendorf and Merson 2014).

Even with successful legislation, it is still prudent for the state to strategise more new schemes and alternative mechanisms to fund the Project aside from the usual course of taxation. The sheer scale of the required funds necessitates more innovations. Deficit financing or public borrowing, which was used to smooth and complement wartime taxation, offer one way to enhance opportunities for climate mitigation finance.

Public borrowing

Borrowing either from public or private banks or through state-issued war bonds provided additional mechanisms to complement wartime taxation. Aside from war bonds, some governments also designed innovative forms of public borrowing such as short-term treasury bills and long-term credit through savings banks, credit unions, and other financial institutions.

In the U.S.A., public borrowing for the war accounted for 27% of total government expenditures from 1942–1945 (Rockoff 1998: 108). The scale of public borrowing climbed from US$40 billion in 1939, or approximately US$685 billion in 2015, to US$279 billion in 1946, or approximately US$3.4 trillion in 2015 (Lumer 1954: 207). The majority of these borrowings were sourced from war bond issues in banks, corporations, and even from ordinary Americans. At the peak of the war in 1944, many Americans purchased celebrity-promoted war bonds such that by the time bond sales ended in 1946, 85 million Americans had acquired more than US$185 billion worth of securities, or approximately US$2.3 trillion in its 2015 value (Tassava 2010).

Wartime borrowing through war bond issuances also reached its all-time high in Australia, where the overall volume reached in excess of AU£1 trillion by June 1944 (Walker 1947: 238–242; in 1944 value). Similarly, public borrowing was also popular in Canada such that between 1939 and 1941, the Canadian Federal Government generated additional new revenues amounting to CAD1.9 billion through bond issues, or approximately US$27 billion in its 2015 value (Plumptre 1941: 152). Canada sold the bonds through government securities supplied by the Bank of Canada, public war loans, security issues by provincial governments, and Canadian private corporations (Plumptre 1941: 153–171).

Axis states also sourced new capital from public debts. In Japan, for instance, the sale of war bonds was instrumental in providing the money needed for the military as early as 1932. Throughout the war, roughly 80% of Japanese wartime government issues were for military purposes (Hara 1998: 257). In Germany, government loans floated on the market between 1935 and 1938 reached close to RM15.6 trillion or approximately US$106 trillion in 2015 (Walker 1939: 129).

Germany also introduced and sold secret state bills of exchange called Mefo bills to supplement funds collected from borrowing and taxation. These ingeniously invented bills of exchange were named after *Metallurgische Forschungsgesellschaft mbH*, a dummy company established in 1933 for munitions productions. Four German blue chip companies whose armaments contracts received limited finance from the government budget or public borrowing took funds from Mefo bills. They drew bills on the dummy company and then cashed them at the Reichsbank, the German central bank. Since they were considered bills of exchange, the true extent of state armaments contracts was hidden. Mefo bills were circulated between 1934 and 1938, and ultimately achieved circulation close to RM12 billion, or approximately US$81 billion in 2015 (Abelshauser 1998: 140).

In contemporary financial architecture, public borrowing through bond issuances offers an attractive instrument since they are familiar products to the investment community. Estimated at US$100 trillion in mid-2013 (Gruic and Schrimpf 2014), bonds represent the largest pool of capital in the world (Burrows 2014), even overshadowing the equities market (Kidney 2015). Large-scale investments required by the Project can, therefore, take advantage of this cache of capital. According to Sean Kidney (2015), institutional investors such as pension funds and insurance companies have global investments of around US$88 trillion, the majority of which are invested in the bond market. In addition, major corporations also have large capital reserves that are waiting for new investment opportunities (Kidney 2015). At the September 2014 United Nations Climate Summit, a cohort of investors representing approximately US$24 trillion of assets under management called for climate action (http://goo.gl/FH4U4q) saying they were ready to provide investment of more than US$5 billion in bonds (Kidney 2014).

For the Project to tap this capital source, institutional investors must be provided with attractive investment opportunity channels to enable them to participate. Thus far, these channels are yet to be opened and delivered at the necessary scale. In 2014, the green bond market has reached an outstanding value of US$53.6 billion (Kidney 2014), which is less than one percent of the total global bond market. Opportunities to attract the cache of funds available from institutional investors can be maximised by issuing climate mitigation bonds that match this untapped supply with the demand for Project investment. These bonds have to create secure, reliable, and predictable long-term assets akin to what institutional investors and even major corporations look for.

In addition to institutional investors, climate mitigation bonds can also capitalise on the growing appetite for 'purpose driven' and 'responsible' finance in the growing world of impact investing. 'Impact investments are investments made into companies, organizations, and funds with the intention to generate measurable social and environmental impact alongside a financial return' (Global Impact Investing Network n.d.). Some financial sector members, including institutional investors, who have already started to shift part of their investment portfolios towards 'socially-responsible' funds, represent additional markets for climate mitigation bonds.

Responsible finance has already gained salience in the world's largest sovereign wealth fund, Norway's Government Pension Fund Global, when it expanded its portfolio to include direct investments in renewable energy assets (World Wide Fund for Nature 2014). The Australian investment fund UniSuper, an industry super fund dedicated to those working in the country's higher education and research sector, provides another example. In 2014, UniSuper snapped up a third of the World Bank's AU$300 million

'Kangaroo Green Fund' offering, the first green bond issued into the Australian market designed to mobilise private sector funding for environmentally focused projects (Vorrath 2014). Mobilising investors such as these is necessary in the new climate finance regime.

To attract institutional investors in purchasing climate mitigation bond offerings, bonds must be simplified and standardised. Although this has already started, especially internationally (e.g. World Bank 2009), the Project's funding requirements necessitate further scaling up.

- *Scaling.* Investors, particularly institutions, demand large-scale investment opportunities. Since the Project calls for utility-scale infrastructure development, investment grade bonds of half a billion dollars upwards must be designed, making them easily secured (Kidney 2012; Burrows 2014). Small-scale technologies, nevertheless, need to be bundled together to make them attractive for investment. Other than institutional investors, small-scale investors such as households, professional and social groups, co-operatives, towns, and cities, as had been illustrated by examples of wartime bond issues, should also be tapped.
- *Advertising.* Public funds must be strategically used to improve the attractiveness of climate mitigation bonds. Widespread and highly attractive promotional activities for advertising mitigation bonds must be made available to institutional, large, and small-scale investors. Bonds could also be made more attractive by reducing tax costs for investors.
- *Providing institutional support.* Financial houses must be set up to aggregate small-to-medium-scale sustainable energy projects. To sort these processes out, sustainable energy project 'warehouses' such as those in the U.S. states of Pennsylvania and Kentucky need to be created (see wheel. renewfund.com). Australia's Clean Energy Finance Corporation, which mobilises capital investment for low-carbon technologies in the country, is another example of a 'warehouse' for sustainable energy projects (see cleanenergyfinancecorp.com.au).
- *Transparency.* Independent third party accreditors, not the bond issuers, should determine the 'greenness' of the bonds to ensure their credentials.

Despite the relative availability and feasibility of funds that can be collected through taxation and borrowing instruments, it still is essential to secure funds beyond these typical mechanisms. The sheer scale of capital needed by the global community to implement the Project justifies the requisite significance of innovative financing strategies.

Complementary climate finance

For the Project to be more cost-effective, existing mechanisms for supporting sustainable energy technology diffusion must be revisited, reviewed, and strengthened. Most of these mechanisms have already been in existence and are empirically tested to work.

- *Expanding and strengthening feed-in tariffs' programmes.* These tariffs, funded by a small increase in electricity prices paid by all electricity end users, are proven strategy for diffusing renewable electricity (IPCC 2014: 29; Couture and Gagnon 2010). They help to cover cost and improve viability by providing renewable energy suppliers and investors with revenue certainty through guaranteed power purchase contracts. For feed-in-tariffs to be effective, however, they should be well designed, meaning they should be gradually reduced (Couture and Cory 2009) and eventually phased out. Experiences in Italy and Spain, for instance, illustrate that too generous or immature feed-in tariffs can be unsustainable. Since these tariffs incur costs for taxpayers and end users, their design must also include means to offset price increases (Sensuss, Ragwitz and Genoese 2008; Lund et al. 2010).
- *Increasing output quotas or renewable portfolio standards.* These administratively effective mechanisms help to increase renewable electricity production by providing renewable producers with incentives to reduce their costs. Unlike feed-in-tariffs, which use public funds, these mechanisms rely on private investments, often with state support (Wiser, Barbose and Holt 2011; Berry and Jaccard 2001). Nonetheless, it is not a fool-proof scheme. It can imbalance prices, especially when sustainable energy projects are concentrated only at locations with high resource efficiency. This situation in turn can lower electricity prices in high generation locations but increase prices in other places.
- *Initiating or expanding regulatory standards.* Establishing or improving performance standards to increase the cost of carbon can contribute to emissions' reduction. The U.S. Clean Power Plan, which sets state-level target emissions for power generation, is one example (United States Environmental Protection Agency 2015).
- *Providing preferential loans and grants, and creating or expanding sustainable energy production tax credits.* Although large-scale renewable energy entities can easily access capital from banks, small-scale, distributed sustainable energy projects such as co-operatives, schools, local governments, community groups, and households are usually less attractive as bankable investments. Thus, they must be supported by public investment, or by some forms of public–private partnerships.

Reforms in sectors where precious funds can be directed towards the Project also need to be undertaken. One way to secure additional revenues is to review existing financial schemes and mechanisms such as direct and indirect public subsidies to fossil-based industries and to shift these to support the Project. Indeed much can be diverted from subsidies to the fossil fuel industry, which, according to the IMF (2013), received approximately US $1.9 trillion in 2011. The lion's share of these subsidies is spent to artificially lower the real price of fossil fuels and nuclear energy, keeping the sustainable energy option off the market, making energy efficiency and conservation less effective, and bolstering inefficient technologies. In total, subsidies for fossil fuels amount to 8.5% of government revenues, or close to 3% of global GDP (IMF 2013). In its 2015 value, this translates to US$2,303 trillion – more than enough to meet global energy transition requirements.

Comparing fossil fuel subsidies and climate finance flows between 2010 and 2012, Oil Change International (2012), found that fossil fuel subsidies eclipsed climate finance in the U.S.A. by 5.25. This means that for every dollar spent on climate change, US$5.25 have subsidised the fossil fuel industry. The ratio is worst in Australia where US$43 were allocated to high carbon industries for every dollar spent on climate. Removing these subsidies and assigning them instead to sustainable energy transition could mean additional, if not substantial, investments for emissions reduction. On a global scale, the IMF (2013) estimates CO_2 emissions could decline by as much as 13% with fossil fuel subsidy removal alone.

The state should also initiate stricter guidelines for fossil fuel divestment by making investors and groups commit to divestment. The state should set the example by divesting all its investments and holdings in fossil fuel, regardless of volume. Public university endowments and public pension funds must be free of any high carbon assets within the Project's first five years. Private funds should be free of fossil fuel investments in less than ten years. Although the direct impacts of divestment on equity are likely to be limited, the indirect, long-term impacts on the value of the targeted firms are made through negative consequences, including tainted reputation and stigma, which weakens business positions (Ansar, Caldecott and Tilbury 2013). In 2014, the stock value of fossil fuel companies was worth approximately US $5 trillion, making the sector one of the world's largest asset classes (Bloomberg 2014). Although part of this stock could be redirected into the Project, most of it will be stranded as it is written off or converted to liabilities in the new sustainable energy regime.

Other huge expenditure items that need revisiting are national budget items apportioned for defence and wars. Joseph Stiglitz estimated in 2008 that the wars in Iraq, Afghanistan, and Pakistan have cost the U.S.A. more than US$3 trillion (Stiglitz and Bilmes 2008) – a cost that they acknowledged in 2010 to be too low (Stiglitz and Bilmes 2010). According to Brown University's Watson Institute for International Studies (2015), the wars costed approximately US$4.4 trillion, and, including future interest costs on borrowing for the wars, the figure would be approximately US$8 trillion through 2054. Australian taxpayers, meanwhile, spent more than AU$3 billion on the Iraq war (Davis and Coorey 2007).

International cooperation

The different contours of national economies and capacities require members of the international community to support each other. To allow every nation to contribute to rapid mitigation efforts, rich countries need to provide poor countries with technology and skill transfer assistance. This is not new, but an affirmation of the 1992 UNFCCC. Likewise, countries that have rich natural sustainable energy resources need to provide those that do not with support through renewable energy trade. International cooperation at wartime provides a lens to view how transnational cooperation can be achieved. The Lend-Lease programme, which began in March 1941, became the principal mechanism used for technical cooperation among Allied nations – and could be called in as a template for cooperation.

The heavy munitions supply that Lend-Lease provided gave many Allied countries a significant boost in their domestic war capabilities (Harrison 1988: 189). Total Lend-Lease exports from 1941 to 1945 were valued at US $43.6 billion in 1945 dollars, or approximately US$576 billion in 2015 (Allen 1946: 250). The British Empire received 69% of this total (US$30 billion in its 1945 value); the U.S.S.R. received 24% (US$10.5 billion); and other Allied countries the remaining 7% (US$3 billion) (Allen 1946: 250, Table 4). Of the US$30 billion worth of military supplies for the British, US$3 billion went to Commonwealth nations: Australia received US$1.6 billion, India US $913 million, South Africa US$296 million, and New Zealand US$271 million (Allen 1946: 252, Table 5, all figures in 1945 dollars). In 1943, Lend-Lease exports to Soviet Russia were valued at around 18% of its national income, which was double their volume in 1942 (Harrison 1988: 189, Table 6). The Lend-Lease figures for Russia remain contentious. Estimates range from US $7.5 billion (Milward 1977: 71) to US$10 billion (Barber and Harrison 1991: 189), to US$11 billion (Allen 1946), and to US$12 billion (Harrison 1996: 132). Regardless of these variations, what is clear is that the munitions sent to the Red Army contributed to the effective prosecution of war in Europe, especially during the intense battles at the Eastern front.

Although domestic manufacturing allowed the Soviets to meet their own munitions needs, the American shipments of trucks, tractors, and tinned foods provided the Red Army with mobility in its westward pursuit of retreating Germans (Harrison 1988: 189). Under Lend-Lease war aid agreements, Russia received more than half a million vehicles, including 77,900 jeeps, 151,000 light trucks, and more than 200,000 army trucks (Overy 2006: 263). Although post-war Stalinist writing ignored the role of Lend-Lease in Soviet victory, Stalin privately viewed the U.S. war aid as vital to Soviet survival and even said that it would have been impossible for the U.S.S.R. to stand against Germany without the Lend-Lease programme (Sokolov 1994: 581).

The Lend-Lease experience suggests that international climate finance can be scaled up. From 2010 to 2012, developed countries provided US$33 billion of climate finance in developing countries, with US$16 billion to US$26 billion reported to have contributed to climate mitigation (UNFCCC 2014). The Green Climate Fund, a fund within the UNFCCC aimed at assisting developing countries in climate adaptation and mitigation, had received pledges of more than US$10 billion for its seed capitalisation by end-2014. Without a formal accounting methodology, however, it remains highly uncertain whether the original Copenhagen pledge of US$100 billion per year will be met. Since current international climate finance infrastructure remains complex and messy, a strengthened approach and arrangement in financing the international dimension of the Rapid Mitigation Project is required.

Assessed, rather than voluntary, contributions based on level of development, technical capacity, and historical and present emissions, may offer the most optimal result for collection and administration of mitigation funds. This can be arranged through a *Multilateral Fund for the Implementation of Rapid Mitigation,* or the Rapid Mitigation Fund, which should be made separate from any future adaptation fund. The structural and administrative design of the Rapid Mitigation Fund could be patterned after the relatively successful *Multilateral Fund for the Implementation of the Montreal Protocol* (Gonzales, Taddonio and Sherman 2015). Replenished every two years, the Rapid Mitigation Fund can be used in financing the conversion of existing high carbon energy systems and technologies, and in paying royalties and patent rights on new technologies in the global south (cf. Muller et al. 2015).

Extra legroom, nevertheless, needs to be provided so that developing countries can fully participate in the Project. This can be done by reducing the strain on their national budgets through some form of debt relief in exchange for their commitments to implement rapid mitigation activities. Based on their actual emissions reduction, 'debt-for-climate' swaps can be designed within the Rapid Mitigation Agreement, or in the absence of one, through bilateral or multilateral climate agreements. The resulting money from the swaps – estimated at US$30 billion per year (Fenton et al. 2014) – should be strictly used to finance mitigation activities and initiatives, especially in vulnerable countries that are also low income and are highly indebted. 'Debt-for-nature' swaps that have been in use since the 1970s with relative success can be used as models for designing the structure of 'debt-for-climate' swaps (Fenton et al. 2014).

Public capital

The extensive role of the state in mobilising climate finance for the Rapid Mitigation Project underscores the extent of the grasp of the state in the financial arrangement, and the degree of public investments on capital formation for the transition. The wartime analogy illustrates how the state can, with policy, legislation and regulation, strengthen the role of public finance in the new climate regime. Public investment overtaking private investment, nonetheless, is not new.

In the U.S.A., for instance, net public investment at the height of war, that is, from 1942 to 1945, was positive US$99.7 billion; whereas, net private investment was negative US$6.2 billion (Higgs 2004: 504). The repercussions of publicly funded mobilisation were huge, with Elberton Smith (1959: 475) viewing it as 'the greatest expansion in [American economic] history – an expansion which went far toward guaranteeing the successful outcome of the war.' Wartime public finance also sent ripples to the overall economy through improved real income, with more than 80% of the increase following the restoration of full-employment performance (Vernon 1994). Overall, the wartime sketch exposes the capacity of public finance to assume a key role for the Project, especially since private finance does not historically have the capacity to support large-scale and aggressive transformations.

Domestic public finance is key in speeding up sustainable energy technology diffusion and for supporting complementary activities such as R&D, labour preparation, and administration (cf. Buchner et al. 2013). To meet the Project's investment requirements and timeline, public funds can be used for paying incremental investment costs and for assuming significant financial risk. Public funds can also pay for capital investments in sectors where private actors are unwilling or unable to bear them, such as capacity building and strengthening, and labour preparation through skilling. Public funds are also essential in altering the returns between high and low carbon investments such as through a carbon price, public borrowing, and other means including subsidies, new taxes, feed-in-tariffs, and regulatory standards.

In a study by the Climate Policy Initiative, public funds for sustainable energy investments stood at US$41 billion, or 16% of the total energy sector investments in 2012 (Buchner et al. 2013). In Germany and China, state entities have been providing public funds to support renewable energy diffusion through loans, grants, and equity for building and strengthening capacity. Direct financing, through aid provision and project-specific grants and loans, is also prevalent in addition to public subsidies through feed-in-tariffs and other power purchase agreements, in both developed and developing countries.

The public sector is also entering the climate finance world as active shareholder so that it can influence investment decision-making in these entities. This is not uncommon since states typically deliver strategic goods and services such as electricity, water, and development aid. In 2013, at least US$42 billion of public money was invested in projects and private entities (Buchner et al. 2013), with public shareholding to support the acceleration of renewable energy penetration accounting for 84% of total investments. In the U.S.A., around 68% of these investments are publicly held; in Germany, the figure is approximately 54% (Buchner et al. 2013). The extent to which the state broadens its scope to support sustainable energy transition, therefore, is already a reality; but, the scope is yet to reach a substantial scale and speed to meet the goal of the Project.

Although public funds remain essential in building financial capital for the Project, the redirection of large volumes of private capital for the transition, as explored earlier in this chapter, is also ultimately required. To access this cache of funds, new financial products must be designed so that private investors, especially institutions, understand the opportunities and risks associated with redirecting their investment into Project needs. Understanding and leveraging these opportunities and risks are essential to unlock a greater capital pool to accelerate climate mitigation.

In addition to the importance of both public and private capitalisation in supporting new supply facilities, it is also key to highlight the benefits accruing from mitigation activities through demand management. Improving end use efficiency and energy conservation directly reduces the pressure on energy supply, which means less need for higher cost energy. Households, the locus of micro-scale innovation in demand side management, therefore, need to be supported with finance as they participate in rapid mitigation activities through effective electricity demand reduction. A complementary, yet key, strategy to achieve energy efficiency is to incentivise landlords in their efficiency investments through some form of grants and tax exemptions or credits.

The wartime mobilisation narrative brings to the fore wider debates on whether financial markets are suitable for coordinating and sustaining the Project's financial needs. The financial market's short-termism, however, is deeply misaligned with the Project's long-term, prudential investment requirements. Wartime fund mobilisation, which underscored the political nature of capitalism, is reproduced in the new imagination for mobilising public funds for the Project, albeit fine-tuned to the needs of modern times. The Pope in his encyclical on climate change highlights this shift:

> economics without politics cannot be justified, since this would make it impossible to favour other ways of handling the various aspects of the present crisis...For 'the current model, with its emphasis on success and self-reliance, does not appear to favour an investment in efforts to help the slow, the weak or the less talented to find opportunities in life'.
>
> (Francis 2015: Paragraph 196)

References

Abelshauser, W. 1998, 'Germany: guns, butter, and economic miracles', in M. Harrison (ed.), *The Economics of World War II: Six Great Powers in International Comparison*, Cambridge University Press, Cambridge, U.K., pp. 122–176.

Allen, R.G.D. 1946, 'Mutual aid between the US and the British Empire', *Journal of the Royal Statistical Society*, vol. 109, pp. 243–277.

Ansar, A., Caldecott, B. & Tilbury, J. 2013, *Stranded Assets and the Fossil Fuel Divestment Campaign: What Does Divestment Mean for the Valuation of Fossil Fuel Assets?* Stranded Assets Programme, Smith School of Enterprise and the Environment, University of Oxford, Oxford, U.K.

Atkinson, R. & Ezell, S. 2012, *Innovation Economics: The Race for Global Advantage*, Yale University Press, New Haven, Connecticut, U.S.A.

Australian Government, Department of the Environment 2014, *Australian National Greenhouse Accounts: Quarterly Update of Australia's National Greenhouse Gas Inventory, September Quarter 2013*, Commonwealth of Australia, Canberra, Australia.

Barber, J. & Harrison, M. 1991, *The Soviet Home Front, 1941–1945: A Social and Economic History of the USSR in World War II*, Longman, London, U.K.; New York, U.S.A.

Bartels, D. 2001, 'Wartime mobilization to counter severe global climate change', *Human Ecology*, vol. 10, pp. 229–232.

Berry, T. & Jaccard, M. 2001, 'The renewable portfolio standards: design considerations and an implementation survey', *Energy Policy*, vol. 29, pp. 263–277.

Bloomberg 2014, 'Fossil fuel divestment: a $5 trillion challenge', *Bloomberg New Energy Finance*, 26 August, http://bit.ly/1qKfFOg.

Bloomberg 2015, 'Nobel laureate economist, Joseph Stiglitz wants to set highly expensive global price for carbon dioxide', *The Economic Times*, 11 July, http://bit.ly/1N8YDJf.

Brown, L.R. 2011, *World on the Edge: How to Prevent Environmental and Economic Collapse*, W.W. Norton & Company, New York; London, U.K.

Buchner, B., Herve-Mignucci, M., Trabacchi, C., Wilkinson, J., Stadelmann, M., et al. 2013, *The Global Landscape of Climate Finance 2013*, Climate Policy Initiative, http://bit.ly/1NDbpOy.

Buffett, W. 2011, 'Stop coddling the super-rich', *The New York Times*, 14 August, http://nyti.ms/1dEZYBh.

Burrows, M. 2014, 'Keynote speech: Investing in sustainable landscapes', Forests Asia Summit 2013, http://bit.ly/1nXJdLW.

Cansier, D. & Krumm, R. 1997, 'Air pollutant taxation: An empirical survey', *Ecological Economics*, vol. 23, pp. 59–70.

Cardozier, V.R. 1995, *The Mobilization of the United States in World War II: How the Government, Military, and Industry Prepared for War*, McFarland & Company, Jefferson, North Carolina, U.S.A.

Center for International Climate and Environmental Research & Climate Policy Initiative 2015, *Background Report on Long-term Climate Finance*, Federal Ministry for the Environment, Nat Conserv, Building and Nuclear Safety, Republic of Germany; Deutsche Gesellschaft für Internationale Zusammenarbeit (GIZ) GmbH, Eschborn, Germany.

Couture, T. & Cory, K. 2009, *State Clean Energy Policies Analysis (SCEPA) Project: An Analysis of Renewable Energy Feed-in Tariffs in the United States*, Technical Report NREL/TP-6A2–45551, National Renewable Energy Laboratory, Golden, Colorado, U.S.A., http://1.usa.gov/1jWNrUM.

Couture, T. & Gagnon, Y. 2010, 'An analysis of feed-in tariff remuneration models: Implications for renewable energy investment', *Energy Policy*, vol. 38, pp. 955–965.

Daly, H.E. 2008, *A Steady-State Economy*, Sustainable Development Commission, U.K., 24 April, http://bit.ly/1j1B32h.

Davis, M. & Coorey, P. 2007, '$3b and rising rapidly: cost of the war to Australian taxpayers', *The Sydney Morning Herald*, 21 March, http://bit.ly/1p59QMr.

Delina, L.L. 2011, 'Asian Development Bank's support for clean energy', *Climate Policy*, vol. 11, pp. 1350–1366.

Delina, L.L., Diesendorf, M. & Merson, J. 2014, 'Strengthening the climate action movement: strategies from histories', *Carbon Management*, vol. 5, pp. 397–409.

Eilert, P., Stevens, A., Hauenstein, H. & McHugh, J. 2010, 'Innovative approaches for reducing GHG emissions: feebates for appliances and buildings', *Proceedings of the 2010 American Council for an Energy-Efficient Economy Summer Study on Energy Efficiency in Buildings*, 15–20 August, Pacific Grove, California, U.S.A.

Engler, M.L. & Knoll, M.S. 2003, 'Simplifying the transition to a (progressive) consumption tax', *SMU Law Review*, vol. 56, pp. 123–138.

Fenton, A., Wright, H., Afionis, S., Paavola, J. & Huq, S. 2014, 'Debt relief and financing climate change action', *Nature Climate Change*, vol. 4, pp. 650–653.

Francis 2015, *Encyclical Letter, Laudato Si' of the Holy Father Francis, On Care for our Common Home*, http://bit.ly/1Gi1Btu.

Frank, R. 2008, 'Progressive consumption tax', *Democracy*, Spring2008, Issue 8, http://bit.ly/1c3nbvY.

Gatrell, P. & Harrison, M. 1993, 'The Russian and Soviet economies in two world wars: a comparative view', *Economic History Review*, vol. 46, pp. 425–452.

German Advisory Council on Global Change 2011, *World in Transition: A Social Contract for Sustainability*, WBGU, Berlin, Germany.

Gibson, J.D. 1941, 'Financing the war', in J.F. Parkinson (ed.), *Canadian War Economics*, The University of Toronto Press, Toronto, Canada, pp. 33–46.

Gilding, P. 2011, *The Great Disruption: How the Climate Crisis Will Transform the Global Economy*, Bloomsbury, London, U.K.

Global Impact Investing Network n.d., '*About GIIN*', http://bit.ly/1BKhpzL.

Gonzales, M., Taddonio, K.N. & Sherman, N.J. 2015, 'The Montreal Protocol: how today's successes offer a pathway to the future', *Journal of Environmental Studies and Sciences*, vol. 5, pp. 122–129.

Government of Denmark 2011, *Our Future Energy*, Copenhagen, Denmark, http://bit.ly/1dcC1XD.

Greenpeace International & European Renewable Energy Council (EREC) 2010, *Energy [R]evolution: A Sustainable World Energy Outlook*, Greenpeace International and EREC, Amsterdam, The Netherlands.

Gruic, B. & Schrimpf, A. 2014, 'Cross-border investments in global debt market since the crisis', *Bank for International Settlements (BIS) Quarterly Review: International Banking and Financial Market Developments*, March, BIS, p. 18.

Haig-Muir, M. & Hay, R. 1996, 'The economy at war', in J. Beaumont (ed.) *Australia's War, 1939–1945*, Allen & Unwin Ltd., St. Leonards, New South Wales, Australia, pp. 107–135.

Hara, A. 1998, 'Japan: guns before rice', in M. Harrison (ed.), *The Economics of World War II: Six Great Powers in International Comparison*, Cambridge University Press, Cambridge, U.K.

Hardin, G. 1968, 'The tragedy of the commons', *Science*, vol. 13, pp. 1443–1448.

Harrison, M. 1988, 'Resource mobilization for World War II: the USA, UK, USSR, and Germany, 1938–1945', *The Economic History Review*, vol. 41, pp. 171–192.

Harrison, M. 1996, *Accounting for War: Soviet Production, Employment and the Defence Burden, 1940–1945*, Cambridge University Press, Cambridge, U.K.

Harrison, M. 1998, 'The economics of World War II: an overview', in M. Harrison (ed.), *The Economics of World War II: Six Great Powers in International Comparison*, Cambridge University Press, Cambridge, U.K., pp. 1–42.

Hassoun, N. & Frank, M. 2010, 'Are debt for climate swaps morally permissible?' Paper 363, Department of Philosophy, Carnegie Mellon University, Pittsburgh, Pennsylvania, U.S.A.

Heath, J. 2014, '$7.6bn-a-year budget cost to chop carbon tax', *The Australian Financial Review*, 15 February, http://bit.ly/1vrdTH8.

Heinrich Böll Stiftung & Overseas Development Institute 2015, *Climate Funds Update*, http://bit.ly/1d74XdS.

Hepburn, C. 2006, 'Regulating by prices, quantities or both: an update and an overview', *Oxford Review of Economic Policy*, vol. 22, pp. 226–247.

Higgs, R. 2004, 'Wartime socialization of investment: a reassessment of U.S. capital formation in the 1940s', *The Journal of Economic History*, vol. 64, pp. 500–520.

IMF (International Monetary Fund) 2013, *Energy Subsidy Reform: Lessons and Implications*, IMF, Washington D.C., U.S.A.

IMF 2014, 'Climate, environment, and the IMF', *IMF Factsheet*, 18 March, http://bit.ly/1o5JtWz.

IGCC (Investor Group on Climate Change) 2014, 'Company emissions fell 7% in the first year of the carbon price', *IGCC Media Release*, 7 March, http://bit.ly/1mLzWo5.

IPCC (Intergovernmental Panel on Climate Change) 2014, *Climate Change 2014: Synthesis Report of the Fifth Assessment Report of the IPCC*, The Core Writing Team, R.K. Pachauri & L. Meyer (eds), IPCC, http://bit.ly/1umDnCQ.

Jacobson, M. & Delucchi, M. 2011, 'Providing all global energy with wind, water, and solar power, Part I: Technologies, energy resources, quantities and areas of infrastructure, and materials', *Energy Policy*, vol. 39, pp. 1170–1190.

Jacobson, M. 2015, personal communication to the author, email, 29 November. Cited with permission.

Jotzo, F. & Burke, P. 2014, 'Direct Action subsidies: wrong way, go back', *Inside Story*, 17 March, http://bit.ly/1tAWJ6h.

Kemp, M. & Wexler, J. (eds) 2010, *Zero Carbon Britain 2030: A New Strategy*, Centre for Alternative Technology (CAT), CAT Publications, Wales, U.K.

Kennedy, D. 1999, *Freedom from Fear: The American People in Depression and War, 1929–1945*, Oxford University Press, New York.

Kidney, S. 2012, 'Bonds best weapon to counter fossil lobby', *RenewEconomy*, 30 January, http://bit.ly/1gYax59.

Kidney, S. 2014, 'USD 2tn of investors back Green & Climate Bonds to tap USD 100tn bond market for climate solutions, call on corps & govts to deliver projects for finance', *Climate Bonds Initiative*, http://bit.ly/1pceBlZ.

Kidney, S. 2015, 'Bonds and climate change', *CFA Institute Conference Proceedings Quarterly*, vol. 32, pp. 44–53.

Kyte, R. 2013, 'Tackling climate change with a robust carbon price', *The World Bank*, 16 May, http://bit.ly/1gfC6fc.

Lin, B. & Li, X. 2011, 'The effect of carbon tax on per capita CO2 emissions', *Energy Policy*, vol. 39, pp. 5137–5146.

Lumer, H. 1954, *War Economy and Crisis*, New York International Publishers, New York, U.S.A.

Lund, H., Hvelplund, F., Ostergaard, P.A., Moller, B., Mathiesen, B.V., Andersen, A. et al. 2010, *Danish Wind Power: Export and Cost*, CEESA Research Project, Department of Development and Planning, Aalborg University, Denmark.

Mayhew, D. 2005, 'Wars and American politics', *Perspectives on Politics*, vol. 3, pp. 473–493.

Milward, A.S. 1977, *War, Economy and Society, 1939–1945*, Allen Lane, London, U.K.

Muller, B., Ngwadla, X.J., Fuller, C., Guoshun, S., Jember, G. et al. 2015, *A Paris Replenishment Cycle for the Contributions to the UNFCCC Financial Mechanism*, Concept Note, Oxford Climate Policy, Wolfson College, Oxford, U.K., http://bit.ly/1Hh7phO.

Nielsen, S. 2012, 'Brazil to issue regulations supporting solar energy, Aneel says', *Bloomberg*, 15 March, http://bloom.bg/1a3hUtY.

Nordhaus, W.D. 1977, '*Strategies for the control of carbon dioxide*', Cowles Foundation Discussion Paper No. 443, Cowles Foundation for Research in Economics at Yale University, New Haven, Connecticut, U.S.A.

Nordhaus, W.D. 1990, 'Slowing the greenhouse express: The economics of greenhouse warming', in H. Aaron (ed.), *Setting National Priorities: Policy for the Nineties*, Brookings, Washington, D.C., U.S.A., pp. 185–211.

Nordhaus, W.D. 1993a, 'Optimal greenhouse-gas reductions and tax policy in the "DICE" Model', *American Economic Review*, vol. 83, pp. 313–317.

Nordhaus, W.D. 1993b, 'Rolling the "DICE": an optimal transition path for controlling greenhouse gases', *Resource and Energy Economics*, vol. 15, pp. 27–50.

Nordhaus, W.D. 2008, *A Question of Balance: Weighing the Options on Global Warming Policies*, Yale University Press, New Haven, Connecticut, U.S.A.; London, U.K.

Nordhaus, W.D. 2015, 'Climate clubs: Overcoming free-riding in international climate policy', *American Economic Review*, vol. 105, pp. 1339–1970.

OECD (Organisation for Economic Co-operation and Development) 2013, 'Carbon taxes and emissions trading are cheapest ways of reducing CO_2, OECD says', *OECD Newsroom*, 11 April, http://bit.ly/1lDj0NM.

OECD 2014, 'Taxes on personal income', *Taxation: Key Tables from OECD*, No.4. doi: 10.1787/tax-pers-inc-table-2013-1-en.

Officer, L.H. 2015, 'Exchange rates between the United States Dollar and forty one currencies', *Measuring Worth*, http://bit.ly/1xVuLth.

Oil Change International 2012, *Fossil Fuel Subsidies vs. Fast Start Climate Finance in Annex 2 Countries*, http://bit.ly/1bPNDtD.

Olmos, L., Ruester, S. & Liong, S. 2012, 'On the selection of financing instruments to push the development of new technologies: application to clean energy technologies', *Energy Policy*, vol. 43, pp. 252–266.

Overy, R.J. 1995, *War and Economy in the Third Reich*, Clarendon Press, Oxford, U.K.; Oxford University Press, New York, U.S.A.

Overy, R.J. 2006, *Why The Allies Won*, Pimlico, London, U.K.

Pearson, N.O. 2013, 'India plans to revive wind-farm tax break, raise subsidy', *Bloomberg News*, 24 June, http://bloom.bg/1fz2Wdd.

Pigou, A.C. 1920, *The Economics of Welfare*, Macmillan and Co., London, U.K.

Pindyck, R.S. 2013, 'Climate change policy: what do the models tell us?' *Journal of Economic Literature*, vol. 51, pp. 860–872.

Pitt & Sherry 2015, 'Electricity emissions update – data to 31 December 2014: Demand down, emissions up – again', *cedex: carbon emissions index*, http://bit.ly/14bZCo1.

Plumptre, A.F.W. 1941, *Mobilizing Canada's Economy for War*, The MacMillan Company of Canada, Ltd., Toronto, Canada.

Prasad, R. 2012, 'Government rolls back tax incentive for wind farms', *The Economic Times*, 3 April, http://bit.ly/1d9CnIm.

Rockoff, H. 1998, 'The United States: from ploughshares to swords', in M. Harrison (ed.), *The Economics of World War 2: Six Great Powers in International Comparison*, Cambridge University Press, Cambridge, U.K., pp. 81–121.

Rosen, R.A. & Guenther, E. 2015, 'The economics of mitigating climate change: What can we know?' *Technological Forecasting & Social Change*, vol. 91, pp. 93–106.

Scrieciu, S.S., Barker, T. & Ackerman, F. 2013, 'Pushing the boundaries of climate economics: critical issues to consider in climate policy analysis', *Ecological Economics*, vol. 85, pp. 155–165.

Sensuss, F., Ragwitz, M. & Genoese, M. 2008, 'The merit-order effect: a detailed analysis of the price effect of renewable electricity generation on spot market prices in Germany', *Energy Policy*, vol. 36, pp. 3086–3094.

Shellenberger, M., Nordhaus, T., Navin, J., Norris, T. & van Noppen, A. 2008, 'Fast, clean, and cheap: cutting global warming's Gordian Knot', *Harvard Law and Policy Review*, vol. 2, pp. 93–118.

Simpson, A. 2011, 'Carbon tax explained', *The Sydney Morning Herald*, 20 July, http://bit.ly/1y5Bhhr.

Skocpol, T. 2013, 'Naming the Problem: What it will take to counter extremism and engage Americans in the fight against global warming', Symposium on the Politics of America's Fight Against Global Warming, 14 February, Harvard University, Cambridge, Massachusetts, U.S.A.

Smith, R.E. 1959, *The Army and Economic Mobilization*, U.S. Government Printing Office, Washington, D.C., U.S.A.

Sokolov, B. 1994, 'The role of lend-lease in Soviet military efforts, 1941–1945', *The Journal of Slavic Military Studies*, vol. 7, pp. 567–586.

Stern, N. 2007, *The Economics of Climate Change: The Stern Review*, Cambridge University Press, Cambridge, U.K.

Stiglitz, J.E. & Bilmes, L.J. 2008, *The Three Trillion Dollar War: The True Cost of the Iraq Conflict*, W.W. Norton & Company, Inc., New York, U.S.A.

Stiglitz, J.E. & Bilmes, L.J. 2010, 'The true cost of the Iraq war: $3 trillion and beyond', *The Washington Post*, 5 September, http://wapo.st/1gYQIdO.

Stine, D. 2009, *The Manhattan Project, the Apollo Program and Federal Energy Technology R&D Programs: A Comparative Analysis*, Congressional Research Service Report for Congress, Washington, D.C., U.S.A.

Tassava, C. 2010, 'WW II', in R. Whaples (ed.), *The American Economy During World War II*, EH. Net Encyclopedia, http://bit.ly/1eoIs6a.

Tietenberg, T.H. 2013, 'Reflections-carbon pricing in practice', *Review of Environmental Economics and Policy*, vol. 7, pp. 313–329.

UNFCCC 2014, *2014 Biennial Assessment and Overview of Climate Finance Flows Report*, UNFCCC Standing Committee on Finance, Bonn, Germany, http://bit.ly/1BeGeoL.

United States Environmental Protection Agency 2015, 'Clean Power Plan for existing power plants', http://1.usa.gov/1VQpq03.

Van Vuuren, D., Edmonds, J., Kainuma, M., Riahi, K., Thomson, A., et al. 2011, 'The representative concentration pathways: an overview', *Climatic Change*, vol. 109, pp. 5–31.

Vernon, J.R. 1994, 'World War II fiscal policies and the end of the Great Depression', *The Journal of Economic History*, vol. 54, pp. 850–868.

Vorrath, S. 2014, 'UniSuper taps World Bank's first Australian Green Bond issue', *RenewEconomy*, 17 April, http://bit.ly/1gFFkJj.

Walker, E.R. 1939, *War-Time Economics, With Special Reference to Australia*, Melbourne University Press in association with Oxford University Press, Melbourne, Australia.

Walker, E.R. 1947, *The Australian Economy in War and Reconstruction*, Oxford University Press, New York, U.S.A.

Watson Institute for International Studies 2015, *The Costs of War Since 2001: Iraq, Afghanistan, and Pakistan*, Brown University, Providence, Rhode Island, U.S.A., http://bit.ly/1GP3Swc.

Whitley, S. 2013, *At Cross-Purposes: Subsidies and Climate Compatible Investment*, Overseas Development Institute, U.K.

Wiser, R., Barbose, G. & Holt, E. 2011, 'Supporting solar power in renewables portfolio standards: experience from the United States', *Energy Policy*, vol. 39, pp. 3894–3905.

Witte, J. 1985, *The Politics and Development of the Federal Income Tax*, The University of Wisconsin Press, Madison, Wisconsin, U.S.A.

World Bank 2009, *World Bank Green Bonds*, http://bit.ly/1d3urJS.

WWF (World Wide Fund for Nature) 2014, 'Move by Norway Sovereign Wealth Fund to invest in renewables could have "global impact"', WWF Press and Media Centre, 13 March, http://bit.ly/1kgMLpl.

World Wide Fund for Nature, Ecofys, & Office for Metropolitan Architecture 2011, *The Energy Report: 100% Renewable Energy by 2050*, WWF International, Gland, Switzerland.

5 Mobilising labour

Winners and losers

The possible impact of the Rapid Mitigation Project on jobs, especially the fear of potential job losses from phasing out high emission, carbon-based industries and sectors, is a concern for many. This is not surprising since retiring fossil fuels means retiring jobs in the sector in favour of a new sustainable energy regime. As always, conflicts related to employment have been fiercely debated.

In countries where fossil-based industry is considered the lifeblood of the national economy, politicians argue in favour of protecting coal and mining industry jobs, and, thus avoid necessary debates about the real impact that both the transition and unmitigated climate change have on jobs and to the economy more broadly. Claims have repeatedly been maintained that shutting coal-fired power plants down can cost miners, truck drivers, and utility workers their jobs. Expectedly, the fossil fuel regime highlights this assumption each time they argue against climate action. For example, the Minerals Council of Australia (MCA), in their 2011 submission to the Federal Government, repeated their 2009 claim that 23,510 jobs will be lost by 2020 and 66,400 by 2030 should a carbon price be introduced in Australia (Concept Economics 2009).

The critique has some validity especially given the scale, intensity, volume, and scope of the required changes in energy systems, which definitely create risks towards some existing jobs. Jacobson et al. (2015) estimate that some 28.4 million jobs in the current fossil fuel, biofuel, and nuclear industries will be lost due to the transition to global 100% wind, water, and sunshine energy. This number represents 0.99% of the total global labour force.

A focus on criticising the perceived weaknesses of the transition to employment, however, is unfair, biased, and unfounded without duly and closely examining the ample opportunities the transition brings. The critiques often fail to mention the benefits of new and additional job creation in new sectors – particularly in the sustainable energy industry, an opportunity to re-consider the meaning of gainful employment, and other potential co-benefits that favour jobs in the sustainable regime. These co-benefits include less reliance on imported fossil fuel, which has economic and security implications for importing countries, reduced health care costs because of avoided pollution, and reduced social, political, economic, and physical climate change impacts. Better lives for the public, following the transition, are unquantifiable benefits that have key implications for strengthening national interest.

Claims about the effects of the transition on the economy over employment have been refuted by many studies, which, by contrast, paint a favourable picture. Bruce Chapman and Kiatanantha Lounkaew (2013: 273), for instance, in assessing the MCA claims above, concluded that the projected job losses over a ten-year time horizon are 'in a statistical sense close to invisible with respect to employment and unemployment stocks, and trivial with respect to aggregate flows in the labour market.' Labour studies in a high renewable energy penetration scenario have also led to conclusions that more jobs can be produced, more than enough to cover job losses in high carbon industries.

Some research has even found that renewable electricity is more job-intensive than fossil generation. For example, Max Wei, Shana Patadia, and Daniel Kammen (2010: 928), who synthesised 15 studies discussing the employment effects of sustainable energy transition, report that 'renewable energy and low-carbon sector generate more jobs than the fossil energy sector per unit of energy delivered.' The study concludes that more than four million job-years can be generated, even by approximately 30% renewable energy technology penetration in 2030 and a 0.37% reduction in annual energy growth rate in the U.S. energy market (Wei, Patadia, and Kammen 2010: 928). A job-year is full-time employment for one person for one-year duration. In a higher renewable energy penetration scenario, such as in the Rapid Mitigation Project, more job-years will most likely be created. Jacobson et al. (2015) project that, globally, close to 24 million 35-year construction jobs and 27 million 35-year operation jobs will be generated during a 35-year transition to renewable energy. Considering the 28 million job losses in fossil fuel, biofuel, and nuclear energy industries, this new job generation results in a net job creation of 22 million 35-year jobs.

The Project offers new job generation in large numbers in replacement industries although, of course, it accepts that jobs will be phased out in high-emission sectors and in wasteful and unnecessary production. With the Project, labour changes are expected to bring large improvement in sectors including manufacturing, research and development, construction and installation, and freight. Operators are required in installed renewable generation power plants, but they are expected to be fewer than those in fossil fuel stations, especially when viewed per unit of delivered electricity. More jobs, nonetheless, open in the freight sector as the demand for transporting biomass and return of ash to croplands intensifies in areas where biofuel is an essential part of the mix. Although many more employment opportunities are created, significant variability will be common because of the rapid introduction and subsequent turnover of generator plants.

Thus far and in real time, renewable energy sector employment is growing. In the state of California, home of the Hollywood film industry, solar industry workers even outnumbered those in the film industry by 11,400 in 2012 (Spross 2013). Also in 2012, there were 31,500 more solar industry workers employed in the U.S.A. than employed by the coal mining industry in the entire nation (Spross 2013). Globally, the International Renewable Energy Agency (IRENA 2014) reported nearly one million new jobs created in 2013, reaching 6.5 million total jobs in renewable energy. IRENA (2015) reports an 18% increase in this figure as the global renewable energy industry employed 7.7 million persons, directly or indirectly in 2014, excluding large hydro, which directly employed another 1.5 million.

In a high penetration renewable energy scenario, Greenpeace International and the European Renewable Energy Council (2010) project approximately 11 million jobs will be created globally because of the transition. In Europe, Greenpeace forecasts 1.2 million new jobs will be generated (Van de Putte et al. 2011).

At the national level, projections for the U.K. stood at 3.4 million jobs (Kemp and Wexler 2010), with new and additional 1.5 million jobs (Allen et al. 2013). In Ireland, the transition will produce some 100,000 new and additional jobs (Connolly and Mathiesen 2014). In Denmark, 30,000 to 40,000 new jobs will be first created as renewables gain entry into the energy system, settling at 15,000 as the transition concludes (Mathiesen, Lund and Karlsson 2011). In Australia, the Commonwealth Treasury (2009) found that an additional 1.8 million renewable industry jobs could be created within 12 years with an additional 4.7 million out to 2050. The Commonwealth Scientific and Industrial Research Organisation (CSIRO) even shows that, under a 100% carbon pollution reduction by 2050, the transition could generate 2.5 to 3.3 million new jobs over the next 20 years, while growing the Australian economy by 29% relative to 2025 (Hatfield-Dodds et al. 2008). A 2015 study by Beyond Zero Emissions shows that the Australian renewable energy industry could generate AU$370 billion worth of jobs in ten years, and could even climb towards AU$1 trillion with the addition of smart homes and buildings, low-carbon land-use, high speed rail and electric vehicle options (Vorrath 2015).

Similar new and additional job generation can be expected at the state level. In the state of Washington, U.S.A., for instance, the transition to 100% renewable energy is projected to create approximately 38,200 40-year construction jobs and 24,900 40-year operation and maintenance jobs (Jacobson et al. 2016). This figure excludes additional jobs in the manufacture and service of storage technologies, hydrogen technologies, electric vehicles, electric heating and cooling appliances, and industrial heating equipment, which according to the authors, are more than enough to cover net losses in heavy emission sectors. In the state of California, the transition to high penetration renewable energy is projected to create 442,000 40-year construction sector jobs, and 190,000 40-year operation jobs (Jacobson et al.

2014a). Not only will employment opportunities arise in the supply sector, but also in demand management, where intensive energy efficiency and conservation programmes are expected to generate new jobs (Wei, Patadia, and Kammen 2010: 923). These are jobs created following the institution of new building codes, appliance and equipment standards, industry improvement, and other demand-side management programmes. They include energy auditors and programme administrators, and implementation, management and support workforce to carry out weatherisation projects, lighting installations, and insulation.

Although the figures showing projected new jobs generated by the transition offer optimistic visions, it still is impossible to predict with certitude the real impact of the transition to net employment. This is especially true since employment is sensitive to many assumptions including future energy price changes and other outcomes of the rapid transition that have repercussions for the broad economy (cf. Dalton and Lewis 2011). Nonetheless, expectations are high that with friendlier public policy on both labour and industry protection, net gains in employment can be generated, as happened in wartime.

New opportunities

Without substantial labour mobilisation, productivity gains in wartime armament production would not have been ensured despite substantial access to capital. Alan Milward (1977: 67) contends the American 'production miracle' would have been impossible without the increased supply of labour and labour productivity.

Following the Great Depression, new streams of work opportunities were created as jobs opened in munitions factories. From 1939 to 1944, the number of workers in munitions factories had increased by 7.7 million (Cardozier 1995: 149). By 1945, there were 11.43 million civilians working in these factories (Rockoff 1998: 101, Table 3.11). The Manhattan Project to build nuclear bombs, alone had employed more than 100,000 Americans (Tassava 2010).

In Canada, the number of employed persons also increased. Close to 880,000 Canadians found new work between 1939 and 1945 with 14% accrued to wartime mobilisation (Milward 1977: 218). In the U.K., 22.2 million persons were employed in 1943, compared to 18.5 million in 1939 (Broadberry and Howlett 1998: 57, Table 2.13). British workers were engaged in armament production and worked in engineering, shipbuilding, metals, and chemical industries. Their number grew from 3.6 million in 1942 to 4.2 million in 1944 (Kaldor 1945–1946: 51). In Australia, the number of munitions factory workers climbed from 534,000 before the outbreak of the war to 753,000 at its height in 1944 (Walker 1947: 148, 402). Other than the expansion in the number of wartime workers described earlier, the ratio of workforce working at war industries and in the armed forces to the total number of the working population, provides a clear perspective to understand the intensity of wartime labour mobilisation (see Table 5.1).

Table 5.1 Labour mobilisation for war, percentage (%) of the working population

		Industrial war workers	Armed forces	Total, wartime workforce
U.K.	1939	15.8	2.8	18.6
	1943	23.0	22.3	45.3
U.S.A.	1940	8.4	1.0	9.4
	1943	19.0	16.4	45.3
U.S.S.R.	1940	8.0	5.9	13.9
	1943	31.0	23.0	54.0

Author's calculation from Harrison (1988: 186, Table 5)

U.K. and U.S. industrial workforce comprised workers in the armament, shipbuilding, engineering, metalworking, and chemical industries. For Russia, these included prisoners of war (POW).

Between 1940 and 1943, the proportion of workforce mobilised for the war in the U.S.A. was the highest among combatant countries. This proportion rose from 8.4% to 19% in four years. The largest mobilisation of industrial war workers during this period, however, occurred in the Soviet Union as the proportion of workforce engaged in war industries soared from 8% to 31% in just three years.

The rapid labour resource mobilisation, from civilian to military pursuits, was possible because almost everybody wanted to work or was looking for new work, and because the state instituted policies and programmes that, in effect, forced able-bodied citizens to work in munitions factories. As a result of deficits in the civilian labour force due to the huge number of working males who volunteered or had been drafted for war, a large number of the working population were conscripted and moved to new working outposts to fill in the dire need for labour especially in new industrial locations.

To fill the necessary workforce for munitions factories, labour supply from industries producing inessential civilian items were redirected into munitions industries (Broadberry and Howlett 1998: 54); thus, affecting other vital economic sectors. In the U.K, for instance, approximately 250,000 workers in consumer industries were conscripted to work for munitions factories (Broadberry and Howlett 1998: 58). The migration of Australian workers to munitions factories shrunk employment in other sectors. Between 1935 and 1945, workers in Australian mines were reduced by 31%; building and construction sector workers were reduced by 48%, and commercial and financial sector workers decreased by 30% (Haig-Muir and Hay 1996: 119).

Despite the migration of workers towards the munitions sector, the volume of manpower remained scarce. Labour scarcity forced governments and industries to tap 'nonconventional' labour source including: retired mechanics, the physically unfit for battle, unemployed youth, and women. The 'new workforce' to be trained with new skills learned tank building, shipbuilding, and machine gun production in factories, colleges, and training centres. In 1942, approximately 90% of the 'new workforce' was trained in American shipyards for their new jobs (Cardozier 1995: 150).

The Rapid Mitigation Project similarly requires additional labour force in manufacturing, installation, construction, operation, maintenance, and management of sustainable energy technologies being rapidly deployed. New labour is also required in providing or strengthening capacities and skills. More jobs will also be required in storage technology R&D, in smart grid development, and in improving the efficiency of existing sustainable energy technologies. In contrast to neoliberal austerity measures aimed at cutting employment, increasing insecurities, and exacerbating inequalities, that persist in today's world, the labour-related measures the Project brings reverse austerity policies by establishing full employment, increasing job security, and raising workers' pay. A new labour reserve, from millions of unemployed persons throughout the world, will be actively recruited to work for the many activities of the Project. As in wartime, they will also be provided with new sets of skills.

Skilling and re-skilling

Although skills provision could be a tough challenge for governments, many skills required in the Project are already available. Most likely, the Project would need new and additional electricians, plumbers, metalworkers, electric power engineers, information technology experts, energy auditors, civil engineers, structural engineers, architects, construction managers, insulation workers, iron and steel workers, and machinists (Cleary and Kopicki 2009). The Project requires a great increase in the number of workers in these trades and professions.

Where skill shortages may loom, the role of the state becomes forefront. The lessons of wartime mobilisation show that labour can be rapidly mobilised and quickly trained in new skills through policy. At the same time, wartime experience also shows several challenges in the absence of appropriate policy to support skilling and re-skilling. Governments must provide policy and programmes to ease the transition especially for those moving out of the fossil sector and other sectors experiencing economic losses through retraining (cf. Saha 2010). The transition requires new vocational, trade, academic, and other training programmes to meet the expanding sustainable energy industry needs, spanning the spectrum from short-term instruction courses to post-graduate academic degrees.

The preparation of a huge labour resource volume for entirely new industrial tasks at the intensity at which they are required can become an arduous task for the state and industries without strategic plans. The development and augmentation of new skill sets were necessary in this new endeavour, since many of the requirements of wartime industry were different from those required in peacetime. To meet this requirement, large-scale training programmes were quickly mounted (*The New York Times* 1942). At wartime, the onus of skilling the 'new workforce' for munitions factories fell upon the shoulders of the state. Nonetheless, the private sector also participated in training and re-training activities by providing instructional programmes for workers.

Early preparations of the labour force for new skills proved to have great advantage. Germany, which made early preparations for the war, provides an illustration. During its rearmament period in the mid-1930s, Germany allo-cated resources to extensive training programmes through industrial voca-tional education across all states. By November 1936, all metalworking and construction businesses with more than ten employees were obliged to create apprenticeships and to organise training programmes (Abelshauser 1998). Although the volume of wartime production was overshadowed by the American production, early preparations in Germany inarguably contributed hugely to the country's wartime efforts.

The situation, however, was different in countries that needed to train their 'new workforce' within the constraints of rapid mobilisation. To compensate for the low-skilled workforce, the state and industries resorted to innovative skilling and re-skilling approaches. In the U.S.A., corporations started rationalising their production techniques by following the Fordist approach. This meant a worker was expected to gain specialisation in a particular skill required in a particular point of production instead of the entire assembly line (Sloan 1990 [1963]: 382).

In Canada, the government itself led its 'new workforce' trainings. Working hand-in-hand with provincial governments, the Federal Government trained more than 10,000 workers per year in new skills. The trainings were done either at vocational schools or industrial plants, where 18-week courses on welding, woodworking, ground mechanic work, engine fitting, and wireless operation, for example, were conducted (Plumptre 1941: 50; Stewart 1941: 78).

In Australia, engineering trade skills were intensified through upgrades in existing skills and new on-the-job technical trainings in technical schools and in factories (Walker 1947: 307). Since education was under the control of state governments in Australia, the Australian Commonwealth Government made an agreement with the States for the use of their factories for skilling and reskilling activities at federal expense. Other policies were also instituted to streamline higher education in the country, including restrictions in admissions to some university courses to a limited number of students (Walker 1947: 307–308).

In light of these experiences, the following strategies could assist governments in addressing the Project's labour dilemmas:

- *Producing labour plans.* Conducting national labour requirement and availability analyses of the number of workforce, the skills they have, and their locations to ascertain surpluses or deficits.
- *Providing guaranteed income.* Providing full wages and benefits for at least three years to allow workers harmed by Project activities to transition

into jobs in the new sustainable energy regime; providing decent pensions with health care for those ready for retirement; providing support for retraining and assistance in finding new jobs to address fears that the Project will result in worker misfortunes.

- *Incentivising future workers.* Incentivising students to opt for courses relevant to rapid mitigation; providing students enrolling and enrolled in rapid mitigation courses with more scholarships, allowances, living expenses, and future tax benefits; providing these students with guaranteed jobs upon course completion by linking them with industries, through on-the-job trainings, as they study.
- *Creating new rapid mitigation learning centres.* Designing new trade, college, and university courses relevant to rapid mitigation, such as energy auditing, machine fitting, electric power engineering, surveying, materials science, civil engineering, structural engineering, architecture, and urban mining/ resource recovery.
- *Expediting training and courses.* Lowering the duration required to finish rapid mitigation degrees, which means revising curricula and dropping non-transition-related courses; providing incentives to those completing their degrees on time.
- *Incentivising R&D.* Providing support and incentives for the R&D of relevant transition technologies at colleges and universities, including the discovery and pilot demonstration of efficient storage for renewable electricity, smart grid, and increasing the efficiency of sustainable energy technologies.
- *Reducing non-relevant and competing courses and degrees.* Reducing enrolments in university courses and degrees meant to support high-emission industries, such as petroleum engineering, nuclear engineering, and some mining courses.

These strategies are mostly social nudges (cf. Thaler and Sunstein 2008). For example, students will most likely opt for a rapid mitigation-related degree given the present and future benefits that accrue from making this choice. Preparations, however, should start as early as primary school, meaning that at their young age, children are taught climate mitigation values. For instance, energy conservation and efficiency programmes are made mandatory at primary schools. Teaching the youth about climate science, its anthropogenic causes, and the required responses would prepare them to make appropriate career choices later in life.

New forms of instruction, such as those provided by internet-based platforms including Massive Open Online Courses (MOOCs), offer additional opportunities for skilling and re-skilling the labour force for the Project. Some MOOC courses can be developed around rapid mitigation courses and taught online including the basics of climate science and energy auditing. Some trade, college, and university courses about the transition can also be done online, making way for the efficient use of physical classroom spaces.

Examples of this approach include programmes directing students to online learning modules covering entry-level concepts before starting formal courses (e.g. Christensen and Horn 2013). By covering basic concepts and competencies online, face-to-face classes can be efficiently spent and made available for higher-order discussion and deep exploration of real-world applications. Of course, not all courses can be taught online. Physical experiments and materials testing, for instance, can only be done at physical laboratories and studios.

The massive changes wartime mobilisation brought on the labour landscape impacted not only the labour sector but also the economy at large. Similar dynamics can be expected with the execution of the Project. At wartime, at least in some democratic, industrial countries, anyone with a desire to work was working, or could find opportunities to work. Full employment relieved a lot of anxieties, especially after the decade of persistently high unemployment characterising the Great Depression. For the next 25 years, reductions in unemployed rates proved to be a long-term phenomenon, having long-lasting economic change that had repercussions in post-war years (Milward 1977: 219).

The resulting women employment in 'men's work' during the wartime period is another long-term impact of the many changes to the labour landscape. At 80% of the entire 'new workforce', the U.K. held the record for highest increase in women's employment during the war with almost all of them either previously unemployed or housewives. In the U.S.A., women comprised half of the 'new workforce' (Milward 1977: 219). By 1945, more than 19 million American women worked outside their homes, up from 14 million in 1940 (Rockoff 1998: 101; Tassava 2010). In Australia, approximately 80,000 women were employed in heavy industries in 1944, whereas practically no women worked in the sector before the war (Walker 1947: 300). As a consequence of increased female employment, their economic conditions vastly improved. With improved family incomes, young single American women and married women, whose husbands were on the battlefields, even returned to school (Goldin 1991).

Protecting the labour force

Despite the impressions of prosperity that wartime mobilisation apparently projects, one must recognise the extraordinary welfare-diminishing changes it brought to many. These changes were excluded in measures of national accounts, yet made a lasting impression on wellbeing. To access the available jobs, millions of Americans, for example, had to relocate in long distant centres of war production such as in far-flung Willow Run and other wartime factories. After bearing the substantial cost of relocation, migrant workers often found themselves crowded into poorer housing units. Transportation, even commuting to work, became difficult for many workers (Cardozier 1995: 150–151; Clive 1979).

Another burden wartime mobilisation brought to the labour force concerns working hours. To ensure the timely delivery of munitions outputs, working hours in industrial factories were increased. For instance, American workers had to work for an average of 47 hours a week in 1944, up from 43.4 hours in 1940 (Rockoff 1998: 100). Wages were also stabilised, meaning no increases were made on income generated from work in munitions factories (Rockoff 1981; Henig and Unterberger 1945). In addition, access to vital resources was also affected. Food supplies, which are critical for survival, were insufficient. Clothing also suffered from deterioration in quality (Rockoff 1998: 94).

Discussions of wartime labour mobilisation are incomplete without mentioning the magnitude and intensity of forced labour, which was systematically instituted through policies of conscription. For example, the conscription of British and Japanese workers to munitions factories led to expansion in industrial production in these countries. The similarities between them, however, end there. While the British conscription programme involved only working adults, the Japanese conscriptions involved children. In 1943, Japanese schoolchildren in their third year of middle school, between 14 and 15 years old and above, were conscripted to work in munitions factories. Many were even sent to active military service. By 1944, conscription in Japan expanded to include the lower years of middle school and the senior class of elementary school, which meant inclusion of 11 and 12 year olds in munitions works. By the end of the war, apan had mobilised approximately 3.43 million schoolchildren (Hara 1998: 255).

Free and forced labour contributions to munitions production, especially by prisoners of war (POWs) in Japan, the U.S.S.R., and Germany, should also be discussed. In Japanese munitions factories approximately 280,000 Korean and 40,000 Chinese POWs were forced to work in military camps and industries (Hara 1998: 254). In Europe, POWs were forced to work in German and Soviet work camps. By 1944, some 7.5 million French and Eastern European POWs worked in German camps (Harrison 1988: 190). By 1945, free labour in Germany comprised 25% of industrial employment and 20% of the total civilian labour force (Abelshauser 1998: 158). In the U.S.S.R., approximately 4.3 million German and Japanese POWs worked in Soviet industries and farms by 1944 (Harrison 1988: 190). By the end of the war, POWs constituted approximately a tenth of the Soviet industrial workforce (Barber and Harrison 1991: 118), without counting the Romanians, Hungarians and Italians as well as non-Russian Soviet citizens such as Ukrainians, Tatars, Volga-Germans, Tadzhik, Ingush, and others forcibly evicted from their homes to work at Soviet munitions factories in remote places as far away as Siberia. (For details of forced labour in the U.S.S.R. during the war, see Dallin and Nicolaevsky (1947: 262–298)).

The worst labour conditions at war should never recur during the execution of the Rapid Mitigation Project. Protecting livelihoods, defending workers' wellbeing, and addressing inequalities should be done in unison with sustainable energy transition. Wartime-like pressures on the labour landscape should be avoided at all cost. The Project shall ensure that strategies are designed to provide full employment and rising living standards.

Learning from the lessons of wartime labour mobilisation, there are essential aspects that must be supported. These include actual worker deployment to industrial regions where proven and demonstrated renewable energy technologies are mass-produced or built. Although this could mean worker relocation as illustrated by wartime labour displacements (Associated Press 1943), policy needs to be provided protecting new, existing, relocated, and migrant workers' rights and benefits. Wartime mobilisation narratives provide lenses through which we can view the challenges labour relocation could bring, and the strategies for easing the transition.

- *Adequate compensation for workers.* Ensuring workers are appropriately and adequately compensated; providing workers in transition industries and those working in far-flung renewable energy rich regions with favourable tax treatments, flexible working hours, access to transport, housing, and amenities on top of financial incentives for relocation.
- *Protecting worker rights and labour unions.* Providing a 'living' minimum wage; strengthening labour rights to collectively organise and bargain to ensure popular participation in the Project and to protect workers from abuse; giving labour unions formal roles in decision-making.

The sordid state of labour rights at wartime provides a way to view the Project as an opportunity for governments and industries to revisit labour policies, not only in mitigation industries, but also across all sectors. The transition should be used primarily as an opportunity to ensure work-life balance. Munitions factory workers were physically and emotionally stressed (*The New York Times* 1943; *The Wall Street Journal* 1942), and aside from having their wages capped, were also forced to work long hours. Policy should be in place to protect workers' general wellbeing during the course of the Project.

Production timetables, for instance, must be designed so that essential goods and services for the transition are efficiently produced and delivered without workers putting in extra hours. Another option is to adopt a four-day workweek, where workers can add an extra two or three hours of work per day during the first four days at work and then take a break on the fifth day. Having an additional day for a weekend means more hours for outside-of-work endeavours. Workers can use this extra time for family, friends, continuing education, hobbies, skills development, caregiving, sports, outdoor recreation, participating in the arts, and volunteering. With their 'additional' time, workers can enjoy quality of life and focus more on activities that bring them enjoyment and satisfaction.

This proposal is theoretically, empirically, and practically sound, as gains from technological progress brought about by the transition should be taken in the form of more leisure, rather than more production (Daly 2008). Juliet Schor (2010) highlights the importance of increased time for leisure, vis-à-vis reduced work-time, for improving quality of life. Schor cited the work patterns of Western Europeans, who put in an average of 270 fewer hours per year than Americans, in establishing how reduced work-time results in improved quality of life. Working less could also mean reduced carbon emissions. Rosnick and Weisbrot (2006) estimated savings of close to 20% of U.S. energy consumption if Americans were to shift to Western European work time patterns.

Maximum income

To save on personnel expenditure and to bolster employee morale during the Project, labour policy regarding maximum income is necessary. This has a relevant precedent in the wartime mobilisation experience when Roosevelt argued that if middle class Americans could put their lives on the line for just US$60 per month, which is about US$875 in 2015, the rich must be required to put in some sacrifice too. In a message to Congress on 27 April 1942, the President stated:

> Discrepancies between low personal incomes and very high personal incomes should be lessened; and I therefore believe that in time of this grave national danger, when all excess income should go to win the war, no American citizen ought to have a net income, after he has paid his taxes, of more than $25,000 a year.
>
> (Roosevelt 1943; cf. Kluckhohn 1942)

This amounts to approximately US$365,000 in 2015. Roosevelt reiterated this in his letter to the House Ways and Means Committee on 15 February 1943:

> I urge the Congress to levy a special war supertax on net income from whatever source derived (including income from tax-exempt securities), which, after payment of regular income taxes, exceeds $25,000 in the case of a single person and $50,000 in the case of a married couple.
>
> (Roosevelt 1943)

In the end, Congress disallowed a full cap, but opted for a 94% top tax rate on income more than US$20,000, approximately US$275,000 in 2015 (Pizzigati 2012).

Considering the scale, scope, and intensity of the Project and its financial requirements, seeking funds from all possible avenues is prudent. A 'super-tax' similar to that proposed by Roosevelt can be levied on compensation in excess of US$275,000.

In 2012, the ratio of executive compensation relative to average worker pay and benefits in the U.S.A. had grown to as much as 1,795:1, meaning for a dollar paid to an ordinary worker an executive receives US$1,795

(Bloomberg News 2013). Taxing high-level salaries, thus, can also result in reducing income inequalities. The policy could also decelerate excessive consumption by high-income persons and the super-rich, which could directly result in some emissions reduction.

The US$275,000 cap, which wartime experience suggests, is one way to determine maximum salary levels. Sam Pizzigati (2004, 1992) advocates for a maximum salary that is ten times the minimum wage, which, in the U.S.A., translates into US$72.50 per hour, or approximately US$139,200 per annum. Using management guru Peter Drucker's argument that CEO-to-worker salary ratio should be below 20: 1, the 1965 ratio in the U.S.A., this means maximum salary can be pegged at US$278,400, which is a level closer to the approved wartime ceiling (Wartzman 2008).

Salary capping and reducing income inequality between executive and ordinary worker pay have already been part of many proposals following the growing divide between the haves and the have-nots and the 2008 Global Financial Crisis. Egypt and France, in 2011, for example, each pursued pay ratios for leaders of their countries' state-owned enterprises (Moustafa 2013; Boxell 2012). Switzerland also passed restrictions on pay for bank executives and banned 'golden parachute' severance packages (Willsher and Inman 2013), although it failed to legislate a proposal to limit executives' pay at a 12: 1 ratio (Copley 2013). In Spain, the manufacturing and retail enterprises belonging to the Mondragón cooperative network limit their managers' pay to five times their lowest income worker's compensation (Herrera 2004).

Capping personal income is also well grounded in the growing literature on wellbeing and happiness. Although money contributes to wellbeing, studies point out that having more of it does not strongly correlate with more happiness. In 2010, Nobel Prize winners Daniel Kahneman and Angus Deaton conducted research on whether money does indeed buy happiness. They found that emotional wellbeing or the emotional quality of personal experience does rise as income improves (Kahneman and Deaton 2010). However, they also found that personal happiness relative to income has a 'ceiling' showing that general happiness is met with an annual income of US $75,000, or about US$82,000 in 2015.

Labour outsourcing

The Project, international in scope but national in focus, has impacts through job leakages and job exports. This means that not all jobs will reside within one country but across multiple countries. Manufacturing sustainable energy technologies, for instance, will most likely be predominantly exported to developing countries where labour cost may be lower, but does not mean that the quality of employment there should be lower as well. The strategies on protecting labour, as discussed in the earlier section, should not be exclusive to high-emission, rich states alone. While manufacturing jobs are exported, the design and development, construction and installation, operation and management of sustainable energy technologies remain onshore; thus, ensuring steady streams of opportunities for domestic labour.

These conditions, however, are heavily dependent on the kind of technology, and the capacity of the labour force itself. For example, turbines, solar panels, or other pieces of equipment can be manufactured in the global south, but installation of these technologies still necessitates local workers. The longer-term operation, management and maintenance work required in running these technologies also require availability of long-term local workers.

Distributed renewable sources, most especially, create 'distributed' employments that have environmental and financial effects including lower initial costs and shorter lead times (Lovins 1976). In developing countries this means local job creation, such as demonstrated by women and youth employment in Bangladesh installing distributed energy (Rashid 2015). Compared with large-scale fossil power plants, which are typically centralised, the penetration of distributed renewable energy technologies in local economies can accelerate development through universal energy access (Sovacool and Cooper 2013).

In closing, the production, installation, operation, and maintenance of sustainable energy technologies are expected to generate positive quantitative and qualitative effects on employment. As demand for these technologies and the necessary skills to produce, construct, install, and operate them mounts, the scale and volume of the required labour force to supply this demand necessitates strategies of skilling and labour preparation. Wartime mobilisation impacts to the contours of labour landscape bring about opportunities for skilling and re-skilling the labour sector in meeting this new demand and assuring that dreadful wartime labour conditions are avoided. With new and additional opportunities for employment expected to rise in the sustainable energy regime, rich and poor countries alike should be able to reap the distributed benefits through new labour creation, job exports, and skills transfer. The labour landscape accruing from the execution of the Project can seek to cut unemployment, improve security, address inequalities, and improve general wellbeing.

References

Abelshauser, W. 1998, 'Germany: guns, butter, and economic miracles', in M. Harrison (ed.), *The Economics of World War II: Six Great Powers in International Comparison*, Cambridge University Press, Cambridge, U.K., pp. 122–176.

Allen, P., Blake, L., Harper, P., Hooker-Stroud, A., James, P. & Kellner, T. 2013, *Zero Carbon Britain: Rethinking the Future*, Centre for Alternative Technology, Powys, U.K.

Associated Press (AP) 1943, 'Manpower lack delays Ford plant', *AP*, 31 January, p.12.

Barber, J. & Harrison, M. 1991, *The Soviet Home Front, 1941–1945: A Social and Economic History of the USSR in World War II*, Longman, London, U.K.; New York, U.S.A.

Bloomberg News 2013, 'Top CEO pay ratios', *Bloomberg.com*, 30 April, http://bloom.bg/1avuX5J.

Boxell, J. 2012, 'France to cap top pay in state groups', *The Financial Times*, 30 May, http://on.ft.com/KZsc3l.

Broadberry, S. & Howlett, P. 1998, 'The United Kingdom: victory at all costs', in M. Harrison (ed.), *The Economics of World War II: Six Great Powers in International Comparison*, Cambridge University Press, Cambridge, U.K., pp. 43–80.

Cardozier, V.R. 1995, *The Mobilization of the United States in World War II: How the Government, Military, and Industry Prepared for War*, McFarland & Company, Jefferson, North Carolina, U.S.A.

Chapman, B. & Lounkaew, K. 2013, 'How many jobs is 23,510, really?', *Australian Journal of Labour Economics*, vol. 16, pp. 259–275.

Christensen, C.M. & Horn, M.B. 2013, 'Innovation imperative: change everything', *The New York Times*, 1 November, http://nyti.ms/1bPE2mD.

Cleary, J. & Kopicki, A. 2009, 'Preparing the workforce for a "Green Jobs" economy', *Research Brief for the John J. Heldrich Center for Workforce Development*, Edward J. Bloustein School of Planning and Public Policy, Rutgers, The State University of New Jersey, New Jersey, U.S.A. http://bit.ly/1x68brn.

Clive, A. 1979, *State of War: Michigan in World War II*, The University of Michigan Press, Ann Arbor, Michigan, U.S.A.

Commonwealth Treasury 2009, *Australia's Low Pollution Future: The Economics of Climate Change Mitigation*, Commonwealth of Australia, http://bit.ly/1fMbltJ.

Concept Economics 2009, 'The employment effects in the Australian minerals industry from the proposed Carbon Pollution Reduction Scheme in Australia', *Report Prepared for the Minerals Council of Australia*, May 2009, viewed 2 February 2014, http://bit.ly/1i71Ab4.

Connolly, D. & Mathiesen, B.V. 2014, 'A technical and economic analysis of one potential pathway to a 100% renewable energy system', *International Journal of Sustainable Energy Planning and Management*', vol. 1, pp. 7–27.

Copley, C. 2013, 'Swiss voters reject proposal to limit executives' pay', *Reuters*, 24 November, http://reut.rs/1hLjxvR.

Dallin, D. & Nicolaevsky, B. 1947, *Forced Labor in Soviet Russia*, Yale University Press, New Haven, Connecticut, U.S.A.

Dalton, G.J. & Lewis, T. 2011, 'Metrics for measuring job creation by renewable energy technologies, using Ireland as a case study', *Renewable and Sustainable Energy Reviews*, vol. 15, pp. 2123–2133.

Daly, H.E. 2008, *A Steady-State Economy*, Sustainable Development Commission, U.K., 24 April, http://bit.ly/1j1B32h.

European Renewable Energy Council (EREC) 2010, *Rethinking 2050: A 100% Renewable Energy Vision for the European Union*, EREC, http://www.erec.org.

Goldin, C. 1991, 'The role of World War 2 in the rise of women's employment', *The American Economic Review*, vol. 81, pp. 741–756.

Greenpeace International & European Renewable Energy Council (EREC) 2010, *Energy [R]evolution: A Sustainable World Energy Outlook*, Greenpeace International and EREC, Amsterdam, The Netherlands.

Haig-Muir, M. & Hay, R. 1996, 'The economy at war', in J. Beaumont (ed.) *Australia's War, 1939–1945*, Allen & Unwin Ltd., St. Leonards, New South Wales, Australia, pp. 107–135.

Hara, A. 1998, 'Japan: guns before rice', in M. Harrison (ed.), *The Economics of World War II: Six Great Powers in International Comparison*, Cambridge University Press, Cambridge, U.K.

Harrison, M. 1988, 'Resource mobilization for World War II: the USA, UK, USSR, and Germany, 1938–1945', *The Economic History Review*, vol. 41, pp. 171–192.

Hatfield-Dodds, S., Turner, G., Schandl, H. & Doss, T. 2008, 'Growing the green collar economy: skills and labour challenges in reducing our greenhouse gas emissions and national environmental footprint', *Report to the Dusseldorp Skills Forum*, June 2008, CSIRO, Canberra, Australia, http://bit.ly/1ehKpoU.

Henig, H. & Unterberger, S.H. 1945, 'Wage control in wartime and transition', *The American Economic Review*, vol. 35, pp. 319–336.

Herrera, D. 2004, 'Mondragón: a for-profit organization that embodies catholic social thought', *Review of Business*, vol. 25, pp. 56–68.

IRENA (International Renewable Energy Agency) 2014, *Renewable Energy and Jobs: Annual Review 2014*, IRENA, Dubai, UAE, http://bit.ly/QA6k0h.

IRENA 2015, *Renewable Energy and Jobs: Annual Review 2015*, IRENA, Dubai, UAE, http://bit.ly/1EhpZDB.

Jacobson, M., Delucchi, M., Bauer, Z.A.F., Goodman, S.C., Chapman, W.E. et al. 2015, '100% clean and renewable wind, water, and sunlight (WWS) all-sector energy roadmaps for 139 countries of the world', 27 November 2015, http://stanford.io/1lvUaVS, accessed 30 November 2015.

Jacobson, M., Delucchi, M., Bazouin, G., Dvorak, M.J., Arghandeh, R. et al. 2016, 'A 100% wind, water, sunlight (WWS) all-sector energy plan for Washington State', *Renewable Energy*, vol. 86, pp. 75–88.

Jacobson, M., Delucchi, M., Ingraffea, A.R., Howarth, R.W., Bazouin, G., Bridgeland, B. et al. 2014, 'A roadmap for repowering California for all purposes with wind, water, and sunlight', *Energy*, vol. 73, pp. 875–889.

Kahneman, D. & Deaton, A. 2010, 'High income improves evaluation of life but not emotional well-being', *PNAS*, vol. 107, pp. 16489–16493.

Kaldor, N. 1945–1946, 'The German war economy', *Review of Economic Studies*, vol. 13, pp. 33–52.

Kemp, M. & Wexler, J. (eds) 2010, *Zero Carbon Britain 2030: A New Strategy*, Centre for Alternative Technology (CAT), CAT Publications, Wales, U.K.

Kluckhohn, F.L. 1942, '$25,000 income limit, ceilings on prices, stable wages, taxes, asked by President', *The New York Times*, 28 April.

Lovins, A. 1976, 'Energy strategy: the road not taken?' *Foreign Affairs*, vol. 55, pp. 65–96.

Mathiesen, B.V., Lund, H. & Karlsson, K. 2011, '100% Renewable energy systems, climate mitigation and economic growth', *Applied Energy*, vol. 88, pp. 488–501.

Milward, A.S. 1977, *War, Economy and Society, 1939–1945*, Allen Lane, London, U.K.

Moustafa, N. 2013, 'Maximum and minimum wage law lacks details, faces obstacles in implementation', *Egypt Independent*, 25 February, http://bit.ly/1hN2YCT.

Pizzigati, S. 1992, *The Maximum Wage: A Commonsense Proposal for Revitalizing America by Taxing the Very Rich*, Rowman & Littlefield Publishers, New York, U.S.A.

Pizzigati, S. 2004, *Greed and Good: Understanding and Overcoming the Inequality that Limits our Lives*, Rowman & Littlefield Publishers, New York, U.S.A.

Pizzigati, S. 2012, 'A bold new labor call for a "maximum wage"', *Too Much: A Commentary on Excess and Inequality*, 25 August, http://bit.ly/KSMV86.

Plumptre, A.F.W. 1941, 'Organizing the Canadian economy for war', in J.F. Parkinson (ed.), *Canadian War Economics*, University of Toronto Press, Toronto, Canada.

Rashid, R. 2015, 'Towards sustainable energy development in Bangladesh: the perspective of renewable energy technology', *Journal of Modern Science and Technology*, vol. 3, pp. 31–39.

Rockoff, H. 1981, 'Price and wage controls in four wartime periods', *The Journal of Economic History*, vol. 41, pp. 381–401.

Rockoff, H. 1998, 'The United States: from ploughshares to swords', in M. Harrison (ed.), *The Economics of World War 2: Six Great Powers in International Comparison*, Cambridge University Press, Cambridge, U.K., pp. 81–121.

Roosevelt, F.D. 1943, 'Letter to the House Ways and Means Committee on salary limitation', *The American Presidency Project*, http://bit.ly/1WrRo4Y.

Rosnick, D. & Weisbrot, M. 2006, *Are Shorter Work Hours Good for the Environment? A Comparison of U.S. and European Energy Consumption*, Center for Economic and Policy Research, Washington, D.C., U.S.A., http://bit.ly/JPhxah.

Saha, D. 2010, *Enhancing state clean energy workforce training to meet demand*, Issue Brief, National Governors Association Center for Best Practices, Washington, D.C., U.S.A., http://1.usa.gov/1Mn3nFZ.

Schor, J. 2010, *Plenitude: The New Economics of True Wealth*, Penguin Press, New York, U.S.A.

Sloan, A.Jr. 1990 [1963], *My Years with General Motors*, Doubleday, New York, U.S.A.

Sovacool, B.K. & Cooper, C.J. 2013, *The Governance of Energy Megaprojects: Politics, Hubris and Energy Security*, Edward Elgar: Cheltenham, U.K; Northampton, Massachusetts, U.S.A.

Spross, J. 2013, 'Solar jobs beat out ranchers in Texas, actors in California, and coal miners nationally', *Climate Progress*, 28 April, http://bit.ly/1bKVIyX.

Stewart, B. 1941, 'War-time labour problems', in J.F. Parkinson (ed.), *Canadian War Economics*, University of Toronto Press, Toronto, Canada, pp. 72–88.

Tassava, C. 2010, 'WW II', in R. Whaples (ed.), *The American Economy During World War II*, EH. Net Encyclopedia, http://bit.ly/1eoIs6a.

Thaler, R.H. & Sunstein, C.R. 2008, *Nudge: Improving Decisions About Health, Wealth, and Happiness*, Yale University Press, New Haven, Connecticut, U.S.A.; London, U.K.

The New York Times 1942, 'Women in training to make bombers', 11 July, p. 16.

The New York Times 1943, 'Foremen strike at Willow Run', 22 December, p. 21.

The Wall Street Journal 1942, 'Supply shortage holds up bids on war housing', 20 June, p. 3.

Van De Putte, J., Short, R., Beranek, J., Thies, F. & Teske, S. 2011, *Battle of the Grids Report 2011: How Europe can go 100% Renewable and Phase Out Dirty Energy*, Greenpeace, Amsterdam, The Netherlands.

Vorrath, S. 2015, 'Australian clean energy jobs could be worth $370bn in 10 years', *RenewEconomy*, 29 September, http://bit.ly/1RL2ueJ.

Walker, E.R. 1947, *The Australian Economy in War and Reconstruction*, Oxford University Press, New York, U.S.A.

Wartzman, R. 2008, 'Put a cap on CEO pay', *Bloomberg Business Week*, 12 September, http://buswk.co/KebzzA.

Wei, M., Patadia, S. & Kammen, D.M. 2010, 'Putting renewables and energy efficiency to work: How many jobs can the clean energy generate in the US?' *Energy Policy*, vol. 38, pp. 919–931.

Willsher, K. & Inman, P. 2013, 'Voters in Swiss referendum back curbs on executives' pay and bonuses', *The Guardian*, 4 March, http://bit.ly/1iE3AIp.

6   Legislations, control, oversight

Bringing 'the state' back

This book argues that the state must coordinate the implementation of the Rapid Mitigation Project. The state, thus, will retain many of the powers that must be summoned in its implementation. The scale, speed, and scope required for executing, administering, and managing the Project rationalise some key changes in the mode of governance to accelerate climate mobilisation. The role of the state in the project entails:

- *Initiating climate policy with long-term impacts, to be undertaken rapidly.* For this to occur, a shift in orientation is key by returning to state planning (cf. Giddens 2011).
- *Distributing powers and responsibilities.* For the Project to be optimally delivered, the state must allocate leadership, activities, and responsibilities between itself, regional and local governments, and civil society (cf. Hirst 2000; Delina 2012).
- *Managing risks and exploiting opportunities in the age of climate consequences.* Where major adjustments in sociotechnical systems are required to achieve rapid mitigation, the state has a key role in providing a structured analysis, design, and execution of policy and responses that address multi-location, multi-sectoral, and multi-scalar qualities of climate impacts and climate action.
- *Encouraging social, political, technological, and economic convergences of multiple actions under the Project.* The large-scale sociotechnical restructuring of the energy system, the first node in a series of activities necessary for achieving a low-carbon, resilient, and sustainable future, entails state-led planning.
- *Interfering with the markets to institutionalise key climate policy.* The Project requires internalising social and environmental costs in the proper pricing of services. The state has the societal mandate to re-order markets that will work towards social and environmental ends.
- *Reining in vested interests that seek to block rapid climate mitigation.* The dominant role of high carbon industries in contemporary societies requires a stronger response from awakened governments, many of which, for long, have been influenced by vested interests.

- *Keeping the Project at the top of the political agenda, and sustaining it in the long-term.* The state has to ensure the sustainability of the Project, a 30–40-year programme at most, until its ambitions are fully realised, despite changes in political leadership. Based on the slow pace of previous energy transitions (Smil 2011), a much stronger role for the state may be essential to implement the Project.
- *Introducing appropriate fiscal architecture that contributes to the funding requirements of the Project.* The scale, scope, and intensity of the required activities necessitate a steady supply of funds. Since not all climate finance should be generated through taxes and public borrowing, the state must design innovative means to maintain the sustainability of Project funding, including securing international support at bilateral and multilateral levels (cf. Delina 2011).
- *Engaging the public.* Public engagement is a crucial asset to activate the role of the state in mobilising dramatic and large-scale rapid mitigation (cf. Levi 1997; Giddens 2011).

The list inarguably asks a lot of the state. I suspect the current neoliberal agenda permeating many democratic governments in capitalist, high emission states will be inadequate to meet these tasks (cf. Francis 2015; Anderson and Bows 2012; Dryzek 1992). The scale, scope, and intensity of the required mobilisation activities to implement the Project demand an alteration of the bureaucracy-capitalist market. Government, itself, must innovate its relationship with the state, markets, and its citizens. The executive-dominated model of governance, which was the approach used in wartime, offers advantages; yet it must be refined within the milieu of contemporary democratic rights and freedoms.

To mobilise essential labour and financial resources for wartime requirements as quickly and as efficiently as possible, profound changes occurred in the administration and direction of the economy, especially in democratic capitalist states. State intervention in the national economy became a necessity, and was greatly increased at the time of war (Lumer 1954: 206). World War II triggered a tectonic shift in governance structures towards something E.M.H. Lloyd, writing in *Experiments in State Control*, predicted just after the conclusion of World War I:

> Another great war will plunge the world into a sort of military communism, in comparison with which the control exercised during the recent war will seem an Arcadian revel. Personal freedom and private property are condemned by the exigencies of a modern war.
>
> (Lloyd 1924: xi)

Over the next three to five years – depending on country – World War II introduced interventionist strategies to control some of personal freedoms and private properties, and the dynamics between agencies of governments.

To initiate control and to ensure rapid mobilisation in democratic states, wartime mobilisation brought about two key changes: the primacy of the state over the market, which led to the suppression of some of the activities of the latter; and the creation by governments of new institutions and the redesigning of existing agencies to fit the requirements of the war.

Notably, although democratic governments adopted central planning to meet the rigours of wartime mobilisation, they were quick to revert to a market economy once the war was over. The period when the state controlled the country's productive apparatus away from the market occurred in a matter of four years in the U.S.A., i.e. between 1942 and 1945, four years in Australia, i.e. between 1942 and 1945, and six years in the U.K., i.e. between 1940 and 1945.

The U.K. transition to wartime central planning came earlier than in the U.S.A. and Australia; hence, this was also the longest period among the three countries. In 1940 and 1941, U.S. and Australian governments intervened in only a few sectors of their respective economies. Both adopted central planning only in 1942, fundamentally in response to Japanese aggression in the Pacific, which started with the December 1941 attack on Pearl Harbor and Manila, both territories under the protection of the U.S. government. As the need to produce munitions intensified, Australia and the U.S.A. began assuming direct control of their economies, thus shifting power and responsibilities away from the markets.

Within the brief period of command-and-control based on central planning, wartime mobilisation in democratic countries comprised two broad forms of rigorous control. The first form involved the direct administration of human, financial, and material resources, which involved the coercion of persons and groups through conscription, rationing of goods, new taxation measures, and restrictions of unessential production. The second form comprised psychological controls designed to encourage 'voluntary' conformity with public policy (Walker 1947; Plumptre 1941).

During the phase of strong executive control and central planning, the state set up production goals, supervised, and managed wartime industries. At the height of these interventions, between 1942 and 1945, the U.S. Federal Government, for example, directly controlled more than 40% of the country's wartime output of goods and services (Lumer 1954: 208). Although the U.S. Federal Government became the operator of these industries, it never took ownership of these industries.

The private sector, although relegated in some ways, was still allowed some complementary roles by being enabled to participate in production contracts (Plumptre 1941: 38), to provide technical skill trainings, especially in its factories and assembly lines, and to contribute its managerial expertise (Walker 1947: 153–154). Despite its indirect roles in mobilisation, the private sector was still able to reap many benefits at wartime. Businesses, especially large monopolies, flourished from the mobilisation because of guaranteed and lucrative contracts, large subsidies, and free-flowing tax rebates (Cardozier

1995: 155; Lumer 1954: 37, 208–210). As large-scale public contracts flowed, opportunities for corruption were also rife, despite the occurrence of war (Poole 2012: 55–59; Fleming 2001: 247).

Central planning in the U.S.A., U.K., and Australia remained in place until 1945, after which the countries all reverted back to capitalism simultaneously in 1946. The surrender of Germany in May 1945 and the defeat of Japan three months later marked the shift away from state control and back to their capitalist orientations.

The story of wartime governance underscores the essential role of central planning in executing large-scale and aggressive mobilisations rapidly. In the post-war world, central planning persisted, thus placing the government as the focal actor in directing the interests of the state. This led to the nationalisation of basic services, and, in many instances, major industries including energy generation and distribution. This governance arrangement provides a precedent about the return to state planning in implementing the Rapid Mitigation Project.

Similarities regarding governance arrangements between wartime mobilisation and the Project also extend to greater state interventionism in climate policy. Although regulations underscore many aspects of the Project, the steering of the macro economy by the state does not mean it will totally handicap the market. What the state does is provide serious checks, particularly on vested interest, while supporting and steering actors relevant to the transition to a new sustainable energy regime. Although the emphasis of the re-appraised mode of governance is on industrial policy, since infrastructure and technology mostly define the transition, the Project equally highlights the social implications and the role of citizens in the transition as it reconciles with and extends democratic rights and freedoms in the new regime.

Planning blueprints

At wartime, the economy was shifted towards greater central planning so that controls could be placed to ensure rapid munitions production and their deployment to battlefields. With victory becoming a state priority, wartime plans were the primary documents detailing not only military strategies but also wartime governance structures and rapid industrial production. Wartime plans, thus, came to be the embodiment of central planning.

Similarly, the Project will require the design of Rapid Mitigation Plans since planning for a future rife with uncertainties remains of great import to limit the risks in the age of climate consequences, which cannot be assessed with precise accuracy anyway (Giddens 2011: 100). Wartime plans provide pictures of how the lessons and blunders of planning can instruct the design and development of contingency plans for the Project.

Wartime plans were concerned with generalities, meaning they were focused on the whole programme of approved projects, and not on the internal execution of a specific production project. The plans laid out implementation strategies and were typically based on the crude matching of available resources to plan for physical output and for coordination. Almost all wartime plans were, as a rule, prepared to ensure continuity even in the absence of direction by a supreme executive. This is essential in keeping the long-term aspect of the Project. For example, Roosevelt's death in April 1945, at the peak of World War II and a month before Nazi surrender, did not hinder the continuation of U.S. Victory Plan enforcement. Wartime plans, overall, were designed to provide not only a logical review and comprehensive picture of commitments and available resources, and how to address gaps as early as possible, but also strategies to ensure continuity.

The state dedicated a major part of its resources to guarantee well-designed master wartime plans. In 1936, the Nazis developed the earliest form of a state plan aimed at mobilisation for another world war. Disguised as a preparation for Germany's self-sufficiency in four years, the Nazi Four-Year Plan also combined and used existing and new instruments to manage the German economy for Hitler's rearmament aims (Abelshauser 1998: 144). Hitler named Hermann Göring as Plenipotentiary to manage the Plan, particularly the rearmament process. The Plan also included strategies that would subordinate parts of the private sector and economic administration for its execution. The essence of the Four-Year Plan called for economic control, and involved components such as wage and price policies, labour resource allocation, and investment regulations through prohibitions, levies, and direct state investment (Abelshauser 1998: 144).

The American wartime plan commenced design when the Germans occupied Poland in 1939. That year, Roosevelt gathered prominent businesspersons and requested them to review the existing Industrial Mobilisation Plan, commonly called the M-Day Plan. The 18-page document was created to serve as a preparatory document for possible U.S. involvement in the war, and to include national aspects of planning, including the establishment of the War Resources Administration in an emergency. On 9 July 1941, Roosevelt asked the Army and the Navy for an extensive plan of all the resources the country needed to defeat its potential enemies. On this day, Roosevelt issued a memorandum directing the Secretaries of War and the Navy to prepare a mobilisation plan to ensure the defeat of America's potential enemies.

The M-Day Plan, along with the plans developed by the Army and the Navy, eventually morphed into the *Victory Plan of 1941*, a major government document produced in September, three months before the attack on Pearl Harbor. The Plan provided the blueprint for the general mobilisation of the U.S. armed forces and for the operational concept by which the U.S.A. fought the war. It covered three vital aspects for implementation: rapid mobilisation of American industries to a wartime output; building up of the

U.S. armed forces; and specific strategies to fight and defeat potential enemies, which they had already identified to be Germany and Japan.

The Victory Plan assigned a highly centralised command-and-control arrangement with the President in charge. During the first weeks when the U.S.A. was formally at war, the U.S. Congress approved the giant Victory Plan. In 1943, the government produced a specific Controlled Materials Plan to complement the Victory Plan and specifically secure balance in munitions' demand. The supplement plan secured this balance by means of a coordinated review of military export and essential civilian programmes, and allotted materials to each claimant agency. It also centralised all wartime administration through a Requirements Committee of the War Production Board.

In Australia, wartime planning was a bit of a struggle so that even at the conclusion of the war a formal master plan had never been formulated (Walker 1947: 35). Nevertheless, Australia produced a document resembling a wartime plan through a 1942 document prepared by a department associated with the War Cabinet Sub-Committee on Manpower. The document contained an informal estimate of 'the total requirements of the services, of war production, and of essential civilian industry, and to weigh these requirements against the available labour force of the nation' (Walker and Foxcroft 1943: 237).

The story of wartime plan preparations and their inherent challenges impart lessons and implications in contingency plan development for the Project. At its crudest, a national plan encompassing and enjoining national, state, and local governments, involves the following activities. The list, although broad, is incomplete to cover the scale of a national Rapid Mitigation Project, but it provides insights into what could be included in the document.

- Establishing a new national institution to serve as a coordinating body to achieve Project ambitions including high renewable energy penetration within the required time.
- Conducting rapid, yet comprehensive, studies on material resources, financial mechanisms, and labour requirements and availability for the Project to ascertain deficits or surpluses.
- Designing plans for ensuring public engagement that go beyond awareness raising.
- Establishing legally binding targets for sustainable energy generation and emissions reduction, according to capacity in every political division such as district, town, city, state or province.
- Establishing a plan to rapidly increase the number of sustainable energy generation power plants at the site of consumption, and at varying distances from where they are used, and to be connected by an increasingly demand-and-supply-responsive electric grid.
- Encouraging local and regional development of sustainable energy systems to foster and create local employment and income generation opportunities through subsidies, grants, and price support mechanisms.

- Supporting installations of different-sized technologies, including distributed sustainable energy generation and back-up emergency sustainable energy power system through a streamlined permit approval process, and incentives.
- Supporting energy storage systems at households and in communities to address grid power losses through incentives.
- Establishing a plan for staged, structured, and systematic phase out of fossil fuel and nuclear power plants through elimination of public subsidies, and properly pricing their services.
- Phasing out laws that give priority access in land-use to mining or drilling for fossil fuels, and providing incentives to landowners whose properties are required for the transition.
- Streamlining planning procedures, approval process, and permit mechanisms to reduce red tape in public contracting, sustainable energy generation projects, and in high-capacity transmission line programmes.
- Supporting increased use of public transport and electric vehicles, while establishing zero-emission standards for all vehicles.
- Disclosing social, environmental and climate impacts to end-users.

Preparing for war starts with the production of wartime plans. For essential rapid mobilisation processes and administrative controls to be legitimate, however, and thus receive formal public mandate, legislation has to be provided. In the U.S.A., Congress provided the executive branch with this power through the *Government Reorganization Act of 1939*. The legislation allowed the President to hire additional confidential staff and reorganise, within limits, the executive branch for two years. The Act created the Executive Office of the President, which extended the reach of presidential control over the executive branch. With an uncooperative Parliament, such an extension may be impossible. Executive-led regulations, therefore, may be used to develop such plans as illustrated by wartime experience.

Despite having wartime plans, governments still faced challenges; national plans for implementing the Rapid Mitigation Project need to note the following challenges:

- *Incomplete information:* Economic and social factors cannot be fully accounted for in plan formulation. Planners, therefore, must be explicit in acknowledging design and plan limitations, and ensuring the inclusion of appropriate means to account for future changes and variations. This necessitates setting up a regular review programme to keep the plan up to date.
- *Human inventiveness:* Mass production requires standardisation, but standardisation promises early obsolescence, thus rendering plans obsolete as well. A regular assessment of the plans is key, including incorporating lessons newly learnt from the execution of the Project component activities in the revisions.

- *Size*: The range of munitions required is so great that consolidating the requirements through a wartime plan demands an army of its own. A national Rapid Mitigation Plan will undoubtedly be presented with similar challenges and there is a high likelihood that an army of planners, designers, and creative thinkers from the technical, physical science, and social science disciplines will be needed.
- *Complexity/scale*: Governments had difficulty contextualising in their wartime plans the extent to which resources could be made available for wartime production. No plan will ever be comprehensive in its scope; thus, options for change and variations should be structurally embedded in the mechanisms for review and revisions.

In the U.S.A., despite provision in the Victory Plan, only in June 1942 did the change of the economy to central planning, state-led production became legal. The stimulus for the shift was obvious: the U.S.A. was at war, and winning at all costs became a state priority. This was done through the issuance of three vital regulations: Priorities Regulations 10 and 11, and Executive Order 9250. The first two regulations, which were issued by the War Production Board in June 1942, expanded executive powers to control materials, allocate them, and prioritise munitions production. Regulation 10 established a method of identifying the final use of all raw materials allocated for mobilisation, while Regulation 11 established the principle of control and allocation of raw materials according to whether their final use corresponded with state priorities. Four months later, another regulation established the Office of Economic Stabilization providing the executive branch with extensive powers including the power to control wages and prices of goods and services, in essence, to control inflation. In effect, these three regulations marked the U.S. Government's interference with the market, hence, a command-and-control system.

The ambit of executive control over the economy was well represented in governments throughout the world. In 1939, as the war raged in Europe, the Australian Parliament began preparing for the eventuality of Australia's involvement in the war. It passed the *National Security Act of 1939*, ushering in the *National Security Regulations*, which authorised the Government to carry out controls. This Act was significant since it made the Government the legislative body on matters regarding the war, not Parliament. This set-up allowed the Government to prepare for the war by enacting crucial legislation on economic control, three years prior to Australia becoming a centrally planned economy in 1942. Crucial legislation and regulations on economic control in Australia followed this timeline:

- 1939 June: *Supply and Development Act* established a new department to control munitions' production, a national register of manpower and property, and alien registration.
- 1939 August: *Defence Act* authorised the Federal Treasurer to completely control all foreign exchange transactions; controlled alien movements;

authorised postal censorship; and other general security measures; and controlled the shipping industry.

- 1939 September: *National Security Act of 1939* empowered the Governor General to regulate 'all matters which are necessary or convenient to be prescribed for the more effectual prosecution of the war'; made the Government, not Parliament, the legislative body on all matters connected with the prosecution of the war; and initiated economic reorganisation.
- 1939: *National Security Regulations*, following the National Security Act of 1939, authorised Ministers to control the production and distribution of goods and services; and specified measures on prices and rent control, acquisition of primary products, export licensing, control of exchange and foreign securities, capital-issues control, and the operations of the Department of Supply and Development.
- 1939 September: *Customs Regulations* under the Customs Act subjected all Australian exports to license; prohibited the exportation of some goods in short supply such as bags and sacks; required gold to be offered only to the Commonwealth Bank; made it an offence to purchase foreign currencies other than through the Commonwealth Bank; and prohibited the export and sale of securities overseas.
- 1939 October: *Capital Issues Regulation* required company formation and any increase in capital to be subject to Treasurer's consent; controlled mortgages; and pegged interest rates chargeable on mortgages.
- 1940: *Labour Regulation* empowered the Minister for Supply and Development to enter into dilution agreements with trade unions, and to arrange industrial training.
- 1940 June: *National Security (Subversive Associations) Regulations* censored Communist papers; declared various Italian societies unlawful; and prohibited the publication and dissemination of 'any unlawful doctrines', which were 'prejudicial to the efficient prosecution of the war'.
- 1940 July: *National Security (Employment) Regulations* required employers to engage only tradespersons having the consent of their previous employer; determined maximum rates for services rendered.
- 1940 December: *Industrial Peace Regulations* enabled the Commonwealth Arbitration Court to deal with any matter that could lead to industrial unrest, in addition to existing disputes.
- 1941 November: *Wartime Banking Control Regulations* instructed banks to avoid public loans without the prior consent of the Commonwealth Bank; required banks to furnish the Treasurer information regarding their business, but not the particulars of individual accounts.
- 1942 February: *Mobilisation of Services and Property Regulations* enabled the Government to require any Australian resident to perform any specified services, or to place his property at the service of the Federal Government at the direction of a Minister. This authority, however, turned out to be symbolic instead of instrumental since sufficient powers for industrial reorganisation were already provided elsewhere, or

more conveniently located in regulations applying to particular industries (Walker 1947: 63).

- 1942 February: *Economic Organisation Regulations* suspended the operations of normal financial incentives over the Australian economy by pegging wages, profits, interests, and prices; subjected transactions in shares and land to government consent; prohibited absenteeism in the workplace (Walker 1947: 63–64).
- 1942 September: Fadden's 'austerity campaign' provided restrictions on racing; introduced new taxation on entertainments and luxury goods; increased borrowing programme.
- 1942: *Black Marketing Act* imposed heavy penalties including summary prosecution for offences against various economic controls.

Although presented through the historical lens of only two countries, the U.S.A. and Australia, the history of formal legislation and regulation issuances instructing governments to execute wartime plans, institute actions to pursue wartime mobilisation, and establish formal controls on almost every sector, illustrate how mechanisms for large-scale mobilisations are accomplished. These experiences offer some possible regulations and/or legislation that governments can introduce to institutionalise the Rapid Mitigation Project. This is inarguably an incomplete list, yet it provides a starting point.

- Legislation reorganising the executive branch and activating all government levels for the overall Project goal and creating a special department or ministry in-charge to design, promote, and implement Project activities.
- Legislation providing appropriate power on the executive branch to design, promote, and implement control measures ensuring rapid implementation of the Project's industrial component, including the manufacture and diffusion of sustainable energy technologies within a stringent timeframe.
- Regulations identifying, controlling, and allocating raw materials required by the Project.
- Legislation and regulations introducing and promoting a new fiscal infrastructure to implement the Project, including:

    a   Legislation realigning budgetary allocations for defence and wars for use in the Project.
    b   Legislation phasing out subsidies for fossil fuel and nuclear power production and inefficient energy use.
    c   Legislation introducing 'polluter pays' principle to reflect external and societal costs of fossil fuels and nuclear power through a carbon price, either via a higher emissions tax or limited allowances in cap-and-trade, or an aggressive hybrid approach that mixes both tax and allowances.
    d   Regulations providing a stable return for sustainable energy investors through price support mechanisms including investment subsidies and grants, feed-in-tariffs, premium or environmental bonus mechanism,

loan guarantees, tax credits, co-investments, and tradable green certificates.

e   Regulations ensuring that investors can rely on the long-term Project stability.

- Legislation and regulations reforming the national electricity market to allow better sustainable energy technology integration, including:

    a   Regulations supporting programmes on retrofitting and/or extending electric grids to conduct sustainable energy from where it is stronger to where electricity is used.

    b   Regulations specifying guaranteed access to the grid by sustainable energy systems at fair and transparent prices.

    c   Regulations ensuring priority access to the grid for electricity generated from sustainable energy sources.

    e   Regulations guaranteeing that grid infrastructure development and improvement costs are borne by the grid management authority and not by sustainable energy providers.

    f   Regulations connecting energy storage to the grid to balance and smoothe power delivery from sustainable energy generators.

    g   Regulations introducing new pricing structures reflecting the full social, environmental, and climate costs of energy production.

    h   Regulations establishing progressive tariffs so that electricity price costs more for those consuming more.

- Regulations introducing incentives that support low carbon transport, including:

    a   Regulations on private car and other transport vehicle efficiency to push manufacturers to reduce emissions by design and technology improvement, and using sustainable energy.

    b   Regulations developing incentives to promote electric car and other efficient low carbon transport vehicle development.

    c   Regulations developing incentives to promote the linking of electric cars to a sustainable energy grid.

    d   Regulations developing, improving, and promoting low emission transport options, such as public and non-motorised transport, walking and cycling, freight transport management programmes, teleworking, and more efficient land-use planning to limit journeys.

- Regulations setting up energy efficiency programmes to limit energy demand, reduce peak loads, and maximise generating power plant's capacity factor, including:

    a   Regulations expanding and enforcing stricter minimum energy performance standards and other energy efficiency regulations in buildings, appliances, power plants, vehicles, and other energy-using equipment.

b   Regulations setting mandatory building codes requiring a set share of sustainable energy technologies and compliance with a limited annual energy consumption level.

c   Regulations siting new buildings that encourage greater population density and, therefore, minimise energy use and emissions from transportation.

d   Regulations introducing large-scale public building retrofit programmes.

e   Regulations offering financial investments to assist in the implementation of energy efficiency measures through tax reduction schemes, investment subsidies and grants, and preferential loans.

- Regulations on meeting the Project's labour requirements and the required competencies for rapid mitigation institutions, including:

  a   Regulations developing strategies and programmes to promote the education of planners, engineers, carpenters, electricians, masons, architects, installers, assembly workers, public transit workers, plumbers, welders, project managers, energy regulators, foresters, workforce training specialists, and other tradespersons and professionals in the supply and demand side of the new sustainable energy regime.

  b   Regulations on teaching and learning, including prioritising of Project-related university courses and degrees.

- Regulations providing grants and other forms of support for research, development, and demonstration at laboratories, colleges, and universities to improve technology viability such as energy storage, smart grid and grid connectivity, increasing efficiency, transport, policy effectiveness, social impacts of technologies, and efficiency of institutional processes for rapid mitigation.

Strong executive control

To prosecute the war in earnest, the state made changes in the bureaucracy. In all combat countries, the entire war mobilisation efforts became the province of the executive branch. In the U.S.A., for instance, wartime departments, boards, commissions, and other institutions were directed to report directly to the Office of the President. This arrangement made the U.S. President a powerful political and economic figure during the war (Dickinson 1997: 118). Similar executive-based arrangements were seen in the U.K., Australia, Canada, and even in the Axis countries of Japan and Germany.

The allocation of wartime power in the U.S.A. to the executive branch was based upon the same *Executive Reorganization Act of 1939*, which explicitly provided wide-ranging Presidential powers to create, establish, revise, and eventually abolish public agencies through Executive Orders. Six years after the enactment of the law – between 1939 and 1945 – around 162 new agencies were created strictly for war purposes (Dickinson 1997: 118; Cardozier 1995: 104). For a list of these agencies, see Appendix 1 of *The United States at War: Development and Administration of the War Program by the Federal Government* (U.S. Federal Government 1945). The proliferation of wartime civilian agencies ushered in growth in the number of workforce in public bureaucracies, thus providing the executive branch a huge army of civilians for wartime mobilisation (Lumer 1954: 209).

The evolution of the U.S. wartime agencies comprised two phases: Phase 1, between 1938 and 1941, or the foundation for defence production; and Phase 2, between 1941 and 1945, or between Pearl Harbor and the end of the Roosevelt Presidency (see Table 6.1). Notably, the U.S. military had its own mobilisation wing, the Army and Navy Munitions Board (ANMB), which acted independently during the early years of the war, but was forced to coordinate its efforts with the civilian mobilisation agencies as the war intensified in 1943.

At a quick glance, it appears that the executive branch held much wartime power. On closer inspection, however, the U.S. President's grip on this power, particularly on mobilisation activities, was never absolute. The activities at the White House during a centrally planned economy suggest an alternative reality regarding the larger role held by the private sector. As shown in Table 6.1, industrialists led vital wartime agencies. For instance, Donald Nelson, a business executive at Sears Roebuck, serves as Office of Production Management (OPM) director between 1941 and 1942 and as War Production Board (WBP) chair from 1942 to 1944. Earlier, General Motors' William Knudsen also directed the OPM between 1940 and 1942. Thus, although the war was a military pursuit, its business orientation persisted.

The Roosevelt Presidency also gave the impression that they were in full and exclusive control of wartime mobilisation. As shown in Table 6.1, however, wartime organisation in the U.S.A. was apparently characterised by strong private sector involvement and overlapping responsibilities across multiple high-level agencies. At many times, these civilian agencies were also in conflict with the military's own mobilisation arm, the ANMB. Competition among these agencies and with the private sector for access to industrial resources, especially during the early years of rapid mobilisation was also rife and evident (Dickinson 1997; Harrison 1988).

As Table 6.1 shows, the structuring of public agencies for wartime mobilisation was a trial-and-error process characterised by frequent changes in their scope and structure. In complex times such as the war, where uncertainties were the norm, this bureaucratic structuring and restructuring appeared to be essential. After periods of learning, nevertheless, the Roosevelt government, with substantial support from managers in the private sector, developed a coherent pattern of war agency specialisation so that a central agency to oversee wartime policy and mobilisation was finally secured with the creation of the Office of War Mobilisation (OWM) in May 1943. This new arrangement

Table 6.1 U.S. civilian agencies for wartime mobilisation

Year	Agency	Statutory authority and structure	Functions	Abolished in
Phase 1: 1939 to Japanese attack on Pearl Harbor				
1939 August	War Resources Board (WRB)	No statutory authority; functioned as an advisory committee; headed by Edward Stettinius Jr, chairman of the U.S. Steel Corporation; reported directly to the President	Collaborated with Army and Navy Munitions Board (ANMB) to formulate economic mobilisation policies; reviewed the M-Day Plan for mobilisation and control of industry in time of war	November 1939. After only two months, Roosevelt dissolved WRB to counter the widespread perception that big businesses dominated the Board.
1940 May	Office of Emergency Management (OEM)	Administrative Order in accordance with Executive Order 8248 (see Roosevelt 1939a); reported directly to the President	As administrative umbrella sheltering all U.S. wartime agencies	November 1944
1940 May	National Defence Advisory Commission (NDAC)	No Chair; reported to the OEM	Provided defence expenditure decisions	October 1941; after 18 months
1940 August	Reconstruction Finance Corporation established the Defence Plant Corporation	Established and chartered by Congress in 1932	Provided loans to the private sector for defence	Defence Plant Corporation dissolved on 1 July 1945; Reconstruction Finance Corporation disbanded in 1957
1940 November	Office of Production Management (OPM)	Executive Order 8629 (see Roosevelt 1941a); chaired by William Knudsen, President of General Motors; reported to OEM	Administered industrial mobilisation	January 1942

Table 6.1 (Continued)

Year	Agency	Statutory authority and structure	Functions	Abolished in
1941 August	Supply Priorities and Allocation Board (SPAB)	Executive Order 8775 (see Roosevelt 1941b); chaired by Donald Nelson, Chair of Sears Roebuck; seven-member Board	Determined the total materials needed for defence and civilian purposes should the U.S.A. enter the war	January 1942
Phase 2: Japanese attack on Pearl Harbor to 1943				
1942 January	War Production Board	Executive Order 9024 (see Roosevelt 1942a); chaired by Donald Nelson	Determined how items were to be rated as priorities; forced manufacturers to accept military contracts; requisitioned private properties; stopped the production of specific goods and services	1945, shortly after the defeat of Japan
1942 October	Office of Economic Stabilization (OES) within OEM until 1944	Executive Order 9250 (see Roosevelt 1942b); headed by James Byrnes; reported directly to the President	Controlled inflation by controlling wages and rationing	1946
1943 May	Office of War Mobilization (OWM) within OEM until 1944	Executive Order 9347 (see Roosevelt 1943); headed by James Byrnes; reported directly to the President	Adjudicated disputes involving war production agencies; coordinated wartime policy	1945

Author's compilation from references cited elsewhere in this book settled early coordination problems among other civilian mobilisation agencies, private sector contractors, and the military's ANMB (Dickinson 1997: 118; Harrison 1988: 181). In contrast to other mobilisation agencies, OWM was headed not by a businessperson but by a politician, James Byrnes, former head of the Office of Economic Stabilisation (OES).

The executive branch took 18 months after the attack on Pearl Harbor to finally transition towards central coordination; this was three years after the creation of its precursor, the structurally weak War Resources Board (WRB). This decision could have been taken earlier if only Roosevelt had considered and implemented the same recommendations made earlier by experienced wartime managers. Bernard Baruch, the main figure of the U.S. industrial mobilisation in World War I, recommended as early as 1939 to Roosevelt that there should be a central agency controlling economic resources should the U.S. involves itself in another world war (Milward 1977: 103–104). The delay showed a lot about Roosevelt's wartime leadership and administrative style. Henry Lewis Stimson, the U.S. War Secretary between 1940 and 1945 wrote in 1971, that the President was the 'poorest administrator [he] ever worked under in respect to orderly procedure and routine of his performance' (Stimson and Bundy 1971: 495). Indeed, it was only when the President yielded some of his executive powers to OWM in 1943 that munitions production intensified. Only by yielding power to specialised wartime agencies, were coordination issues in an obviously bloated bureaucracy and competition between civilian and military mobilisation agencies, typical of pre-Pearl Harbor mobilisation agencies, substantially reduced (Dickinson 1997).

The executive branch, along with top industrialists, became the central actors for wartime mobilisation. Their concentrated wartime power allowed them stronger control, especially with resource mobilisation (Plumptre 1941; Walker 1939: 75). The powers of what were then called 'war czars' included prioritising and rating munitions and even extended to forcing manufacturers to accept military contracts; requisitioning private properties for wartime mobilisation; and stopping the production of specific goods and services, especially those competing with war essentials (Dickinson 1997). Strong executive control also went beyond this to include the issuance of regulations on rationing of basic goods and services. In the U.S.A., the locus of these powers was initially located in industrialist Donald Nelson's WPB and then, from 1943 onwards, with politician James Byrnes's OWM. For four years, 1942–1945, these agencies centrally governed wartime mobilisation and production in the country.

Notwithstanding the early conflicts between the military's ANMB and civilian wartime agencies, the central structure and dominance of the executive branch proved to be efficient in organising and coordinating the actors involved in munitions production and mobilisation. The reach of these Executive Branch-based civilian agencies extended to military agencies, the expanded bureaucracy, material suppliers, and the private sector. These essential agencies were structured so that they reported only and directly to the President. They were also placed a notch above other regular peacetime agencies in executive branch departments. Although some may see this arrangement as unacceptable in a democratic setting, its utmost importance in an emergency became apparent, especially as the need for munitions intensified.

WPB and OWM provide structural models to pattern an agency at the executive branch to coordinate the implementation of the Rapid Mitigation Project. Learning from the lessons on the delays in creating a central agency for wartime mobilisation and minimising potential conflicts among public agencies early on, this agency should also be created as a special cabinet-level ministry directly and regularly reporting to the chief executive. Following wartime lessons, the agency needs to be administratively and structurally placed a notch higher than other conventional ministries. In what could be called the *Ministry for Rapid Climate Mitigation*, planning and coordinating functions can be delegated.

Planning

- Providing a timeline for achieving Project ambitions at the national, regional, state, and local levels that meets the required rate of mitigation.
- Conducting material, technology, labour, and financial requirement studies for the Project at all government levels.
- Advising the chief executive of priority legislations and regulations required to implement the Project in earnest.
- Assessing sustainable energy potential, capacity, and limitations at all government levels.
- Assessing electricity grid requirements including the identification of new transmission line routes that will connect sustainable energy generation power plants to end users.
- Setting renewable energy targets and energy efficiency production goals and priorities at all government levels.
- Devising social nudges to accelerate climate mitigation including those aimed at decelerating personal and public consumption behaviours.
- Setting up activities for ensuring greater public engagement at all government levels.
- Securing public contracts for the various activities.
- Instituting efficient and transparent contracting procedures.
- Reducing red tape in public contracting.

Coordinating

- With the Treasury to organise funding for the Project and its activities pursuant to new legislation and regulations outlined earlier (also see Chapter 4).
- With Labour Ministry to implement and monitor labour strategies for the Project pursuant to new legislation and regulations outlined earlier (also see Chapter 5).

- With Education Ministry to implement skilling and re-skilling strategies (also see Chapter 5).
- With the Treasury and Education Ministry to increase funding for specific aspects of education, training and retraining (also see Chapter 5).
- With other branches of government at all levels for the effective and efficient Project implementation.

An important wartime lesson concerns having an overly powerful executive branch to coordinate the Rapid Mitigation Project. Overall, the wartime mobilisation experience caused considerable nervousness about executive power (cf. Rosenbloom 2001; Davidson 1990), since with a dominant executive the legislative branch was indubitably rendered weak. At the end of the war, this arrangement, however, made sense since it allowed for easy dissolution of public bodies that had just been rendered obsolete without repealing legislation or initiating a new law just to dissolve it (Dickinson 1997: 118–119). Not all wartime agencies, however, were repealed. There had been some organisations that stayed for good such as the House and Senate Appropriations Committee, the Federal Bureau of Investigation's General Intelligence Division, the Bureau of the Budget, the Council of Economic Advisors, and the Central Intelligence Agency (Mayhew 2005: 486). Nevertheless, the U.S. Congress recognised that they had provided the executive branch with excessive wartime power. Realising that such an arrangement is prone to abuse, Congress enacted *The Administrative Procedure Act of 1946* to essentially limit executive power. During the same year, Congress also passed *The Legislative Reorganization Act of 1946* to strengthen a congressional committee for executive oversight. In 1947, Congress also sent to the states the *Twenty-Second Amendment* establishing a term-limit for presidents (Mayhew 2005: 479), which was formally ratified in 1951. Since then, U.S. Presidents can only serve two terms.

A powerful executive branch with too much control of the Project could easily lead to abuse, if not a tyrannical regime. Following the lessons of post-war legislative activities to rein in a powerful executive branch, a countervailing public agency, with power to provide adequate check-and-balance on the executive branch, is indispensable as the state-led Rapid Mitigation Project is implemented.

Countervailing power

Legislation should provide a mandate to an institution to act as a countervailing power to executive government and the special ministry. This institution should also provide the public with the means to judicially examine executive decisions regarding Project implementation, meaning it also has to be provided with legal powers to investigate, sue, and prosecute corruption, and other power abuses in a special court. This institution, which can be called the *Rapid Mitigation Ombudsman*, must be independent of the executive branch and made answerable to Parliament and the public. To safeguard its independence, this institution should be funded through a separate legislated budget. Its functions should include, but not be limited to:

- Reviewing the transition timeline prepared by the Rapid Mitigation Ministry specifying the period when executive control starts and ends, and periodically reviewing said timeline, as well as progress towards decarbonisation.
- Conducting regular audits of the Ministry and other agencies involved in the Project at all government levels.
- Auditing and scrutinising government and executive actions, especially those of the Ministry, and providing periodic reports to Parliament and the public.

Several examples from existing contemporary institutions in democratic states can be used as models in designing the structure of the Rapid Mitigation Ombudsman. These include the Office of the Auditor-General and the Office of the Ombudsman itself. The Office of Auditor-General ensures the public that government entities operate and account for their performance. They conduct financial performance and long-term plan audits, carry out public enquiries, provide advice to public agencies, and support better service performance information. An Ombudsman handles complaints against government bodies, investigates, and inspects. Although these two offices investigate all complaints of maladministration, their powers are also limited. For example, the Commonwealth Ombudsman in Australia is prevented from investigating actions of a government Minister, actions of police, actions of a judge, and other actions of a few government authorities as specifically provided in *The Ombudsman Act 1976*. More legal powers than those held by some Auditors-General and the Ombudsman, therefore, are needed for scrutinising Project activities and its institutions.

The short time-horizon of democratically elected governments introduces risks to the agencies of the Project – political changes, in particular, which are prevalent in many contemporary institutions. Since the Project takes at least a decade, in its optimistic scenario, and four decades for many on a global level to accomplish, it is necessary to maintain and sustain the independence of these two agencies, and its plans, strategies, and activities. The Project and its two agencies, thus, should be institutionalised through legislation or regulation to shelter them from possible termination by a change of government. Insulating them from political changes, pressures, and shifts in policy direction ensures Project implementation and continuity regardless of the political party in administration. Some institutions in contemporary democracy assume these particular arrangements including Central Banks, elements of the judiciary and, as mentioned earlier, the Office of the Ombudsman.

Over time, Central Banks have been given increasing independence as a means to improve long-term economic performance. Since a politically susceptible Central Bank may encourage 'boom and bust' as politicians pressure them to boost economic activities before an election, Central Banks must be free from political influence. This way, political manoeuvres are avoided, thus securing the long-term national economic advantage. Independent central banks can be called in as examples. The European Union, for instance, afforded explicit independence to the European Central Bank through Article 130 of *The Lisbon Treaty* (2007). In the U.K., the Parliament has granted independence to the Bank of England through *The Bank of England Act 1998*.

Central Bank independence means its objectives, operations, and management structures are independent from any intervention from politicians, and even from the state itself. They are independent because they set their own policy objectives without responding to any pressure from the government of the day. Operationally, they are independent because they determine the best means of achieving their policy objectives including the timing and choice of mechanisms and instruments used on their own without political pressure. They are also independent because they run their operations without intervention from governments, and can, sometimes, fund themselves as commercial banks do. Following the Central Bank example, the two agencies of the Project can also be made independent in terms of their policy objectives, operations, and management structures. Nevertheless, their independence can only be best secured if they have their own legislated budgets.

It is necessary that the two mitigation agencies stick to their vital mandate, which is to implement the Project and to provide check-and-balance. Swaying away from addressing the root causes of anthropogenic climate change is likely to occur when governments, instead of implementing the corrective approach of rapid mitigation, opt for band-aid approaches, which are likely in emergency events.

As climate impacts intensify, governments will be most inclined to succumb before strong pressures from vested interests and genuinely concerned persons to direct their policies and resources towards band-aid approaches such as adaptation and geoengineering instead of rapid mitigation. Adaptation is of course necessary, but it has limited long-term effectiveness without mitigation. In the short-term, it is, indeed, easier for governments to create the appearance of effective action by funding sea walls, flood controls, dams and improved wildfire protection, among others, instead of funding rapid mitigation.

The response made by the State Governor of New Jersey following Hurricane Sandy in 2012, the deadliest and most destructive during the Atlantic hurricane season that year, offers one lucid example. After Sandy, Governor Chris Christie refused to engage with policy questions surrounding climate change, and even called climate change an 'esoteric question':

Now maybe, in the subsequent months and years, after I get done with trying to rebuild the state and put people back in their homes, I will have the opportunity to ponder the esoteric question of the cause of this storm. Right now I'm dealing with people who are out of their homes, out of their businesses because of the storm and, candidly, I don't have time to deal with it.

(See Reitmeyer and Linhorst 2013)

The statement made by Christie provides a preview of what politicians may do when governments are faced with a climate emergency. This example highlights the necessity of strong political will, where governments are enjoined to keep focused on the mandate of the Project. This also underlines the need to insulate the two institutions away from political pressure. Nevertheless, even if there is an independent institution acting as a check-and-balance agency, environmental and social justice non-government organisations, along with the media, should continue to provide countervailing forces to possible misuse of government power (cf. Delina, Diesendorf and Merson 2014; Diesendorf 2009).

Although it is crucial that governments are watched by an independent audit agency so that they focus solely on Project aims, 'watching the watchers' is another essential consideration since the Rapid Mitigation Ombudsman occupies an essential place for efficient and corruption-free Project implementation (cf. Del Villar 2003). To maintain full adherence to the rule of law, avoidance of institutionalised corruption, and maintain integrity within this agency, a range of accountability mechanisms should be in place, including: clear processes for appointment and removal of its officers; codes of conduct and guidelines with a regulatory effect on their operation; regular Parliamentary oversight; and scrutiny by other accountability agencies, such as the conventional Ombudsman, anti-corruption commissions, and Auditors-General.

In closing, 'the state,' as emphasised in this chapter, has the experience and capacity to coordinate efforts to mitigate climate change at the scale, scope, and speed required. Strategies for the Project need to be created, determined, and implemented across multiple levels of government to produce an impact commensurate with the scale, scope, and intensity required to address the root anthropogenic causes of climate change. At any rate, the governance apparatus, mechanisms, and strategies for rapid climate mitigation outlined in this chapter revive the key role of the state in large-scale, transformative, and aggressive resource mobilisation and sociotechnical transition. In the age of climate consequences, where addressing the climate issue demands a straightforward approach, governments may be compelled to adopt stronger roles as key actors to coordinate the activities for rapid mitigation. The mobilisation for climate mitigation emphasises a revitalised role for the state – structures many are familiar with that have been demonstrated to have similar capacity as they did in wartime mobilisation. At a time when contemporary capitalism seems to fail in protecting the public, the state has a role to play.

References

Abelshauser, W. 1998, 'Germany: guns, butter, and economic miracles', in M. Harrison (ed.), *The Economics of World War II: Six Great Powers in International Comparison*, Cambridge University Press, Cambridge, U.K., pp. 122–176.

Anderson, K. & Bows, A. 2012, 'A new paradigm for climate change', *Nature Climate Change*, vol. 2, pp. 639–640.

Cardozier, V.R. 1995, *The Mobilization of the United States in World War II: How the Government, Military, and Industry Prepared for War*, McFarland & Company, Jefferson, North Carolina, U.S.A.

Davidson, R. 1990, 'The advent of the modern Congress: the Legislative Reorganization Act of 1946', *Legislative Studies Quarterly*, vol. 15, pp. 357–373.

Delina, L.L. 2011, 'Asian Development Bank's support for clean energy', *Climate Policy*, vol. 11, pp. 1350–1366.

Delina, L.L. 2012, 'Coherence in energy efficiency governance', *Energy for Sustainable Development*, vol. 16, pp. 493–499.

Delina, L.L., Diesendorf, M. & Merson, J. 2014, 'Strengthening the climate action movement: strategies from histories', *Carbon Management*, vol. 5, pp. 397–409.

Del Villar, K. 2003, 'Who guards the guardians? Recent developments concerning the jurisdiction and accountability of Ombudsmen', *Australian Institute of Administrative Law Forum*, No. 36, pp. 25–53.

Dickinson, M.J. 1997, *Bitter Harvest: FDR, Presidential Power and the Growth of the Presidential Branch*, Cambridge University Press, Cambridge, U.K.

Diesendorf, M. 2009, *Climate Action: A Campaign Manual for Greenhouse Solutions*, University of New South Wales Press, Sydney, Australia.

Dryzek, J. 1992, 'Ecology and discursive democracy: beyond liberal capitalism and the administrative state', *Capitalism Nature Socialism*, vol. 3, pp. 18–42.

Fleming, T. 2001, *The New Dealers' War: FDR and the War Within World War II*, Basic Books, New York, U.S.A.

Francis 2015, *Encyclical Letter, Laudato Si' of the Holy Father Francis, On Care for our Common Home*, http://bit.ly/1Gi1Btu.

Giddens, A. 2011, *The Politics of Climate Change*, 2nd edn, Polity Press, Cambridge, U.K.

Harrison, M. 1988, 'Resource mobilization for World War II: the USA, UK, USSR, and Germany, 1938–1945', *The Economic History Review*, vol. 41, pp. 171–192.

Hirst, P. 2000, 'Democracy and governance', in J. Pierre (ed.), *Debating Governance – Authority, Steering and Democracy*, Oxford University Press, Oxford, U.K.

Levi, M. 1997, *Consent, Dissent, and Patriotism*, Cambridge University Press, New York, U.S.A.

Lloyd, E.M.H. 1924, *Experiments in State Control at the War Office and the Ministry of Food*, Clarendon Press, Oxford, U.K.

Lumer, H. 1954, *War Economy and Crisis*, New York International Publishers, New York, U.S.A.

Mayhew, D. 2005, 'Wars and American politics', *Perspectives on Politics*, vol. 3, pp. 473–493.

Milward, A.S. 1977, *War, Economy and Society, 1939–1945*, Allen Lane, London, U.K.

National Security Act 1939, Commonwealth of Australia, http://bit.ly/1soJs11.

Plumptre, A.F.W. 1941, 'Organizing the Canadian economy for war', in J.F. Parkinson (ed.), *Canadian War Economics*, University of Toronto Press, Toronto, Canada.

Poole, R. 2012, 'When everybody loved Congress', *American History*, pp. 55–59.

Reitmeyer, J. & Linhorst, M. 2013, 'Sandy recovery, not climate, on Governor Christie's radar', *North Jersey.com*, 5 February, http://bit.ly/19doQ7m.

Rosenbloom, D. 2001, '"Whose bureaucracy is this, anyway?" Congress' 1946 answer', *Political Science & Politics*, vol. 34, pp. 773–777.

Roosevelt, F.D. 1939a, *Executive Order 8248, Reorganizing the Executive Office of the President*, 8 September 1939, Washington, D.C.

Roosevelt, F.D. 1941a, *Executive Order 8629, on the Office of Production Management and the Office for Emergency Management*, 7 January 1941, Washington, D.C.

Roosevelt, F.D. 1941b, *Executive Order 8875, Establishing the Supply Priorities and Allocations Board*, 28 August 1941, Washington, D.C.

Roosevelt, F.D. 1942a, *Executive Order 9024, Establishing the War Production Board*, 16 January 1942, Washington, D.C.

Roosevelt, F.D. 1942b, *Executive Order 9250, Establishing the Office of Economic Stabilization*, 3 October 1942, Washington, D.C.

Roosevelt, F.D. 1943, *Executive Order 9347, Establishing the Office of War Mobilization*, 27 May 1943, Washington, D.C.

Smil, V. 2011, *Energy Transitions: History, Requirements, Prospects*, Praeger, Santa Barbara, California, U.S.A.

Stimson, H. & Bundy, M. 1971, *On Active Service in Peace and War*, Octagon Books, New York, U.S.A.

The Administrative Procedure Act of 1946, U.S. Congress, http://bit.ly/XLOtrN.

The Bank of England Act 1998, Parliament of the United Kingdom, http://bit.ly/MMjWV9.

The Executive Reorganization Act of 1939, U.S. Congress, http://bit.ly/1BUxwe0.

The Legislative Reorganization Act of 1946, U.S. Congress, http://bit.ly/1p8pEkZ.

The Lisbon Treaty 2007, European Union, http://bit.ly/MMiTof.

The Ombudsman Act 1976, Commonwealth of Australia, http://bit.ly/1A1Ghid.

U.S. Federal Government 1945, 'Appendix I: The War Agencies of the Executive Branch of the Federal Government', in *The United States at War: Development and Administration of the War Program by the Federal Government*, http://bit.ly/1dpdSbX.

Walker, E.R. 1939, *War-Time Economics, With Special Reference to Australia*, Melbourne University Press in association with Oxford University Press, Melbourne, Australia.

Walker, E.R. 1947, *The Australian Economy in War and Reconstruction*, Oxford University Press, New York, U.S.A.

Walker, E.R. & Foxcroft, E.J.B. 1943, 'War administration in Australia', *Public Administration Review*, vol. 3, pp. 223–239.

7 Dilemmas, implications

Convergences

The similarity and parallel special conditions between wartime mobilisation and the Rapid Mitigation Project appropriately highlight the analogy, especially when viewed through the following lenses.

International cooperation

The burden of winning the war was shared across belligerents. Alliances in both Axis and Allied states were formed such that those with more access to resources and the capacity to rapidly mobilise provided some forms of assistance to those with less capacity. In the Allied bloc, we saw this alliance occurring through the Lend-Lease Programme. The Rapid Mitigation Project requires a similar degree of multilateral cooperation including international trade of sustainable energy technology and renewable energy itself, skills and technology transfer, funding assistance for both mitigation and adaptation, and some mechanisms for compensation following damages caused by a climate-related event. Wartime cooperation was evident in the agreement of unconditional surrender, which leaders of the Allied bloc forged at Casablanca, the Lend-Lease agreement regarding munitions transfer, and post-war reconstruction. The Casablanca Agreement of unconditional surrender provides a similar arrangement on how to lock-in countries in a new rapid emissions reduction treaty, including the benefits of technology transfer and capacity strengthening from participation, the burdens of trade sanctions, and international censures for non-participation and non-cooperation. Since a universal climate agreement is highly unlikely to occur without credible stimuli, international cooperation may still be coordinated bilaterally, such as the China–U.S. climate change deal, or multilaterally.

Rapid sociotechnical transitions

Wartime mobilisation required the imposition of massive and rapid social, industrial, technical, structural, political, and economic changes. World War II brought forth high demand for new products, such as tanks, bombs, and various kind of munitions, the rapid expansion of capital funds, the increased productivity of labour and management, and the extraordinary institutional arrangements coordinating the execution of large-scale, aggressive, and transformative sociotechnical changes. In high likelihood, similar scale, scope, speed, and intensity of sociotechnical transition is needed for an accelerated approach to climate mitigation to transition the economy, and first its energy systems, to a low-carbon society. The transition requires the extensive deployment of sustainable energy technologies, the need for mobilising capital funds, new skills, labour resources, and institutional arrangements to coordinate the required changes.

Availability of technology

The majority of munitions deployed on a large scale during the war by all combatant countries were largely based on designs or prototypes developed prior to the outbreak of hostilities. What the state did was to coordinate efforts to manufacture these technologies, and diffuse them widely. Similarly, almost all of the sustainable energy technologies to be diffused are already commercially available. Of course, there are still research and development opportunities in the low-carbon scenario, including shoring up renewable energy power storage, smart grids, and increasing efficiency and capacity factors of existing technologies. Nevertheless, the capacity of the state to provide and coordinate resources for research and development of novel technologies during the war – as for the Manhattan Project to develop the atomic bomb, for instance – shows that the state has the capacity to coordinate the mobilisation of resources to develop similarly novel technology for storage and international connectivity, more particularly.

Massive public investment

The necessary investment for the Rapid Mitigation Project calls for increased scale of available public finance and the speed at which it is collected. Wartime fiscal policy innovations, seen through intensified taxation and public borrowing, are most likely to recur, albeit with modifications, to meet the scale and speed requirement of rapid mitigation finance. Taxation on high incomes, as implemented during the war, is also seen to be a prominent funding mechanism in Project execution. The 'burden of war' as allocated equitably at wartime also describes the equitable distribution of resources during the Project. Significant changes in ways we spend for things are also expected in the new regime. Innovation in existing funding mechanisms needs to be shored up to maximise opportunities for revenue collection that is fair, just, and equitable.

Increased employment opportunities

The conditions at wartime, where full employment was secured, is most likely replicated, or at least approached to a closer degree, by the Project as a result of intensive labour mobilisation strategies. Unlike labour conditions during the war, however, the transition to a low carbon economy paves the way for universal employment and improved labour conditions that aim at achieving quality of life, rather than deteriorating it.

Production controls

The staged, systematic and structured retirements, moratoria, and shutting down of high carbon production activities and technologies, including coal-fired and nuclear power plants, in the Rapid Mitigation Project are reminiscent of automobile industry production controls, for example, during wartime mobilisation. By contrast to the automobile industry, which saw substantial improvements in new production during post-war years, however, high carbon and unsustainable industries will be things of the past in a highly sustainable society following the Project. By 2050, high carbon systems have to be history.

Expansion of new industries

The expansion of the sustainable energy industry and other sectors in a low carbon economy is most likely to follow similar trajectories to munitions factories and accomplished through massive public funding, subsidies, and contracts distribution, among other strategies. Although munitions factories were shut following the conclusion of the war, the low carbon industry and sectors will persist in the new age of highly sustainable societies. Distributed sustainable energy micro-generation that is community-oriented and highly democratic will be the norm of the time, along with controlled grids that link utility-scale renewable energy to end-users.

Central planning

National governments will coordinate the Rapid Mitigation Project just as they did at wartime. The Project, following the structural design of the U.S. Office of War Mobilization and War Production Board, suggests the creation of a similarly structured agency called the Rapid Mitigation Ministry, which, like its wartime analogues, is placed a notch higher than usual ministries and provided with powers to coordinate rapid mitigation efforts at all levels of government. Learning from the lessons of wartime mobilisation arrangements, the Project calls for ways to provide checks-and-balances on the work and activities of the executive branch, particularly its special ministry, through the creation of an auditing body called the Rapid Mitigation Ombudsman.

Divergences

As with any comparisons, the analogy between mobilising for war and mobilising for rapid climate mitigation are never perfect. Broadly, the divergences are seen in the following lenses.

Timeframes and rates of deployment

The Rapid Mitigation Project, depending on national capacity and resources, is envisioned as taking 10–40 years to implement. By contrast, the timeframe at which democratic combatant countries transitioned their economies into central planning to rapidly mobilise for war was, at most, only five years, after which they reverted to their market orientations quickly.

The timeframe of the Project considers that energy technology diffusion takes time since 'there are physical limits to the rate at which new technologies can be deployed' (Kramer and Haigh 2009: 568). Vaclav Smil (2011) emphasises this limitation in his critiques of rapid energy transitions, arguing that the change requires at least three generations, or 60 years, to accomplish. Smil's (2011) observation is based on his studies of historical energy transitions and the massive and expensive cost of energy production, processing, transport, and distribution. Smil emphasised his position to this author, writing:

> There can be no rapid transition either to new sources of primary energy or to new materials: inertia of existing complex systems, their expensive capitalization, scale of the needed replacements and many inherent problems with alternative conversions and materials make any rapid shifts (that is changes that could be accomplished in less than several decades, or on the order of two generations) impossible.
>
> (Smil 2013, personal communication)

Other writers have also reported that aggregate energy transitions – those involving an entire economy – could even take centuries, since they depend on the switch in fuels and technologies for multiple energy services in different sectors (see Fouquet 2010; Allen 2009; Mokyr 2009). Nevertheless, a three-generation timescale is debatable, especially in the context of the rapid innovation and the declining costs of sustainable energy technologies, which have accelerated their contemporary diffusions.

Wind capacity, for example, has been growing at 20% to 30% per year and solar photovoltaic (PV) at 30% to 40% per year for decades on a global scale (Worldwatch Institute 2013; Global Wind Energy Council (GWEC) (2013). GWEC (2013) reported that 45 GW of wind capacity had been installed globally in 2012, a six-fold increase from 7 GW a decade earlier. The Worldwatch Institute (2013) reports that solar PV installed capacity grew by 41% between 2011 and 2012. Between 2007 and 2012, the Institute also reported that the installed PV capacity grew by an order of magnitude from 10 GW to 100 GW (Worldwatch Institute 2013).

Such high rates of growth are possible because wind and solar technologies are manufactured in factories and the installation is generally standardised and rapid. The wartime story of industrial mobilisation had similar undertones, which makes the analogy more sensible. Sustainable energy technologies in contemporary times are more akin to information technology (IT) than they are to central fossil fuelled or nuclear power stations, which they are replacing (Gilding 2015). Paul Gilding (2015) argues that IT and sustainable energy technologies follow a closely similar business pattern 'where prices keep falling, quality keeps rising, change is rapid and market disruption is normal and constant.' This pattern is in contrast to fossil-fuelled technologies, which follow a pattern where prices increase as demand expands because new fossil reserves cost more to develop (Gilding 2015).

Despite differences on timing, there is some common ground. As Smil (2011) points out, the Project could never be realised as quickly as one decade as proposed by, for example, Al Gore (2008) for the U.S.A., and Wright and Hearps (2010) for Australia. The Project assumes the timeframe for a full transition to renewable energy will take well in excess of ten years, a position shared by some (e.g. Anderson 2013; Diesendorf 2010). The Project, under circumstances of strong state intervention, will still likely require a more than one decade window for developed countries, and may extend to 40 years at the global level.

Trigger events

The American wartime mobilisation intensified only with the formal entry of the U.S.A. to World War II following the Japanese attack on Pearl Harbor. The attack provided a visceral and physical trigger event for the U.S.A. to embark on an intensified mobilisation. Some writers have argued that humans need to be surprised to trigger an accelerated approach to climate mitigation (cf. Wagner and Zeckhauser 2012). Climate impacts, however, are a series of or parallel events in contrast to the single trigger event provided by Pearl Harbor. They are also not location-exclusive, although more of these impacts are expected in coastal communities and equatorial countries. Moreover, the impacts can be extremely catastrophic, given the 'fat tail' distributions of climate risks (Weitzman 2009).

The use of climate impacts as trigger events for accelerated climate mitigation, thus, is problematic since governments may instead opt for securing the survival of citizens first instead of embarking on rapid climate mitigation, which is a long-term work. Climate tipping points can also trigger governments to employ short-term responses such as mega-adaptation, intense border security control, and even risky geoengineering. Nevertheless, the spatial and temporal uncertainties surrounding the occurrence of large-scale climate tipping points and the intensity and scale of resulting devastations should galvanise the argument for early and accelerated climate action, not the other way around. Taking the Project as an insurance against the huge risks of climate impacts is much more sensible than taking ineffective action.

Technology mix

The technology mix of the Rapid Mitigation Project relies heavily on renewable energy coupled with greater energy efficiency. This portfolio is different from the munitions portfolio during the war where all kind of armaments, including the devastating atomic bomb, were deployed. Fossil gas, new nuclear energy, and geoengineering are excluded in the technology portfolio because of their risks, and the time required for their construction and diffusion (see Chapter 2). The saliency of these competing technologies, nonetheless, are likely to increase especially in a political environment where demand to consider all possible technological options ramps up. Several crucial climate policy players, China and India included, invest substantially in nuclear energy expansions, for instance. In addition, China and India, as well as the U.S.A., Australia, and South Africa, still have substantial coal reserves and politically powerful coal industries. These interests are expected to lobby for pursuing the nuclear option and coal with carbon capture and storage (CCS).

Geoengineering strategies also represent another probable inclusion in the technology mix because of their theoretical potential to technically and quickly control the climate. Under the circumstances of a dramatic catastrophic scenario, policymakers and the public might insist they cannot afford to wait as the sustainable energy transition unfolds in more than one decade. Having, we assume, already crossed at least one catastrophic tipping point, policy-makers will be more motivated to avoid crossing another. There would, therefore, be no shortage of proponents to press geoengineering options as solutions. Some would again likely argue for the potential of geoengineering to significantly mitigate climate impacts without necessarily transforming the global economy (e.g. Keith 2013). With high likelihood, therefore, some policymakers could end up seizing on geoengineering as a backstop to buy time for the sustainable energy transition to take hold.

Political reluctance

Political ineffectiveness means many governments will be reluctant to support the Rapid Mitigation Project. Many growth-orientated governments, especially in the developed world and in emerging economies, may object to the execution of the Project since it questions consumer cultures. Some governments are even captives of fossil fuel interests (Pearse 2007; cf. Diesendorf 2009: 85), and many may rebuff the idea citing challenges regarding free-riding.

Climate mitigation has also been stymied by a generational dilemma since the threat of unmitigated climate change is long-term but the action required is short-, medium-, and long-term. Unlike the threat of war, which was imminent and to which politicians, when convinced, responded with decisiveness, climate change represents a long-term threat to those who have always thought about short-term election cycles. It is, therefore, unlikely, that governments will adopt the Project without strong countervailing pressure for action from the public, robust social, political, technical and economic incentives to undertake these activities, a legally binding international climate agreement, or a combination of the above.

In the same vein, although the legal arrangements of contemporary democracy contain provisions for governments to access extraordinary powers in an emergency, these powers are unlikely to be invoked by politicians unless a threat is properly justified, becomes imminent, and there is strong support for emergency-like action from a large majority of the population. As with wartime, the government-led Rapid Mitigation Project will most likely be implemented only when life-threatening situations become more apparent and affect a large majority of the population. Nonetheless, this remains unguaranteed.

Susceptibility to coercion

There also lurks the fear of a coercive government, even with a multi-party transition cabinet, in a powerful executive branch provided with access to emergency and extraordinary powers. The Project, therefore, could end up as a warrant for heavy-handed government intervention in national and even global economic activity, and perhaps control of personal activities (cf. Oreskes 2011: 224).

Despite legislation on the Project's timeframe, the presence of a Rapid Mitigation Ombudsman, and the availability of other avenues for redress, there could be no guarantee of a return to a state of normal democracy at Project conclusion. History tends to support this scenario. Brian Martin (1990) analysed post-crisis political affairs and found that voluntary termination of emergency powers does not always occur. State executives often defend their 'right' to remain in position as long as possible, despite constitutional requirements to prevent the extension of authoritarian regimes. In some historical episodes, terminating emergency power was only possible after strong and widespread public condemnation, huge public protest (e.g. the deposition of Ferdinand Marcos in the Philippines in 1986), or a violent revolution.

Corruption and oligarchy

The potential for corruption arising from an oligarchy may persist in the Project's timeframe. Wartime experience suggests the danger of creating a similar situation where few privileged persons, mostly industrialists, were provided easy access to guaranteed contracts and other wide-scale powers ensuring their prosperity even at wartime through friendly and protective institutional arrangements (Cardozier 1995). The War Production Board, which became the primary U.S. government agency for wartime mobilisation between 1942 and 1945, fell into the hands of business leaders. Throughout the war, the name of the industrialist Donald Nelson became synonymous with wartime mobilisation. Other businesspersons also successfully secured key posts in governments including prominent roles in the administration of powerful civilian agencies. The revival of oligarchic governance is, therefore, likely but with greater consequences than what was experienced at wartime considering the scale, scope, and timeframe of the Project. With few persons in power, decision-making, coordinating, and administering Project activities could destroy representativeness in democracy.

Limited public engagement

The exclusivity of state-led mobilisation tends to disregard the value of public engagement in the execution of climate mitigation activities and programmes. In many ways, this arrangement – without mechanisms for participation and engagement – could undermine democratic fundamentals including the ability of the public to actively participate and engage in issues of public importance. The strong leaning towards macro-level actions generated at and flowing from top to bottom could also diminish, marginalise, and exclude the importance of local and community actions. Since the means of diffusing sustainable energy technology will be accomplished also through distributed micro-generation – not only in centralised, large-scale approaches – the state should use the period of transition to enlarge democratic participation of households and local communities in transition-related programmes.

As with any other public programme, there is also no guarantee of support for the Project from a large majority of the population. For these strategies to succeed, the state must rely to a great extent on the public's willing cooperation. The wartime mobilisation experience was different since there was – at a time before support inevitably slumped – strong public support for mobilisation programmes such as wartime bonds, rationing, and victory gardens. Wartime experience suggests public support for this kind of programme might not last beyond five years, and with constant ongoing threats. Since the Project requires at least ten years, at most 40 years to implement, an accelerated approach to climate mitigation is likely to fail without strong support from citizens.

The state should, therefore, ensure that the public adequately supports and engages with the Project. At the very least, citizens should be informed about the Project, its rationale, and its repercussions before it is implemented. This entails explaining the need for urgent action, and obtaining a mandate for a specified period of at least one decade for the creation of the two institutions and for the kind of strategies to be implemented. Merely 'informing the public', however, does not guarantee strong and lasting public support, and could even backfire. For a successful and sustainable policy implementation, citizens must be given the opportunity to participate in and engage with the development of the policies, as partners and not mere receivers.

The limits of the book

Although this book offers some non-technical solutions that achieve rapid emissions reduction, and critically analyses and interrogates these strategies, it offers no silver bullet. And while the scenario developed and presented here sounds promising, it has the potential to become 'black box'-like and can conceal potential conflicts and negative consequences (cf. Trutnevyte, Stauffacher and Scholz 2011; Berkhout 2006). For a vision to be effective, it needs to be socially viable and analytically sound (Trutnevyte 2014). The rapid mitigation scenario, which is a product of a *Gedankenexperiment*, has its strengths and weaknesses, and although modelled and projected to be economically, technically, and politically plausible, can hardly be considered the best vision.

The contingency strategies and plans developed and reported as scenarios are generic. Mitigation strategies are produced generally for governments in high-emission countries but without considerations of their specific capacities for and ongoing advances in technological innovation, manufacturing, and diffusion. This book acknowledges that every country, state, or province, town or city has distinct natural endowments that it can or cannot tap. For instance, mid-latitude countries generally have high solar potential, and those at high latitudes generally have high wind potential. Countries have also diverse political, economic, social, and cultural arrangements that must be considered. An American Rapid Mitigation Project may be different in execution and governance from a Chinese programme. China, however, in high likelihood, can adopt the suggested contingency plan quicker than other high-emission states in democratic governments since its powerful single-party central government may already have the political inclination to do so.

The changes in technology provided by sustainable energy transition do not represent the whole solution to the climate challenge. Changing high-emission technologies only addresses one driver of environmental destruction, which at some conceptual level also includes growth in economic activity and population (cf. Dietz and O'Neill 2013; Daly and Farley 2004; cf. Feng et al. 2015). Decelerating consumption and addressing population growth are as essential as changing unsustainable energy systems; thus, they too must be included when designing rapid mitigation strategies. Partly, this book provides some of the strategies, but does not claim an exhaustive and comprehensive exploration. Deeper analysis also suggests climate change is but an externality of the socio-political condition we, since the dawn of Industrial Revolution, are in. This means that addressing climate change will most likely require a tectonic social shift that goes beyond a mere technofix. Some writers have already argued for a review of the neoliberal agenda (e.g. Klein

2014; Anderson and Bows 2012). Again, although this book tackles some of these issues, it does not claim to be a comprehensive exposition of such a shift.

In addition, the technologies and activities for sustainable energy deployment outlined in this scenario are not completely emission free. In many ways, they too contribute to carbon emissions, especially during mining the raw materials and in the manufacturing processes. Rare earth elements essential to sustainable energy technology development include: dysprosium, whose high magnetic strength is used in hybrid and electric vehicles and in wind turbine generators; europium used in compact fluorescent lamps; neodymium used in high-strength permanent magnets for electric vehicles and wind turbines; terbium for LED lighting; yttrium also for lighting; cerium for batteries in hybrid and electric vehicles and also for efficient light bulbs; indium, a critical component of copper indium gallium diselenide solar panels; lanthanum for batteries in hybrid vehicles; and tellurium for cadmium-telluride solar panels (Arent et al. 2014, Appendix A). To say sustainable energy technologies are zero emission technologies, therefore, is erroneous. Moreover, mining and processing these elements have social, institutional, political, and environmental implications that must be accounted for in the Project conception, design, and implementation. For all the life cycles of the technologies that are dependent on these elements, however, emissions are much less than those of fossil fuel technologies (Moomaw et al. 2011). In the long-term, as energy inputs become increasingly renewable, life-cycle emissions from sustainable energy technologies are expected to decline and reach close to zero.

Possible conflicts and negative consequences can arise from implementation of the Project. I acknowledge these conflicts by providing some practical examples. For instance, the renewable energy vision in a region in Austria, despite its noble objective, polarised the public when this vision was mainstreamed in local discourses (Spath and Rohracher 2010). Those critical of certain technologies were branded an 'annoyance' when in fact their insights on the likely negative consequences of these technologies could have been used to increase the legitimacy of the vision (Spath and Rohracher 2010: 454). Similar contestations can be expected, especially when the Project goes to scale.

Social and environmental impacts on source countries, mostly in the tropics, include deforestation and relocation of indigenous peoples (Scholz 2011), which could cause conflicts, if not effectively addressed. Note also that any combustion sources, such as corn ethanol, cellulosic ethanol, soy biodiesel, algae biodiesel, biomass for electricity, and other biofuels have limits in their potential to fully reduce GHG emissions to near zero. In addition, they can also have significant land-use, water-use, or resource availability issues (Jacobson 2009; Delucchi 2010). According to some studies, even the most climate-friendly and ecologically acceptable sources of ethanol, such as unmanaged, mixed grasses restored to their native, non-agricultural habitat can cause air pollution mortality on the same order as diesel or gasoline (Jacobson 2007; Anderson 2009; Ginnebaugh, Liang and Jacobson 2010). At any rate, these resources can be sustainably grown, harvested from crop residues, and processed making them better alternatives than climate change-inducing fossil fuels.

This book's focus on state-led approaches, activities, and programmes can miss an essential strand in climate mitigation: citizen and/or grassroots-organised activities. The book has neither discussed nor critically analysed the emergence of many citizen-led approaches on climate mitigation, which have been largely successful at various levels and have already gained traction. The ongoing transitions in communities, towns, and cities as I argue in my contingent researches, are key in climate mitigation narratives (e.g. Delina, Diesendorf and Merson 2014). Stronger public engagement strengthens the position that governments do not have all the solutions for climate change; instead, it underlines that for a complex challenge such as climate change, multiple, multilevel, and plural sets of approaches are essential. While large-scale centralised options are held as key in the rapid transition, small-scale, distributed approaches may be essential, especially in scaling.

State-led policy and strategies, without due consideration of the diverse social processes, would stand weakly as an effective approach for rapid mitigation. Nevertheless, I have decided to focus the orientation of this book on the key role of the state, since, among other reasons, this locus of action has the experience and capacity to accomplish large-scale, aggressive, and transformative policy and programme management. This brings about the need for an entirely new volume that specifically deals with how collaborative activities between governments, whichever level they may be, and civil society, where citizens are ensured of their active engagement in the process, become key strands in the climate mitigation narrative.

Despite this book's promise to rapidly decarbonise the global economy through aggressive strategies to transition energy systems, one key limitation also needs to be acknowledged: the combined inertia of the carbon cycle and the human economy. This means the current generation and, most likely, the next would not see most of the benefits of reduced climate change if the envisaged Rapid Mitigation Project is implemented today. The carbon cycle's inertia dictates even aggressive emissions reduction now has few effects since climate impacts have a high likelihood of occurring anyway. Cutting emissions only limits climate risk for future generations, yet it increases current costs – with pain felt most strongly by today's poor. The Project, therefore, once implemented, should be taken more as an insurance mechanism to hedge against future physical, social and natural impacts.

This book also has its limitations regarding its methods. Although comparative analysis and qualitative scenario building approaches are complementary, each has their own methodological challenges, which, early on this book, I have acknowledged (see Introduction chapter). I accept, therefore, that finding more improved data collection and analysis methods to overcome these limitations, and to extend the exploration and debates on what ought to constitute an accelerated approach to climate mitigation, is a vital component for future studies.

References

Allen, R.C. 2009, *The British Industrial Revolution in Global Perspective*, Cambridge University Press, Cambridge, U.K.

Anderson, K. 2013, 'Avoiding dangerous climate change', The Radical Emissions Reduction Conference, 10–11 December 2013, The Royal Society, London, U.K., http://bit.ly/1bvfVsj.

Anderson, K. & Bows, A. 2012, 'A new paradigm for climate change', *Nature Climate Change*, vol. 2, pp. 639–640.

Anderson, L.G. 2009, 'Ethanol fuel use in Brazil: air quality impacts', *Energy and Environmental Science*, vol. 2, pp. 1015–1037.

Arent, D., Pless, J., Mai, T., Wiser, R., Hand, M., Baldwin, S. et al. 2014, 'Implication of high renewable electricity penetration in the U.S. for water use, greenhouse gas emissions, land-use, and materials supply', *Applied Energy*, vol. 123, pp. 368–377.

Berkhout, F. 2006, 'Normative expectations in systems innovation', *Technology Analysis and Strategic Management*, vol. 18, pp. 299–311.

Cardozier, V.R. 1995, *The Mobilization of the United States in World War II: How the Government, Military, and Industry Prepared for War*, McFarland & Company, Jefferson, North Carolina, U.S.A.

Daly, H.E. & Farley, J. 2004, *Ecological Economics: Principles and Applications*, Island Press, Washington, D.C., U.S.A.

Delina, L.L., Diesendorf, M. & Merson, J. 2014, 'Strengthening the climate action movement: strategies from histories', *Carbon Management*, vol. 5, pp. 397–409.

Delucchi, M. 2010, 'Impacts of biofuels on climate, land, and water', *Annals of the New York Academy of Sciences*, vol. 1195, pp. 28–45.

Diesendorf, M. 2009, *Climate Action: A Campaign Manual for Greenhouse Solutions*, University of New South Wales Press, Sydney, Australia.

Diesendorf, M. 2010, 'Ambitious target does not quite measure up', *Ecos*, vol. 157, p. 30.

Dietz, R. & O'Neill, D. 2013, *Enough is Enough: Building a Sustainable Economy in a World of Finite Resources*, Berrett-Koehler Publishers, San Francisco, California, U.S.A.

Feng, K., Davis, S.J., Sun, L. & Hubacek, K. 2015, 'Drivers of the US CO_2 emissions 1997–2013', *Nature Communications*, doi: 10.1038/ncomms8714.

Fouquet, R. 2010, 'The slow search for solutions: lessons from historical energy transitions by sector and service', *Energy Policy*, vol. 38, pp. 6586–6596.

Gilding, P. 2015, 'Don't be fossil fooled – It's time to say goodbye', 13 July, http://bit.ly/1HY4hLl.

Ginnebaugh, D.L., Liang, J. & Jacobson, M. 2010, 'Examining the temperature dependence of ethanol (E85) versus gasoline emissions on air pollution with a largely-explicit chemical mechanism', *Atmospheric Environment*, vol. 44, pp. 1192–1199.

Global Wind Energy Council (GWEC) 2013, *Global Wind Statistics 2012*, GWEC, Brussels, Belgium, http://bit.ly/1adSutq.

Gore, A. 2008, *A Generational Challenge to Repower America*, http://bit.ly/1bRDQlB.

Jacobson, M. 2007, 'Effects of ethanol (E85) versus gasoline vehicles on cancer and mortality in the United States', *Environmental Science and Technology*, vol. 41, pp. 4150–4157.

Jacobson, M. 2009, 'Review of solutions to global warming, air pollution, and energy security', *Energy and Environmental Science*, vol. 2, pp. 148–173.

Keith, D. 2013, *A Case for Climate Engineering*, The MIT Press, Cambridge, Massachusetts, U.S.A.

Klein, N. 2014, *This Changes Everything: Capitalism vs. The Climate*, Simon & Schuster, New York, U.S.A.

Kramer, G.J. & Haigh, M. 2009, 'No quick switch to low-carbon energy', *Nature*, vol. 462, pp. 568–569.

Martin, B. 1990, 'Politics after a nuclear crisis', *Journal of Libertarian Studies*, vol. 9, pp. 69–78.

Mokyr, J. 2009, *The Enlightened Economy*, Penguin Books, London, U.K.

Moomaw, W., Burgher, P., Heath, G., Lenzen, M., Nyboer, J. & Verbruggen, A. 2011, 'Annex II: methodology', in O. Edenhofer, R. Pichs-Madruga, Y. Sokona, K. Seyboth, P. Matschoss, S. Kadner et al. (eds), *IPCC Special Report on Renewable Energy Sources and Climate Change Mitigation*, Cambridge University Press, Cambridge, U.K; New York, U.S.A., pp. 973–1000.

Oreskes, N. 2011, 'Metaphors of warfare and the lessons of history: time to revisit a carbon tax', *Climatic Change*, vol. 104, pp. 223–230.

Pearse, G. 2007, *High and Dry: John Howard, Climate Change and the Selling of Australia's Future*, Penguin, Cambelwood, Victoria, Australia.

Scholz, R.W. 2011, *Environmental Literacy in Science and Society: From Knowledge to Decisions*, Cambridge University Press, Cambridge, U.K.

Smil, V. 2011, *Energy Transitions: History, Requirements, Prospects*, Praeger, Santa Barbara, California, U.S.A.

Smil, V. 2013, personal communication to the author, email, 17 May. Used with permission.

Spath, P. & Rohracher, H. 2010, '"Energy regions": the transformative power of regional discourses on socio-technical futures', *Research Policy*, vol. 39, pp. 449–458.

Trutnevyte, E. 2014, 'The allure of energy visions: are some visions better than others?' *Energy Strategy Reviews*, vol. 2, pp. 211–219.

Trutnevyte, E., Stauffacher, M. & Scholz, R.W. 2011, 'Supporting energy initiatives in small communities by linking visions with energy scenarios and multi-criteria assessment', *Energy Policy*, vol. 39, pp. 7884–7895.

Wagner, G. & Zeckhauser, R.J. 2012, 'Climate policy: hard problem, soft thinking', *Climatic Change*, vol. 110, pp. 507–521.

Weitzman, M.L. 2009, 'On modeling and interpreting the economics of catastrophic climate change', *The Review of Economics and Statistics*, vol. 91, pp. 1–19.

Worldwatch Institute 2013, 'Growth of global solar and wind energy continues to outpace other technologies', *Vital Signs Online*, 30 July, http://bit.ly/1ep15qR.

Wright, M. & Hearps, P. 2010, *Australian Sustainable Energy: Zero Carbon Australia Stationary Energy Plan*, University of Melbourne Energy Research Institute, Melbourne, Australia.

Conclusion

Unmitigated climate change poses physical, ecological, social, economic, and institutional threats. Ineffective mitigation has already impacted many lives and disrupted social orders; we can anticipate prolonged human misery in *the age of climate consequences* as more climate-related impacts push societies to the brink of unimaginable crises. Several historical examples have shown how climate change and social crises are closely intertwined. To avoid warming beyond +2°C – which does not necessarily mean a safe threshold – mitigation should be rapid and cognizant of the scale and scope required to transition away from high carbon infrastructure. Global greenhouse gas (GHG) emissions must peak by 2020, be reduced to close to zero by 2040 or 2050, and continue to dive into negative levels by 2100 to avoid major impacts from climate change. The climate challenge, therefore, has temporal and structural properties, which means that addressing it requires dramatic, aggressive, and large-scale innovations in technological, industrial, and socio-economic arrangements.

While these narratives sound burdensome, climate action, in many respects, is rife with opportunities and benefits. These, however, are possible only if action is taken soon.

The challenge to address climate change is brought to the fore by rigorous scientific observations and measurements showing emissions from human activities have not been effectively curtailed. Atmospheric GHG concentrations have already reached a level never before breached by human civilisation. Yet, response to the challenge remains ineffective, lacklustre, and does not measure up.

After more than 20 years, the internationally agreed United Nations Framework Convention on Climate Change (UNFCCC), advances in scientific knowledge and observations, the availability of technological solutions to change energy systems responsible for most of the emissions, and the record-breaking extreme events impacting lives have proved unable to successfully reverse our collective understanding that climate action needs to be rapid and stringent. The near-futile response to curbing emissions can be ascribed to the relentless pursuit of high carbon-based industrialisation driven by tenacious free markets and intense globalisation, which persist in many countries' primary development orientation. Free-riding in international agreements also remains a challenge for achieving collective and meaningful mitigation. The neoliberal agenda underpinning this posture has hijacked many governments, which shrunk not only in size but also in power to regulate and coordinate efforts to address societal challenges – including the most important challenge of our time, climate change.

To maximise opportunity to harvest potential benefits of climate action – including minimising the burdens of climate change – these systemic challenges need to be addressed aggressively.

Of the many drivers of human-induced climate change, burning fossil-based fuels to generate electricity and heat and to power transportation is the biggest contributor to global GHG emissions. Quickly changing these technologies and effectively transitioning to sustainable energy through a *Rapid Mitigation Project* will likely lead to substantial emissions reduction, thereby minimising future impacts. Fortunately, the technological means to accomplish most of the sustainable energy transition are already commercially available, demonstrated to be effective, and are decreasing in price. This is where huge opportunities can be found; hence, this book's principal orientation.

Other suggested options to abate emissions, such as nuclear energy, fossil gas, and geoengineering, promise on paper to deliver emissions reduction, but could only crowd out investment for renewable energy sources and delay their diffusion. In addition, these competing technologies are environmentally and socially risky and expensive. Compared to commercially available sustainable energy technologies, they also take much longer to construct. For rapid emissions reduction, therefore, the technical options provided by sustainable energy technologies – not nuclear power, fossil gas and geoengineering – offer the most optimal option.

This book complements many quantitative modelling and other technical works showing the plausibility of high sustainable energy penetrations at the state, national, regional, and global levels. With technological strategies already addressed robustly by others, this book provides the non-technical approaches on state-led mobilisation for rapid GHG emissions reduction. This book contributes to sociotechnical transition scholarship as one of a few to envision a transition in the context of a challenging timeframe and rate of mitigation. In occupying this niche, this book is also the first, to the best of my knowledge, to discuss, examine, and critique the socio-technical interface between mobilising for war and mobilising for climate mitigation.

Although the technology is already available, diffusing it, especially in the *scale, speed and scope* that concurs with the requirements for an accelerated approach to climate mitigation, has long been delayed. Policy to support its diffusion in many countries remains below par. Short-termism, free-riding, political myopia, and the political power of vested interests collude to prevent many governments from providing leadership and coordination to initiate policy and deploy programmes aimed at rapid mitigation. The neoliberal

paradigm, which is deeply entrenched in the governance of many contemporary democracies, has also tolerated ineffective climate response. Only
a paradigm shift in the mode and arrangements of governance can make
rapid climate mitigation proceed at the required speed. This entails bringing
the state back into core contemporary governance architecture and
strengthening its pivotal role in climate policy.

This book used a *Gedankenexperiment* through a thinking-aloud protocol
in envisaging a qualitative scenario where the state re-assumes its original
purpose: to protect citizens against harm. This arrangement is not new.
Indeed, the state has been a pivotal actor when markets failed, and in creating
new spaces for new kinds of markets to thrive. This book underscores the
role of the state in paving a new pathway for a sustainable regime that not only
addresses anthropogenic climate change to its core but also opens up new
opportunities for envisioning democracy and social goods, and in reaping
other co-benefits of the transition. This pathway involves activities for rapid
mitigation through sustainable energy transition.

To track this new course, the transition calls for a structured and organised
mobilisation of financial and labour resources and the re-alignment of the state's
political, social, and institutional arrangements and mechanisms to allow the
rapid diffusion of demonstrated and proven climate mitigation technologies.

To contribute to the discussion about how we can accomplish this task, this
book presented a review of World War II mobilisations to provide evidence
on the capacity of the state to implement aggressive, large-scale, transformative,
and rapid mobilisation processes. These historical moments are also used as
a model for envisaging *legislation, control, and oversight* mechanisms necessary
for the state to pursue effective mobilisation.

This book has shown that generic strategies for mobilising finance and
labour for rapid mitigation are attainable. Since wartime mobilisation illustrates
the capacity of many national governments to provide leadership necessary to
mobilise vital, yet limited, resources, this book offers lessons on the processes that would ensure less cumbersome and thus more effective state-led
mobilisation.

In implementing the Rapid Mitigation Project, innovations in governments
are essential, underscoring the priority need to provide 'new' and additional
power to the executive branch. These political innovations, however, can
only materialise if a series of events occur that create a visceral need for such
extraordinary action. In the scenario developed, the driver for a state-led,
centrally coordinated Project is assumed to be more severe than what drove
the U.S.A. to join the Great War in 1941.

Following insights from behavioural studies, catastrophic climate events
such as the West Antarctic Ice Sheet collapse, or similar large-scale black
swan events – which are quite likely to occur – may provide the stimuli for
the scenario to eventuate. Although I am not particularly at ease using this
scenario, behavioural studies suggest that it could be the only driver for
mitigation that could deliver required emissions reduction. The scenario

assumes that a *Rapid Mitigation Agreement* is forged either following these not-so-bright events.

Unlike previous and contemporary climate agreements, however, this new agreement has built-in strong sanctions on non-participation, while underlining the many potential incentives for participation. There is no guarantee that a legally binding and stringent agreement such as this will be forged – even with catastrophic stimuli. Multilateral level politics, despite the relative success of the Paris climate summit, remain complex and messy, and fraught with uncertainties.

This book's spatial focus has been on nation-states and multiple levels: states or provinces, cities or municipalities, and local communities. The scenario assumes the suspension of some aspects of free markets in favour of state planning akin to pre-1970s welfare states. In terms of supporting the large-scale transition, the leading role of the state in mobilisation for climate action is key in fixing market failures to address it, while actively shaping and creating new markets for the sustainable energy regime. The locus of action is large-scale emissions reduction from the energy sector – the largest contributor to anthropogenic GHG emissions.

In this revitalised role, governments provide leadership and coordinate a programmed mobilisation project involving structured, systematic, and staged phase-out of fossil-based technologies, especially fossil-fuelled power stations and motor vehicles, systematically replacing them with demonstrated and commercially available sustainable energy technologies. In accomplishing the transition, this book provides some financial, labour, and governance strategies. The strategies are generic in design, since they are intended to be general guidelines in developing state-oriented rapid mitigation programmes.

Using the lessons provided by the climate-war analogy, the following parallel strategies for the accelerated approach to financial mobilisation can be envisaged.

- Instituting a rapidly increasing price on GHG emissions.
- Providing financial incentives to sectors working on emission abatements.
- Reviewing existing financial schemes, including the institutionalisation of climate mitigation bonds.
- Revising universal income taxation in favour of progressive consumption tax.
- Abolishing fossil subsidies and realigning non-transition related expenditures.

To prepare the necessary requirements for labour, strategies developed include:

- Conducting labour requirement and availability analyses.
- Incentivising education and training relevant to rapid mitigation.
- Ensuring quality of life with a progressive labour policy.

The strategies for rapid mitigation following a wartime mobilisation model entail a stronger form of governance, where the executive branch of government coordinates a predominantly top-down approach to mitigation. The long-term challenge of climate mitigation necessitates insulating rapid mitigation institutions from party political pressure and changes in government administration. For the Project to work and following wartime insights, governments must create new specialised public institutions and endow them with necessary mobilisation powers. Two special institutions are suggested:

- A special cabinet-level Ministry for Rapid Mitigation to coordinate and implement the Project.
- A check and balance institution, called the Rapid Mitigation Ombudsman, to audit the Ministry's works and powers.

The strategies arising from using wartime mobilisation as model for rapid climate mitigation highlight the use of political and economic tools and approaches that may be unfamiliar to the modern, deregulated mode of government in capitalist, neoliberal, democratic states. The Project's assertion of a revitalised welfare state with national public planning and strong command-and-control regulations strongly counters the prevailing neoliberal system. The political and social picture in the envisaged Project, however, appears to be less foreign. This picture closely resembles the mode of governance during the war, as well as in democratic welfare states from post-war until mid-1970s.

In coordinating organisational resources for mobilising labour and finance, governments are brought back as central political actors. The state has proven structures and arrangements that could provide a critical context for legitimising collective decisions for rapid mobilisation. It maintains political, legal and economic arrangements that hold societies in order. The return to welfare state and central planning in executing rapid mitigation, nonetheless, should always be reconciled with democracy by extending, instead of constraining, freedoms. This has to be non-negotiable.

The sheer scale and scope of mobilisation for war seem to be commensurate with the urgency requirements of the accelerated approach to climate mitigation. This, among others, rationalises the analogy, but it does not lend perfection to it. With *dilemmas and implications* surrounding the analogy carefully examined, this book has offered critical insights on the relevance, utility, and appropriateness of its contingency plan, and the institutional arrangements of the plan.

This book addresses the question: can previous wartime mobilisations provide a model for contemporary policies to quickly, yet effectively, reduce GHG emissions? Stating it another way: Is wartime mobilisation a suitable policy model for rapid mitigation? Although replicability is difficult to study, the theoretical, policy, practical, institutional, and social implications of the underlying question – Can climate change be mitigated in a way that its impacts are reduced? – are too essential to avoid.

Although there is much to learn from wartime experience, state-led strategies for rapid mitigation have serious limitations. These challenges include lesser likelihood for:

- Governments to adopt aggressive mitigation policies such as those proposed in the Project in the absence of life-threatening events that can be directly linked to climate change.
- Governments to initiate the Project, considering existing power relations between the state and wealthy private interests.
- Politicians to support emergency measures for fear of losing corporate support and, in countries with large fossil fuel reserves, tax revenues.
- Politicians to support any policy on tax increase, especially on the scale required by the Project since it could mean losing public support and votes.
- Governments to give up their power once it is granted to them.
- Governments to put more public resources into rapid mitigation especially in events of life-threatening situations where overall sentiment tends more towards adaptation and, possibly, geoengineering.
- The public to provide full support for a government-led, centrally controlled climate action.

Even when legislative mandates are provided for stronger executive governments, this arrangement – unless provided with strong mechanisms for review – could still lead to:

- A coercive government.
- The weakening of democratic processes.
- Possible absence of long-term public support.
- The danger of having unaccountable government executives.
- The possibility of governments taking alternative solutions such as geoengineering and large-scale adaptation, which promise to address the climate challenge, but unnecessarily and indirectly address its root causes.

In scrutinising the wartime mobilisation analogy, challenges, shortcomings, and limitations have surfaced, theoretically and methodologically. This book, nonetheless, demonstrates that scholars, policymakers, and the public can take a reasoned look at the relative replicability of some episodes in human histories, even though comparing them with modern and future challenges remains contentious and imperfect. At the very least, this book suggests that the analogy could be used to inform, incite, and excite contemporary visions for rapid climate mitigation. It also sets a new agenda for debates in a Post-Paris climate regime.

Restructuring the existing socio-economic arrangements for rapid climate mitigation, as shown in this book, is indeed more complex than fighting a world war. If implemented, these strategies are just the first wave of a truly effective climate mitigation strategy. The second wave must involve embedding these strategies in institutions, not only within the political structures of governments but also – and most importantly – within the social and cultural structures that are shaping human societies.

This book's limitations open avenues for future research. These include: improving methods; widening scope; exploring opportunities for iterative learning; investigating new modes of governance; applying the generic strategies in national contexts; and envisaging a strengthened role for citizen-based rapid climate mitigation approaches.

First, historical and contemporary comparisons are never exact. Although comparative analysis can be used to extract lessons, the similarities, parallels, and analogies identified in this book are never universal. The climate change challenge is unique and, inarguably, more complex than any other problem to have engulfed humanity, including world wars. On a per country basis and even within the state itself, responses to climate change will also be expectedly unique. Future research about developing climate mitigation strategies, therefore, needs to employ other innovative research methods that take complexities and varieties into account.

Second, climate change impacts are not solely a function of inappropriate technology. Although this book's main focus has been on envisioning strategies for the rapid diffusion of technological alternatives to high carbon technologies through sustainable energy transition, which is essential in rapid mitigation, it does not claim that technological transition alone would be sufficient. Strategies need to be envisioned in agriculture and forestry sectors, and in realms of excessive consumption, population growth, and economic inequalities. Holistic analysis of accelerated approaches to climate mitigation encompassing multiple sectors and trajectories remains valid.

Third, human innovations, be they technical or social or a combination, are highly uncertain, unpredictable, and contentious processes. There will never be a predetermined, single pathway to mobilise for rapid climate mitigation. Since an iterative robust decision-making could help in reducing uncertainty over time, thereby increasing the likelihood of success, opportunities for iterative learning that could be embraced within governmental policymaking need to be part of future research inquiry. Other social tools and technologies that the state can use to strategise mitigation approaches, which allow iterative learning to thrive, should also be explored.

Fourth, the complexity of designing rapid mitigation strategies leads to the question of the performance and suitability of current governance arrangements and, in effect, the construction of paradigms that define our way of life to deliver quick emissions reduction. The aggressive measures required by the accelerated approach to climate mitigation through stronger governments described in this book, if implemented, will likely place some form of pressure on democracy, both in temporal and spatial terms; thus, innovations to make political and institutional arrangements stronger while strengthening democracy have be envisaged.

Fifth, the strategies for affecting rapid mitigation developed in this book are generic at best. Although there are inherent challenges with the applicability of these strategies to a specific country, the results provide overarching insights, frameworks, or guidelines that could inform, incite, and excite future research in this domain, particularly in the future design of national strategies that consider distinct country capacities. This involves envisioning a national Rapid Mitigation Project that values different political, economic, social, and cultural orientations and takes into account divergent natural endowments and capacities in governing sociotechnical transitions, innovations, and diffusion. More specific research questions in future studies also include envisaging the Project in the context of a low-emission, developing country.

Sixth, this book's focus on state-led approaches, activities, and programmes fails to discuss key strands in climate mitigation, particularly those that are citizen and/or grassroots-organised. This book does not examine in detail the emergence of citizen-led approaches, many of which have been successful at various levels. Stronger public engagement will surely strengthen a position that governments alone do not have all the solutions for climate change. Echoing that, state-led strategies alone cannot strongly stand as an approach for rapid mitigation without due consideration of diverse and dynamic social processes. Collaborative activities between the state and civil society have to be designed.

I accept some will question either the technical, social, or political assumptions involved in producing this book's contingency strategies. As I have argued, many of these strategies are unattractive, controversial alternatives – especially if viewed in a predominantly market-oriented frame of mind. Many of these strategies, I concede, are highly idealised and utopian – even for progressives. For liberals, they can be considered intrusive.

To this end, I invite the reader to consider a short *Gedankenexperiment*. When climate impacts hit in a scale, scope, and intensity we are not expecting, the state will still surely expand its power, and most possibly intrude into our private lives. In such an event, there will be two alternatives: a confused government responding to forced migrations, famines, and conflicts; or an organised government with a bounded set of contingency plans that could be activated with some oversight built in to address not only the devastations but also their human drivers. The choice is yours.

Index

For Product Safety Concerns and Information please contact our EU
representative GPSR@taylorandfrancis.com Taylor & Francis Verlag GmbH,
Kaufingerstraße 24, 80331 München, Germany

Printed and bound by CPI Group (UK) Ltd, Croydon, CR0 4YY
08/05/2025
01864511-0003